Arbitraging Japan

Arbitraging Japan

Dreams of Capitalism at the End of Finance

Hirokazu Miyazaki

UNIVERSITY OF CALIFORNIA PRESS
Berkeley · Los Angeles · London

University of California Press, one of the most distinguished university presses in the United States, enriches lives around the world by advancing scholarship in the humanities, social sciences, and natural sciences. Its activities are supported by the UC Press Foundation and by philanthropic contributions from individuals and institutions. For more information, visit www.ucpress.edu.

University of California Press
Berkeley and Los Angeles, California

University of California Press, Ltd.
London, England

Library of Congress Cataloging-in-Publication Data

Miyazaki, Hirokazu.
Arbitraging Japan : dreams of capitalism at the end of finance / Hirokazu Miyazaki.
p. cm.
Includes bibliographical references and index.
ISBN 978-0-520-27347-4 (cloth : alk. paper)
ISBN 978-0-520-27348-1 (pbk. : alk. paper)
1. Stockbrokers—Japan—Case studies.
2. Investment analysis—Japan—Case studies.
3. Arbitrage—Japan—Case studies. 4. Finance—Japan—Case studies. I. Title.
HG5774.3.M59 2013
332.60952—dc23

2012027300

Manufactured in the United States of America

22 21 20 19 18 17 16 15 14 13
10 9 8 7 6 5 4 3 2 1

In keeping with a commitment to support environmentally responsible and sustainable printing practices, UC Press has printed this book on Rolland Enviro100, a 100% post-consumer fiber paper that is FSC certified, deinked, processed chlorine-free, and manufactured with renewable biogas energy. It is acid-free and EcoLogo certified.

For Annelise and Xavier

Contents

Acknowledgments

This book is based on longitudinal ethnographic field research among Japanese financial market professionals in Tokyo completed between 1998 and 2011. It seeks to recapture these professionals' excitement about techniques of finance and the capacity of those techniques to transform economy and society. My research was assisted by a grant from the Abe Fellowship Program administered by the Social Science Research Council and the American Council of Learned Societies in cooperation with and with funds provided by the Japan Foundation Center for Global Partnership. The initial phases of the project were supported by the American Bar Foundation, and more recent research trips to Tokyo were made possible by research funds generously provided by Cornell University.

Special thanks are due to Jacquelyn Ball, Laura Cocora, Alexander Gordon, Davydd Greenwood, Vinny Ialenti, Annelise Riles, Jennifer Shannon, and Chika Watanabe for reading the entire manuscript and generously offering line-by-line comments. I also benefited a great deal from detailed comments on individual chapters provided by the following people: Tom Boellstorff, Walter Cohen, Tony Crook, Yuji Genda, Douglas Holmes, Naoki Kasuga, Webb Keane, Donald MacKenzie, Bill Maurer, Katrina Moore, Adam Reed, and Richard Swedberg.

Over the last ten years, I have presented versions of the argument I develop in this book at various seminar series, workshops, and conferences. I thank all who attended and commented on my presentations, especially Allison Alexy, Michael Allen, Anne Allison, Masahiko Aoki, Diane Austin-Broos, Frank Baldwin, Brett de Bary, João Biehl, Luc

Boltanski, James Boon, John Borneman, Laura C. Brown, Timothy Choy, Jean Comaroff, John Comaroff, Veena Das, Elizabeth A. Davis, Brett de Bary, Joseph Dumit, Lieba Faier, James Faubion, James Ferguson, Paul Festa, Melissa Fisher, James J. Fox, Bryant Garth, Carol Greenhouse, Chris Gregory, Jane Guyer, Ghassan Hage, Koichi Hamada, Abdellah Hammoudi, William Hanks, Yonosuke Hara, Karen Ho, David Holmberg, Waheed Hussain, Miyako Inoue, Reginald Jackson, Casper Jensen, Jennifer Johnson-Hanks, Margaret Jolly, Mamoru Kaneko, William Kelly, Christopher Kelty, Shuhei Kimura, Sharon Kinsella, Karin Knorr-Cetina, Naveeda Khan, Junji Koizumi, Eisei Kurimoto, Benjamin Lee, Haiyan Lee, Vincent-Antonin Lépinay, Michael Lynch, Neil Maclean, Ramah Mckay, George Marcus, Francesca Merlan, Yuval Millo, Timothy Mitchell, Koji Miyazaki, Henrietta Moore, Atsuro Morita, Fabian Muniesa, Karen Nakamura, Victor Nee, Ryoko Nishii, Michio Nitta, Katsuro Niwa, Emiko Ohnuki-Tierney, Aihwa Ong, Takashi Osugi, Morten Pedersen, Trevor Pinch, Mary Poovey, Alex Preda, Michael Pryke, Nigel Rapport, Kathryn Robinson, Janet Roitman, Carolyn Rouse, Hugh Ruffles, Minako Sakai, Naoki Sakai, Steve Sangren, Ryan Sayer, Teruo Sekimoto, Michael Silverstein, Kenneth Singleton, David Slater, Rogers Smith, David Stark, Hirokazu Takizawa, Sachiko Tanuma, Philip Taylor, Nigel Thrift, Takuya Toda-Ozaki, Ikuya Tokoro, Matt Tomlinson, Greg Urban, Katherine Verdery, Jeff Weintraub, Kazuo Yamaguchi, Shinji Yamashita, Sylvia Yanagisako, Tomiko Yoda, and Alexei Yurchak.

A workshop organized for me in July 2010 by Naoki Kamiyama, then managing director and chief equity strategist at the Tokyo office of Deutsche Securities was also a valuable opportunity for me to present my work to financial market professionals.

Daisaku Yoshida, an editor for *Chuokoron,* a monthly Japanese opinion magazine, helped me present the core argument of the book in a two-part essay published in the February 2012 and March 2012 issues of the magazine. The process of writing this essay allowed me to sharpen my argument considerably.

The chairs of Cornell University's Department of Anthropology—David Holmberg, Nerissa Russell, and Andrew Willford—and deans of Cornell University's College of Arts and Sciences have been generous in granting me extra funding and time away from teaching over the last ten years. I would not have been able to complete my field research and this book without their support.

I thank Stan Holwitz for taking interest in the project in the first place. Reed Malcolm patiently waited for the completion of my manuscript and sustained my work through his timely and generous intellectual interventions. I am profoundly indebted to Reed and two anonymous reviewers for their deep engagements with my ethnographic analysis. I have gained substantially from their penetrating comments, and I am very grateful for their generosity. At the final stage of the project, Emily Park made the manuscript significantly more readable. I cannot thank her enough for her careful and thoughtful work.

I thank all who have participated in my ethnographic research in Tokyo since 1998. I especially would like to thank those traders I call Aoki, Ibuka, Ishida, Koyama, Sasaki, Tada, and Tanaka for their patience, guidance, and friendship. Their continuous critiques of my writings about them have enriched my understanding of their lives and careers. I also thank Tokyo Stock Exchange officials, former Osaka Stock Exchange officials, and others who participated in my research for their time and generosity. Needless to say, views and opinions expressed in the book, and errors that may be found, are entirely mine.

I also would like to add a special note of thanks to my uncle, Takeji Yamashita, a retired securities analyst at a major Japanese securities firm who published *Kabushikishijo no kagaku* (The science of stock markets), an early Japanese effort to approach financial markets in scientific terms (Yamashita 1987). He introduced me to a number of securities industry insiders at the beginning of this research project.

My mother, Keiko Miyazaki, has shown keen interest in this project since its inception. It was one of her close friends who introduced me to the manager of a derivatives unit inside a securities firm where I later conducted field research. Without this introduction, the project would never have taken off.

The scope of my original project went beyond the approximately forty former members of the proprietary trading team of a securities firm on whom I have focused my research over the last ten years. I also have studied Japanese commodity futures merchants, exchange officials, and industry insiders involved in the establishment of the market for Japanese government bond futures in 1985, and more recently, credit derivatives specialists and their responses to the crisis of Tokyo Electric Power Company following the earthquake, tsunami, and nuclear power plant accident in March 2011.

This project has been part of my long-term collaboration with my partner, Annelise Riles. Whereas my work has focused on derivatives traders, fund managers, and structure finance specialists, her work has focused on central bankers, regulators, and lawyers involved in the regulatory infrastructure of financial transactions in Japan. In this sense, *Arbitraging Japan* is a companion volume to her book *Collateral Knowledge: Legal Reasoning in the Global Financial Markets* (University of Chicago Press, 2011). My book's connection to her work goes well beyond this research collaboration, however. Her scholarship has been the single most important source of inspiration for my work.

I would not have been able to bring this project to completion without Annelise and my family's encouragement and generous support. I completed a first draft of this book around the time of the birth of our now six-year-old son, Xavier, who has patiently waited for the manuscript to be completed while he finished numerous "books" of his own containing fantastically creative letters and pictures. I dedicate this book to these two best friends and soul mates of mine.

Unless otherwise noted, all names of persons and corporations are fictitious. I also have modified certain aspects of individuals to protect their privacy.

Portions or wholes of the following previously published essays are reproduced, with or without modifications, in this book with the permission of the copyright holders:

"The Temporalities of the Market." *American Anthropologist* 105, no. 2 (2003): 255–265.

"The Materiality of Finance Theory." In *Materiality*, ed. Daniel Miller, 165–181. Durham: Duke University Press, 2005.

"Economy of Dreams: Hope in Global Capitalism and Its Critiques." *Cultural Anthropology* 21, no. 2 (2006): 147–172.

"Arbitraging Faith and Reason" (commentary on Jane Guyer, "Prophecy and the Near Future: Thoughts on Macroeconomic, Evangelical and Punctuated Time"). *American Ethnologist* 34, no. 3 (2007): 430–432.

"Between Arbitrage and Speculation: An Economy of Belief and Doubt." *Economy and Society* 36, no. 3 (2007): 397–416.

"Kin'yu-jinruigaku kara mita kin'yu no 'owari': Toreda no nijunen to 'nihonteki' gakushu no genkai" [The "end" of finance as seen through the anthropology of finance: Traders' experience of the last twenty years and the limits of 'Japanese'-style learning]. *Chuokoron*, February 2012, 164–175.

"Kin'yu-jinruigaku kara mita kin'yu no 'owari': Fukakutei de fukachina sekai wo hikiukeru giho" [The "end" of finance as seen through the anthropology of finance: The art of embracing an uncertain and unknowable world]. *Chuokoron*, March 2012, 162–173.

Introduction

"The subprime crisis revealed a simple fact, that is, that finance is nothing but a fraud [*inchiki*]," Tada, a former derivatives trader at a major Japanese securities firm, told me at a small Roppongi, Tokyo, bar in July 2009. He went on to frame the notion of fraud in terms of arbitrage, a trading strategy seeking to profit from a difference in the prices of an asset in two different markets: "As it has turned out, finance was the arbitrage of knowledge gaps between those who know [those in the financial industry] and those who don't [the public], not arbitrage between markets, and this fact has been revealed." Tada noted that financial market insiders like himself had known this all along, but now that the fraudulent nature of finance had been disclosed, he believed that no further innovation in financial technologies would be possible. That is, the difference in knowledge that financial innovation has exploited and has sought to perpetuate has been eliminated, and arbitrage of this kind would no longer be allowed. For Tada and many of the other financial market professionals I have met in Tokyo since the late 1990s, the era of finance—the era in which financial market professionals were regarded as movers and shakers of economy and society—has ended.

What does this sense of the end of an era, widely shared among financial market professionals, mean for the future of capitalism, whose creative and destructive force finance has demonstrated repeatedly over the last three decades? What does it mean for financial market professionals, whose careers and lives have been driven by utopian imaginaries and dreams of economic, social, and personal transformation inspired by techniques and theories of finance? What does it mean for critics of capitalism, who have long predicted the burst of financial markets and their underlying deceptive and destructive logics? And what is specific about the Japanese inflections of all these questions?

In order to answer these questions, I turn to the dreams that have manifested themselves in the careers and intellectual trajectories of members of a small derivatives trading team originally founded inside a major Japanese securities firm in 1987. The category of derivatives includes a wide range of financial instruments intended to disperse, manage, and profit from risks of all kinds. The value of derivatives "derives" from another asset (usually called an "underlying asset") or an assemblage of such assets whose exposure to risks derivatives seek to manage. Some of these instruments, such as stock index futures and options, are traded in standardized forms at exchanges, while other kinds of derivatives, such as currency swaps and credit derivatives, are contracts arranged privately for specific parties ("over-the-counter derivatives," or OTC derivatives). Derivative products take apart and recombine known risks associated with their underlying assets and repackage them into tradable forms, although these processes of decomposition and recombination typically create new risks along the way and often lead to further repackaging. These products have created a new set of secondary markets that in turn have forged new flows and linkages between previously unconnected markets.

For Tada and the other derivatives traders whose professional careers and personal lives I chronicle in this book, the techniques and theories of finance—particularly the relativist logics and sensibilities of arbitrage, a cornerstone of financial economics and derivatives trading—have served as sources of inspiration for highly reflexive conceptions of their own power to change the world for the better. These traders' dreams and intellectual adventures embody the energy, speed, and utopianism of financial innovation since the 1980s, as well as the social and personal costs of that innovation.

At the same Roppongi bar, Tada, whom I have known since 1997, had previously shared with me his pioneering experiences of introducing the techniques of arbitrage to Japan's stock markets (see chapters 2 and 3) and his later dreams of arbitraging a whole range of mispriced goods and services in Japan, from golf club memberships to hospital fees (see chapter 4). Some of Tada's dreams of arbitraging Japanese markets of all kinds ended badly during the tumultuous first decade of the twenty-first century, in which neoliberalism and the associated faith in the power of money produced mixed economic and social effects. If arbitrageurs ultimately eliminated arbitrage opportunities in their own conception, however, by the summer of 2009, Tada seemed to have embraced the possibility that finance itself had come to an end (see chapter 5). Before turning to the details of Tada's and other derivatives traders' philosophical elaborations of arbitrage in their professional and personal lives, however, I consider the particular significance of taking seriously Japanese derivatives traders' dreams, imaginations, and thoughts at the moment at which finance globally has produced spectacularly broad destructive effects.

FINANCE AS PHILOSOPHY: AN ETHNOGRAPHY OF THINKING

In *The Crash of 2008 and What It Means: The New Paradigm for Financial Markets,* the speculator and philanthropist George Soros outlines a "new paradigm" for the regulation of financial markets (Soros 2009). This new paradigm draws on Soros's long-standing critique of neoclassical economics and its underlying assumption of equilibrium. Soros's proposal is based on what he calls the "theory of reflexivity," a general theory of the recursive relationship between ideas and the world: "The theory of reflexivity seeks to illuminate the relationship between thinking and reality. . . . Misinterpretations of reality and other kinds of misconceptions play a much bigger role in determining the course of events than [is] generally recognized" (Soros 2009: 10–11). From this standpoint, Soros insists, "the behavior of financial markets needs to be interpreted as a somewhat unpredictable historical process rather than one determined by timelessly valid laws" (p. 53). Soros's theory of reflexivity "recognizes the uncertainties associated with the fallibility of both regulators and market participants. The prevailing paradigm acknowledges only known risks and fails to allow for the consequences of its own deficiencies and misconceptions. That lies at the root of the current turmoil" (p. 79).

Soros's critique resonates with some of the major insights of various ongoing efforts to take the global financial crisis as an opportunity to reconsider the theoretical assumptions of economics, the role of the government in the market, and the nature of money and capitalism (see, e.g., Akerlof and Shiller 2009; Krugman 2008; Stiglitz 2010). For example, in their book *Animal Spirits: How Human Psychology Drives the Economy, and Why It Matters for Global Capitalism,* George Akerlof and Robert Shiller redeploy John Maynard Keynes's notion of "animal spirits," which in *The General Theory of Employment, Interest, and Money*, Keynes identifies as a major source of market insatiability and an inevitable and necessary force in all forms of human decision making: "A large proportion of our positive activities depend on spontaneous optimism rather than on a mathematical expectation, whether moral or hedonistic or economic. Most, probably, of our decisions to do something positive . . . can only be taken as a result of animal spirits—of a spontaneous urge to action rather than inaction, and not as the outcome of a weighted average of quantitative benefits multiplied by quantitative probabilities" ([1936] 1997: 161). In Akerlof and Shiller's view, "economic crises, like the current financial and housing crisis, are mainly caused by changing thought patterns. . . . [The current crisis] was caused precisely by our changing confidence, temptations, envy, resentment, and illusions—and especially by changing stories about the nature of the economy" (Akerlof and Shiller 2009: 4). Akerlof and Shiller's argument departs from the conventional economic assumption that "people rationally pursue their economic interests" (p. 3); they draw attention to other "noneconomic motivations" (p. 3), or "intangibles" (p. 4), which in their view are "real motivations for real people" (p. 174). Akerlof and Shiller propose to put this "restless and inconsistent element" (p. 4) at the center of economic analysis and embrace all the distinctively human complexity resulting from it (pp. 175–176).

In my view, Soros's critique exceeds the efforts of Akerlof and Shiller and other prominent economists to offer a new vision of the economy that is more realistic and therefore more humanistic. What I have in mind is Soros's motivation for writing the book itself. Soros offers an autobiographical account of his "philosophical explorations" (Soros 2009: 18) and of the influence of Karl Popper's philosophy—especially the proposition that human "understanding is inherently imperfect" (p. 17)—on his trading and philanthropic practices. In Soros's own account, the main goal of his book is to demonstrate the validity of his philosophical system, his theory of reflexivity. Soros has repeatedly claimed in his writings that this theory of reflexivity has guided both his speculative and philanthropic activities, and that it has much more general implications (see, e.g., Soros 1998: ix). In his view, the theory offers a "new philosophical paradigm for understanding human affairs in general and financial markets in particular" (Soros 2009: 223). In this context, his attention to financial markets is merely an illustration of the theory (see p. 230).

Underlying Soros's intellectual exploration is his grand personal dream of becoming, and being recognized as, a philosopher. Soros laments that his first attempt to present his philosophy in *The Alchemy of Finance,* published in 1987 at the height of his career as a speculator, "was dismissed by many critics as the self-indulgence of a successful speculator" (p. 19) despite his strong desire "to be taken seriously as a philosopher" (p. 21). Soros's ultimate goal is to reinject philosophy into public debates about economy and society: "Philosophy used to occupy a preeminent position before scientific method took its place. . . . It may be appropriate to restore philosophy to its preeminent position" (p. 223).

The current debate about the regulation of financial markets concerns how to incorporate diverse human interests and motivations, both rational and irrational, into economic analysis. Apart from the work of Akerlof and Shiller, a number of similar efforts are under way from a variety of theoretical perspectives. For example, in his recent synthesis of game theory and comparative institutional analysis, the economist Masahiko Aoki points to the competition to demonstrate one's intelligence among Wall Street investment bankers. In Aoki's view, what was critical was that "there was no ceiling to this social rat race, even though an extra million dollars might not have mattered to them for its own sake" (Aoki 2010: 138):

> The economic game and the social game were linked in such a way that the rules of the economic game, the reward to financial engineers according to their short-term financial performance, generated a rat-race culture among them in the social game, on one hand, and playing the social game encouraged them to take economic actions that generated economic risks endogenously, on the other. The primary fault may have been in the ways that incentive contracts were designed, but it was the mind-sets of the people absorbed in that culture that eventually led to the spectacular failures of some major financial service houses. (p. 138)

Aoki's attention to the fetishization of intelligence among Wall Street investment bankers resonates with many academic and popular accounts of Wall Street generally (see, e.g., Ho 2009; Lewis 1989) and the world of derivatives trading more specifically (see, e.g., Lewis 1999; Lowenstein 2000; see also Tett 2009a).

However, Soros's contention that his engagement with Popper's philosophy has informed both his trading and philanthropic practices suggests that it is not enough to see market participants as decision makers with multiple interests and motivations. Of course, Soros is an exceptional figure. He is a highly successful and controversial trader who has been widely accused of causing and profiting from the currency crises in Southeast Asia in 1997 (see, e.g., the exchange between Malaysian Prime Minister Mahathir Mohamad and Soros [Mahathir and Soros 1997]). As a philanthropist he is also an influential public figure. But in my view, as a trader and financial market professional, Soros is not as unique as is often assumed in terms of his intellectual scope and ambition.

Arbitraging Japan responds to Soros's long-standing insistence on the philosophical significance of his theory of reflexivity, not by endorsing his theory of reflexivity or his somewhat anachronistic vision of the relationship between philosophy and science (cf. Latour 1987, 1993), but by taking his frustration seriously. That is, this book seeks to demonstrate that, like Soros, many traders (and other financial market professionals) are not simply decision makers but also *thinking subjects* engaged in dialogue with a variety of broader intellectual debates and projects. In the context of their daily work, financial market professionals habitually reflect on and debate the complexity of the markets they seek to interpret and navigate; the inadequacy of the models, theories, and strategies they deploy in their work; and the possibility of adopting other ways of apprehending market phenomena.

This view departs from the long-established practice of regarding professional traders as irrational, rational (see, e.g., Friedman 1953; Keynes [1936] 1997: 147–164; see also Iwai 2000: 16–25), or even "hyper-rational" (Abolafia 1996: 23) actors in economics and economic sociology. In my observation, many financial market professionals have a much more expanded and complex vision of the market and the world. In this context, thinking gravitates not toward simplification but toward the embrace of ambiguity, complexity, and the ultimate unknowability of the world (see also Amartya Sen's discussion of "commitment" [1977]).

There is no denying that the action (and inaction) of financial market professionals at times appears to have resulted in catastrophic economic damage. Yet how should we respond critically to this fact? The shift from decision making to thinking as a focus of analysis is intended to broaden the scope of critical inquiry to include the various intellectual engagements of financial market professionals as part of the immediate context in which their decisions, and the consequences of those decisions, are understood and evaluated. The aim of this exercise is to bring two kinds of thinking subjects—producers of critiques of capitalism and consumers of their ideas, including myself—together on the same ethnographic plane, as cotheorists and cocritics of capitalism loosely connected with one another. My ultimate goal is to explore where dialogue and collaboration may take place between social theorists and financial market professionals.

In this book, I use an anthropological perspective based on my own longitudinal ethnographic research to illuminate certain financial market professionals' distinctive modalities of knowing, reasoning, and engaging with the world. Anthropological research generally pays close attention to specific actors' own categories and the practical uses to which those categories are put. In his well-known essay "The Way We Think Now: Toward an Ethnography of Modern Thought," Clifford Geertz presents three methodological components of an ethnographic inquiry into thinking: "the use of convergent data; the explication of linguistic classifications; and the examination of the life cycle" (Geertz 1982: 25). A similar set of methodological concerns about data, categories, and temporal frameworks informs my ethnography of thinking in, about, and for financial markets. The focus of my ethnography is a small yet significant group of mostly male Japanese derivatives traders originally assembled in the late 1980s within a major Japanese securities firm in Tokyo, which I call Sekai Securities. During the course of my longitudinal study, completed between 1998 and 2011, I gathered a broad spectrum of information. My data ranges from the team's internal records concerning trading strategies, product development, and regulatory concerns to firsthand ethnographic observations of the traders' professional relationships and career decisions. In private conversations over drinks, the traders also shared with me their complaints, personal dreams, and seemingly random thoughts on a variety of topics, from the nature of money to spiritual and extraterrestrial matters. My goal has been to observe each trader's thinking in the vicinity of his professional trading practices, where his professional and personal lives converge and diverge. This is also where I have sought to observe the ways in which various ideas and beliefs, economic and otherwise, shape, animate, and constrain decisions, thoughts, and imaginations.

The starting point of every good ethnographic account is a rigorous examination of salient categories in the lives of the subjects of ethnographic inquiry. The category of arbitrage, a central category of financial economics and a widely deployed trading strategy, quickly emerged as an exceptionally salient category in the professional and intellectual lives of Sekai Securities traders.

Arbitrage, sometimes called "relative value trading," is ideally risk-free or low-risk trading in which traders aim to capitalize on economically significant variations in the market's valuation of what the traders regard as equivalent or linked assets. Typically, arbitrage entails the simultaneous buying and selling of a single security at two different geographical locations, such as silver traded in New York and silver traded in Tokyo, or of two economically related securities, such as a basket of stocks traded in the cash market and futures contracts on those stocks, when there is a significant price difference between them. Arbitrage assumes that there is an economically fair price difference between economically related or linked assets, and deviation from that difference becomes an arbitrage opportunity. The vast majority of arbitrage operations entail much less obvious sets of assets brought into arbitrageable relationship. Only by foregoing precision could such a relationship be identified and serve as the starting point of an arbitrage operation. This makes arbitrage more ambiguous. In fact, arbitrage is driven by layers of ambiguity. Such ambiguity allows arbitrageurs to extend the idea of arbitrage to various objects and operations. Whatever assets are at stake, however, the strategy remains the same: arbitrageurs seek to generate profit by simultaneously buying low and selling high and subsequently reversing the trades and unwinding the positions when the prices converge.

Throughout the book, I carefully examine the ambiguous and constantly shifting conceptual boundaries of the category of arbitrage vis-à-vis the broader category of speculation. In fact, the slippery distinction between the two categories is a central ethnographic problem I address. The overall goal of my study is to demonstrate the complexities, intricacies, and subtleties of thinking afforded by the sensibilities of arbitrage.

The longitudinal study I have completed has allowed me to observe not only the changes in Sekai Securities traders' thinking over time but also arbitrage as a trading strategy, trading as a profession, each trader's confrontation with the peculiar temporalities of the market, and broader social trends, such as Japan's neoliberal socioeconomic reform. My examination of the traders' thinking is therefore based on an analysis of intersecting temporal orientations manifested in the trajectories of the traders' professional and personal lives over more than a decade.[1]

My ethnographic account follows a long tradition of anthropological attention to the parallel between anthropologists' and their interlocutors' ways of analyzing, critiquing, interpreting, knowing, modeling, and theorizing (see, e.g., Bateson [1936] 1958; Geertz 1973; Holmes and Marcus 2005; Leach [1954] 1970; Marcus 1998, 2007; Maurer 2003a, 2005a, 2005b, 2005c, 2006b; H. Miyazaki 2004b; Riles 2000, 2011; Shore and Wright 1999; M. Strathern 1988, 2000).[2] This allows for engagement with financial market professionals as coanalysts, cointerpreters, and cotheorists of economy and society, and even as cocritics of capitalism, as well as the possibility of exploring substantive intellectual dialogue and collaboration with financial market professionals on Wall Street and elsewhere (see also Riles 2010, 2011). I suggest that an entryway to such dialogue and collaboration should be found in ethnography.

The anthropology of finance is by now a well-established field (see Elyachar 2005; Fisher 2010; Fisher and Downey 2006; Hertz 1998; Holmes 2009; Holmes and Marcus 2005; Lee and LiPuma 2002; LiPuma and Lee 2004; Maurer 1995, 1999, 2002a, 2002b, 2005b, 2005c, 2006a, 2006b; H. Miyazaki 2003, 2006b, 2007; Miyazaki and Riles 2005; Riles 2004b; Roitman 2005; Zaloom 2006; see also O'Barr and Conley 1992 for a notable pioneering study), and it has recently been reenergized by the global financial crisis of 2007 to 2008 (see, e.g., Ho 2009; Riles 2010, 2011). In the aftermath of this global financial crisis of unprecedented scale, an ethnographically informed analysis of the workings of financial markets and their sociocultural consequences is an urgent anthropological task. To the extent that the anthropology of finance is different from journalistic accounts, insider exposés, or theoretically driven critiques of capitalism, however, a brief discussion of the intellectual background of the present study may be helpful here.

Since the late 1990s, Michel Callon, Karin Knorr-Cetina, Donald MacKenzie, and other leaders of the social studies of science have turned their analytical attention to finance. The result is the interdisciplinary field known as the social studies of finance (see, e.g., Callon 1998a, 1998b; Callon, Millo, and Muniesa 2007; Knorr-Cetina and Preda 2005; Lépinay 2007a, 2007b, 2011; MacKenzie 2006, 2009; MacKenzie, Muniesa, and Siu 2007a; Preda 2009; see also Mitchell 2002; Thrift 2005). This field proposes a view of market action as a networked configuration or arrangement of financial (and economic) theories, computer technologies, calculative devices, mathematical formulas, documents, institutional and organizational features, and humans (Callon 1998b). What underlies this view is a proposition that the arrangement of human and nonhuman entities into specific configurations sets the boundaries of economic action. Karin Knorr-Cetina and Urs Bruegger, for example, have studied international currency trading rooms in Zurich, analyzing the formation of global sociality and reciprocal relationality, based not on face-to-face interactional relationships but on global currency traders' shared attention to the information on their computer screens (Knorr-Cetina and Bruegger 2000, 2002).

The debate concerning the "performativity" of economic theory (see, e.g., Butler 2010; Callon 1998b, 2005, 2010; MacKenzie 2006, 2009; D. Miller 2002; see also H. Miyazaki 2005b) is particularly relevant to the present study. Michel Callon uses the case of a French rural strawberry market in which a network of calculative devices, including introductory textbook economic theory, created a space where otherwise socially embedded human actors act as self-interest-maximizing economic actors (Callon 1998a, 1998b). Donald MacKenzie extends Callon's insights to his historical study of the way the Black-Scholes options pricing model, a standard formula for pricing options, came to be shared by Chicago options traders and in turn made the prices conform to the pricing model (MacKenzie 2006):[3] "Economic agents such as Chicago option traders are not just 'naked' human beings, nor simply human beings embedded in social networks. Their 'equipment' matters" (MacKenzie 2009: 4; see also Callon, Millo, and Muniesa 2007).

This attention to the place of theories and formulas in the market and the economy deliberately departs from a dominant view of economic anthropology and sociology originating from the work of Bronislaw Malinowski and Marcel Mauss (but see my discussion in chapter 6). As MacKenzie, Muniesa, and Siu note, "Economic sociology and anthropology should focus on how markets are constructed and maintained (and on the role of economic theory, material devices, procedures, physical architectures, linguistic codes, and so on, in the construction and functioning of markets), rather than focusing simply on demonstrating ways in which concrete marketplaces differ from economists' 'abstract' markets" (MacKenzie, Muniesa, and Siu 2007b: 8).

The anthropologist Daniel Miller, who proposed in 1998 to study how economics as a discipline had become so powerful that it had begun to shape the world through a class of phenomena he called "virtualism" (D. Miller 1998; see also Carrier and Miller 1998a), has suggested that Callon's attention to the role of economic theory reifies economic theory and therefore loses its critical edge: "Callon writes from the basis of an economists' [*sic*] vision, which has at its heart the assumption that most transactions within the capitalist word [*sic*] are indeed market transactions and that his task is to understand the mechanisms that allow them to work as markets. As a result, Callon follows the economists in mistaking a representation of economic life for its practice" (D. Miller 2002: 219).

In response, Callon has sought to articulate his own vision of the role of critique: "Talking of the performativity of economics means assuming that agency is distributed and that concrete markets constitute collective calculative devices with variable, adjustable configurations. It also means that the role of critique is limited to clarifying differences and local asymmetries in order to raise the open question of experimentation with new forms of organization" (Callon 2005: 3). In Callon's view, Miller "thinks . . . that anthropology aims to tell the (almost whole) truth on man in society, and that by telling that truth it combats the illusions masking the strength of the powerful" (p. 18). Callon, by contrast, seeks to illuminate those ambiguous and fragile moments in which a new configuration of theories, technologies, and human interests emerges: "I, on the other hand, think that anthropology can only participate, along with the actors, or rather with certain actors in a position to produce small differences, in showing that other worlds are possible and that humans in society (in markets) have multiple and uncertain forms that emerge through trials. It is up to social scientists to recognize the moment when, still fragile and enigmatic, they appear" (pp. 18–19).

It is with this spirit of coparticipation and collaboration that I approach arbitrage, the focus of my ethnographic inquiry, and its theoretical, technical, and aesthetic components. I discuss the use of the category of arbitrage among a group of Japanese traders specializing in arbitrage operations in the Japanese financial markets since the late 1980s. I examine the expected and unexpected, mundane and not-so-mundane, and secular and nonsecular thoughts, imaginations, and dreams inspired by theories and techniques of arbitrage.

To be clear, I am not claiming that the practices of these particular arbitrageurs can be generalized to all arbitrageurs. On the contrary, my goal is to demonstrate the importance of ethnographic attention to the specific uses to which categories of economic analysis are put in particular ethnographic settings. By drawing attention to the particular way the idea of arbitrage has inspired a broad range of thought experiments and imaginations in a Japanese securities firm's trading room, I suggest that theories and techniques of finance could serve as a source of inspiration for a critique of capitalism.

A JAPANESE EXPERIMENT AND ITS COMPARATIVE SIGNIFICANCE

The global financial crisis of 2007 to 2008 has made Wall Street a primary target of public criticism and the focus of the debate about how to regulate financial markets. A premise of this book is that this debate would benefit from an ethnographically and historically informed comparative perspective. Yet turning to a relatively little-known experiment with derivatives trading in a Japanese securities firm at the moment in which Japan is increasingly irrelevant in economic policy debates in the United States demands an explanation. The time in which the Japanese economy and corporations offered a model to emulate is long gone. Paul Krugman recounts how the Japanese government mishandled the Japanese economy after the burst of the bubble economy in the early 1990s, leading it into the two decades of recession widely known as "the lost two decades": "The failures of Japan are every bit as significant for us as its successes. What happened to Japan is both a tragedy and an omen" (Krugman 2008: 56–57). Likewise, a recent *New York Times* article reports that many economists "are now warning of 'Japanification'—of falling into the same deflationary trap of collapsed demand that occurs when consumers refuse to consume, corporations hold back on investments and banks sit on cash. It becomes a vicious, self-reinforcing cycle: as prices fall further and jobs disappear, consumers tighten their purse strings even more and companies cut back on spending and delay expansion plans" (Fackler 2010).

The poverty of the hitherto dominant comparative analytical framework positing Japan as a model for the United States to follow is evident in the radical discursive shift in mainstream American economic writings from the idea of "Japan as Number One" (Vogel 1979) to "Japan's 'lost decade or two decades.'" A few notable efforts have been made to carve out an analytical space between the culturalist celebration and dismissal of Japanese models. These range from the Stanford University economist Masahiko Aoki's long-standing and influential effort to build a universal framework for comparative institutional analysis focusing on various features and properties of Japanese and Euro-American firms (see, e.g., Aoki 1988, 1994) to the attempt by Ikujiro Nonaka and Hirotaka Takeuchi to generalize the process of institutional learning based on Japanese manufacturing companies' experiments in product research and development (Nonaka and Takeuchi 1995).

My present endeavor follows the spirit of these ambitious efforts with a slightly more modest goal. I aim not to construct a universal model but to offer a comparative framework for understanding how ideas that seem purely economic, such as those originating from theories and techniques of finance, shape broader action, thought, and imagination. Here I follow an enduring concern in the humanities and humanistic social sciences with the intersections of economic, literary, and other cultural forms (see, e.g., Maurer 2005c; Poovey 1998, 2008; Shell [1982] 1993a). The immediate impetus for setting this objective, however, is my frustration with the narrowness of the current debate about financial markets and their regulation, which is preoccupied with the question of rationality versus irrationality and the idea of a free market versus the need for government interventions in the market. Instead of treating financial market professionals as rational, irrational, or hyperrational decision makers, this book seeks to depict them as complex actors who can be rational, irrational, and hyperrational at different points in time. More importantly, I reveal these financial market professionals to be thinkers caught up in historically specific institutional, intellectual, and sociocultural configurations of ideas about individualism, freedom, the state, money, capitalism, and life more generally. This study examines the way different sociocultural and historical configurations can open and close different aspects of economic ideas.

I approach my objective from two interrelated vantage points. First, I draw attention to the daily comparative work of Japanese financial professionals themselves (their comparative assessment of the practices of Japanese securities firms with those of Euro-American investment banks) and the distinctive intellectual space that this daily comparative work generates in their professional work (see also Choy 2011; Riles 2000, 2011). Although the basic ideas and operations underlying derivatives trading have existed in the Japanese rice markets since the eighteenth century, the kinds of derivatives contracts and associated theories and techniques examined in this book originated in the United

States and were introduced to Japan in the context of the deregulation of Japan's financial markets after the mid-1980s. Japanese government bond futures contracts were launched at the Tokyo Stock Exchange in 1985. In 1987, the Japanese government lifted the ban on financial futures trading in overseas markets previously imposed on Japanese institutional investors. In September 1988, futures contracts on Japan's premier stock indexes, the Nikkei 225 and TOPIX, were launched at the Osaka Stock Exchange and the Tokyo Stock Exchange respectively. The Osaka Stock Exchange and the Tokyo Stock Exchange launched options contracts on the Nikkei 225 and TOPIX, respectively, in 1989. These newly established stock index futures and options markets ostensibly afforded investors in the Japanese financial markets tools for hedging the risks of the Tokyo Stock Exchange–traded stocks' downward turns as well as new tools for speculation.

The introduction of these theories and techniques was part of the negotiation between the U.S. and Japanese governments over the U.S. trade deficit and the deregulation of the Japanese markets through the Japan-U.S. Yen-Dollar Commission in 1984 (see, e.g., Nakanishi 2002: 180), but it was also part of a global trend spearheaded by Wall Street investment banks that its Japanese counterparts eagerly followed at the height of Japan's bubble economy (see, e.g., Rosenbluth 1989). The deregulation program followed the Japanese stock market bubble of the 1980s and associated development of Japanese securities firms' general belief in their capacity to "catch up with and overtake" their Euro-American counterparts. The peculiar temporal location of Japanese securities firms relative to Euro-American investment banks largely defined Japanese financial market professionals' daily comparative work (see chapter 3).

The Japanese securities firm I call Sekai Securities established its proprietary trading team in 1987. It employed a number of engineers and scientists from manufacturing firms and graduate programs and assigned them to derivatives trading–related units. In the chapters that follow, I examine the Sekai derivatives team's efforts to learn to trade derivatives and experiments with theories and techniques of finance associated with derivatives trading, as well as the consequences of those efforts and experiments. The Japanese traders I came to know exercised a significant degree of relativity and reflexivity in the midst of economic instrumentality and rationality, and they engaged philosophically and strategically with theories, concepts, and techniques of financial derivatives trading.

I also seek to examine the historically specific significance of Japanese engagement with financial theories and techniques, the deregulation of financial markets, and neoliberal reform programs more generally (see Borovoy 2010; H. Miyazaki 2010b; see also Fourcade-Gourinchas and Babb 2002).[4] The enthusiasm with which certain Japanese, like many of the Sekai Securities traders who participated in my research, recognized the power of money and of the market underlying the Japanese government's neoliberal reform programs in the late 1990s and the early 2000s seems simultaneously old and new. The idea of "new" capitalism certainly highlighted a new kind of ethos and ethics. Neoliberal reform programs, such as the privatization of Japan's postal and postal savings services, had significant political effects, and, more importantly, promoted a particular brand of individualism, expressed in terms of the ideas of risk and responsibility (*risuku to jikosekinin*) (see chapter 4). But the figure of the "individual" (*kojin*) emerged vis-à-vis the communalist and group-oriented large corporation (*daikigyo*) in the media, and the debate that ensued revisited the long-standing problematic of individualism (*kojinshugi*), self (*jiko*), and subjectivity (*shutaisei*), or the lack thereof, in Japanese society (see, e.g., Koschmann 1996). These historically specific cultural dimensions of the appeal of neoliberalism were important elements of Sekai traders' career trajectories (see Greenhouse 2010; Ong 2006; cf. Harvey 2005). During this period, Sekai traders' attitude toward work seems to have changed radically, as the relationships between individuals and corporations, individuals and society, and individuals and the nation were reworked explicitly in the name of "reform" (*kaikaku*) and the "market" (*shijo*).

With this view of new individualism, there was pervasive talk of Japan's defeat (*haisen*) in its financial war with the United States (see chapter 3). Japan's financial "big bang," officially launched in 1996, took effect in the late 1990s with a series of drastic deregulation measures, such as the deregulation of over-the-counter derivatives trading. By the mid-1990s, Sekai Securities also had shifted its energy from an effort to train its own traders and derivatives specialists and create a Japanese version of Wall Street–style investment banking inside the Japanese firm, at any cost, to an effort to hire away experienced traders and derivatives specialists from Euro-American firms. In particular, the Sekai derivatives team attempted to globalize its operations by employing a team of French derivatives specialists. Yet a series of scandals in the early 1990s, such as those related to the firms' compensation of a few important clients for their loss in the stock markets, had weakened Sekai and other major firms considerably in financial terms, thus preventing their ultimate success in this goal. Sekai Securities terminated its derivatives operations in 1998, and many of Sekai's derivatives traders left the firm.

Overall, these comparative (United States versus Japan) and historically specific contexts profoundly affected the way Japan's pioneering derivatives specialists encountered derivatives and other theoretical and technical developments in the global financial markets of the 1980s and 1990s. For them, derivatives not only have offered a tool for transforming Japanese financial markets and the Japanese economy at large but also have afforded a critical vantage point on the nature of Japanese capitalism and Japanese society more generally. My ethnographic analysis of a small group of Japanese derivatives traders' practical and intellectual engagements with theories and techniques of finance, therefore, aims to answer more general questions: to what extent could theories and techniques of finance serve as a source of inspiration for the critique of finance and capitalism, and to what extent do theories and techniques of finance override various sociocultural and historical specificities?[5]

In this project, I examine whether the extensible logic of arbitrage can be sustained as an explicit alternative to other modes of explanation, partly to see what kind of thought, imagination, and dreams arbitrage inspires in arbitrageurs and partly to see how theories and techniques of finance resonate with critical theory, spirituality studies, and even less mainstream intellectual pursuits such as "ufology" (UFO studies). In this sense, this project is an experiment of a sort in replicating the analytical work of a particular group of actors to its limits. In doing so, I suggest that the boundaries of finance as an ethnographic subject cannot easily be confined to the practice of financial trading.

DERIVATIVES, DOCUMENTS, AND DREAMS

In my effort to take traders' intellectual endeavors and intellectual trajectories seriously, I begin each of the five chapters with a document or a book and an associated genre of writing that had particular significance at one stage of Sekai traders' careers. These include a handout for a training session for new employees, a report commissioned by an exchange, a popular book about trading strategies, an Excel spreadsheet calculation, and a business plan. My analysis focuses not only on the content and form of these documents and books but also on the way these genres of writing point simultaneously to arbitrage's infinitely extensible potential and its ambiguities, limits, and endpoints, or in more theoretical terms, the idea of capitalism as a perpetual movement and the idea of capitalism as a movement coming increasingly closer to its own endpoint.[6] These documents also encompass both arbitrageurs' professional commitments to the practice of arbitrage and their personal dreams partially inspired by the idea of arbitrage. In other words, I approach these documents as crystallizations of arbitrage's capacity to eliminate and to extend its users' expansive potential. An extension of arbitrage generates a simultaneous viewing of arbitrage's infinitely open future (in which arbitrage serves as the dominant principle at work) and fast approaching endpoint (in which no arbitrage can be detected). I seek to retain the mutually incompatible possibilities that everything is arbitrage and nothing is arbitrage. In this sense, my account of arbitrage aims to capture the intertwined nature of arbitrage with its absence, on the one hand, and of the logics of finance and personal lives, on the other hand, as manifested in arbitrageurs' extensions of the category of arbitrage.

My attention to documents and various genres of writing in the arena of financial derivatives trading is partially inspired by the important efforts of Vincent-Antonin Lépinay, Bill Maurer, and Annelise Riles to bring into sharp focus form filling, record keeping, legal documentation, research, and other practices known as "middle-office" and "back-office" work, as opposed to traders' "front-office" work (see, e.g., Lépinay 2007b; Maurer 2005a, 2005c, 2006b; Riles 2010, 2011; see also Riles 2000, 2006 on more general ethnographic attention to documents). However, my interest in writing, reading, and research practices engaged by Sekai traders reflects the ethnographic specificity of their workplace. Many dimensions of the Sekai workplace distinguish it, but three are particularly relevant to my analysis. First, as I examine in chapter 3, Sekai traders' predominant modality of engagement with theories and techniques of finance was learning. Second, as a result of the experimental and less specialized nature of the team, Sekai traders were engaged in a wider range of activities than their Euro-American counterparts. Third, Sekai traders' reading practice had much to do with Japan's culture of reading and what Marilyn Ivy and others have noted as the strong influence of sociocultural theorization available through the media on daily conversation and work practice (see, e.g., Ivy 1993, 1995). The influence of the economist Katsuhito

Iwai's popular book on the Sekai derivatives team described in chapter 1 is an example of this pervasive phenomenon.

My ethnographic attention to documents and books also has much to do with the way I conducted ethnographic fieldwork inside the Sekai derivatives team. A quick account of my location in the team may be helpful here. Following a pilot study that Annelise Riles and I conducted during the summer of 1997, I initiated ethnographic field research inside the Sekai Securities trading room in the fall of 1998.[7] Since our first encounter in the summer of 1997, Tada, the head of Sekai's derivatives trading team at the time, had demonstrated an unusual degree of interest in and curiosity about my research project, and he immediately began to arrange interviews for me. When I returned to Tokyo in the fall of 1998, Tada allowed me to visit him and his team daily. The Sekai Securities trading center was located in an office complex approximately 1.2 kilometers southeast of Kabutocho, Tokyo's securities industry district, where the Tokyo Stock Exchange is located. Tada gave me a desk space next to him at the very back of a large room, one-third of which was occupied by Tada's team. Tada's desk faced the entrance to the room. Two female assistants sat at desks placed sideways in front of Tada. Several senior traders occupied other desks in front of Tada's, but the majority of traders in Tada's team worked in a separate trading room on another floor that they shared with traders from other sections of the firm. As a result, Tada's floor was relatively quiet. There were two small, segmented areas for conferencing purposes at the right side of Tada's desk. Occasionally different groups within the team met there to discuss their trading strategies, but I was usually allowed to use one of these areas.

For obvious reasons, my access to proprietary information was limited, and my movement within the firm was also constrained. I was not allowed to see either the team's trading logs or trading proposals, but I was given access to the team's extensive library of books on derivatives trading and financial economics, located near the entrance of the room. Tada initially suggested that I focus my research on the team's founding years, and I was able to discuss those years with the team's current and former members. I also accessed some internal documents related to the team's engagement in the lucrative Nikkei 225 arbitrage operation from the late 1980s until the early 1990s and its negotiations with stock exchanges and government authorities.

At the time of my fieldwork, Tada's team shared a large room with Sekai's research center and another unit of the firm. The head of the research center was Tada's longtime colleague and friend, Numata, who had participated in the founding years of Sekai's derivatives team. Numata also arranged a number of interviews with researchers under him. Their common mentor and the team's founder, whom I call Aoki in this book, was in his early fifties and was at that point one of Sekai's top executives. Aoki had his own office on another floor. Tada arranged two long interviews with Aoki during my time at Sekai in 1998. Toward the end of my stay, however, Aoki, Tada, and Tada's team were all embroiled in an internal debate about the future of their firm. Eventually, the firm's management decided to join an American conglomerate. As a result, Aoki and his traders, like Tada, left the firm at the beginning of 1999.

I rarely spent time with traders who had their desks in a different room during trading sessions. All the traders under Tada, and various other figures involved in derivatives trading and research at Sekai Securities, were willing to discuss their work with me over lunch and after work. A total of approximately forty former Sekai employees participated in the project. My subsequent research from 1999–2000, 2001, 2003, 2005, 2007, 2008, 2009, 2010 and 2011 consisted largely of long semistructured individual interviews and conversations with key figures. Typically, these conversations lasted for two to four hours and took place at coffee shops, restaurants, bars, and nightclubs.

Like documents and books, what Sasaki and other Sekai traders routinely referred to as "dreams" (*yume*) quickly emerged as an ethnographically significant object. In the Japanese business world, storytelling is an important genre of speech that has a particular temporal orientation and arrangement of participant roles. Typically delivered in monologue form by a senior to a junior while drinking and eating late into the night, this speech consists of a retrospective account of the senior's reflection on his career (see also Allison 1994; Kondo 1990). The account always has a slight moral overtone. It also usually culminates in a revelation of the speaker's dreams for the future. The dreams are presented as if they were secrets, truthful presentations of who one is. As a relatively young anthropologist, I was routinely cast into the role of the junior listener to the dreams of my senior informants. Dreams were sometimes intertwined with books in the traders' accounts of their professional and personal intellectual trajectories.

Stories constitute an integrative part of any organizational life (see, e.g., Frost et al. 1985; Frost, Nord, and Krefting 2004; Wilkins 1989), and the ambiguity they afford serves both organizationally productive and unproductive purposes (see, e.g., March 2010; March and Olsen 1976). However, the focus of my analytical attention is not so much on these traders' organizational experiences as on traces of techniques and sensibilities of finance in their respective intellectual trajectories. In this respect, my goal is closer to Martha Banta's analysis of stories of Taylorism. Reflecting on the challenges she faces in writing about Taylorism without reproducing its own "totalizing" tendency, Banta notes that her historical analysis of Taylorism "is a history that continues to replicate itself in our own desire to gain totalizing control over literary structures, by whose means we might gain control . . . over the systematized worlds in which we speak, make money, wield power, love, live, and die" (Banta 1993: xi). Banta's strategy focuses on analyzing stories surrounding Taylorism in order to recapture its "totalizing" tendency without reproducing it in her analysis. Here Banta relies on stories' inherent propensity for complexity, messiness, and excess (see also Stewart 1996). Yet, in the case of finance theory, and arbitrage more specifically, its presumably "totalizing" tendency is undermined by its explicit fictionality and associated tendency to cancel itself out. Arbitrage and arbitrage opportunities could be found everywhere and nowhere. In analyzing stories of arbitrage, I seek to recapture the simultaneous totalizing presence and self-canceling absence of arbitrage and its sensibilities in traders' work and life (cf. H. Miyazaki 2005a).

In this book, therefore, I do not use documents and dreams as analytical categories. They were the most salient ethnographic artifacts that emerged from my field research in Tokyo, and I use them to illustrate how Japanese arbitrageurs' commitment to arbitrage worked. In each chapter, I draw attention to two or more specific purposes that each document served; often, a work-related document reflected a personal dream of its drafter as well as an official professional purpose.

In chapter 1, "Shakespearean Arbitrage," I offer a concrete image of the relationship between techniques of finance and traders' dreams and intellectual trajectories as manifested in a handout created by Sasaki, a mathematician turned trader, for a training session for new members of his derivatives development team. This document contains both an important insight about finance—the centrality of arbitrage in derivatives trading—and Sasaki's personal dream of contributing to academic knowledge about financial mathematics. I analyze the significance of what I call a "bibliographical autobiography" in light of arbitrage's self-canceling tendency as evidenced in the way arbitrageurs exploit and eliminate arbitrage opportunities and ultimately themselves. Sasaki's reading of an analysis of William Shakespeare's *The Merchant of Venice* by the economist Katsuhito Iwai illustrates that tendency. In this sense, Sasaki's document has a similar shape to Soros's book. Both are anchored partially in theories and techniques of finance and partially in their respective intellectual trajectories. Both men's dreams are simultaneously internal and external to financial markets.

Building on the centrality of arbitrage in Sekai traders' professional and personal trajectories, in chapter 2, "Between Arbitrage and Speculation," I show how the paper that Sasaki coauthored with Aoki in 1990 concerning the economic role of index arbitrage in defense of their index arbitrage operations served another purpose for Aoki: the training of Sasaki in logical thinking. Rationality, in the sense of logicality, was an important element in Aoki's effort to introduce the notion of arbitrage to his team. Central to the idea of arbitrage as the basis of the pricing of derivatives products is the idea that market participants must act rationally in the sense that they seize arbitrage opportunities when they find them. Without this assumption, arbitrage is impossible. At the same time, this assumption gave rise to a particular conception of the agency of arbitrageurs. For the arbitrageurs I knew, arbitrage was both their individual action and the market mechanism itself. I discuss the implications of this circular logic inherent in arbitrage for their commitment to rationality.

In chapter 3, "Trading on the Limits of Learning," I discuss the way Sekai traders read the Wall Street securities analyst Jack D. Schwager's book *Market Wizards: Interviews with Top Traders* (Schwager [1989] 1993). This was the most frequently referenced book in Sekai traders' conversations with me. Generally, *discipline* is a popular term in the world of trading, but in the Sekai Securities trading room, it was explicitly related to Schwager's book. Indeed, discipline is one of the most important lessons Schwager draws from his interviews with highly successful U.S.-based traders. My point, however, is that Sekai traders' interest in the idea of discipline in Schwager's book points to their paradoxical fascination with their American counterparts as those from whom they simultaneously need to learn and differentiate themselves. The chapter draws particular attention to Sekai traders' collective experience of learning, a celebrated virtue and a dominant modality of being in the Japanese corporate world, as a hindrance to arbitrage operations and the discipline they demanded. Confronting the limits of learning as a modality of engagement with the market, the Sekai arbitrageurs who participated in my research project began to apprehend America as a signifier of a new form of subjectivity.

Chapter 4, "Economy of Dreams," is about Aoki's successor, Tada, and his fascination with the kind of transparency that he believed money would bring to his relationship with himself. The starting point of my discussion is a spreadsheet Tada created in January 1999, after his trading team was disbanded, to compute his own market value. As a result of this calculation, Tada took a greater risk than he had ever taken in his career and quit Sekai Securities to join an independent investment fund. I trace the trajectory of Tada's changing views on the relationship between money and what he termed "self-realization." I examine his heroic effort to arbitrage every possible inefficient market in Japan and the relationship of this effort to his own personal dreams, which included making enough money to retire early and bicycle around Japan.

In chapter 5, "The Last Dream," I discuss a business plan Aoki crafted in his effort to raise money for a hypnotherapy clinic that would specialize in addressing the psychological problems of Japanese youth. The business plan as a genre of writing became salient in the early 2000s, in the midst of the rise of the culture of venture capitalism in Japan. As a former antiwar student activist turned derivatives trader, Aoki sought to revisit his youthful passion to change Japan and tackle what he saw as the negative consequences of Japan's uncompromising pursuit of economic growth. The focus of my discussion is the debate concerning this project between Aoki and Tada, who helped Aoki draft the business plan. The debate ultimately points to the two financial market professionals' complex views on the role of belief in the market and in life, and the possibility of an exit from finance and capitalism. Using this debate and the contrast between the two men's seemingly different dreams of an exit from their work, I bring to light a particular kind of commitment emerging at the intersections of arbitrage and arbitrageurs' lives, a commitment to keep in view both an endpoint to their work and the endlessness of their work.

Finally, in chapter 6, "From Arbitrage to the Gift," I juxtapose arbitrageurs' engagements with capitalism with recent Japanese academic critiques of global capitalism and point to the differences between them. I focus on the economist Iwai's 2000 essay, written in response to the Asian currency crisis and the failure of the hedge fund Long-Term Capital Management, and on the Marxist literary critic and philosopher Kojin Karatani's 2003 book, *Transcritique on Kant and Marx*, originally written in Japanese between 1998 and 2000, and their respective commentaries on the global financial crisis of 2007 to 2008. Here I seek to demonstrate that these critics of capitalism have extended speculation and its accompanied leap of faith as their method and the object of their critique. In contrast, I consider what a theory of capitalism would look like if it were built not on speculation, but on arbitrage. In particular, I contrast the speculative leap of faith in those critiques of capitalism with the ambiguous faith and skepticism entailed in arbitrage. For the self-designated arbitrageurs I have studied, arbitrage is predicated on both a faith-like commitment to its technique and a deep skepticism of itself. My larger project is to consider the implications of this double vision inherent in arbitrage for what might be termed academic arbitrage.

What is unique about Iwai, one of a handful of economist turned humanist public intellectuals in Japan, and Karatani, a highly influential literary critic, is the particular sociocultural and intellectual locations they occupy in Japan's public culture.[8] Here I am extending the method of bibliographical biography to link Sekai arbitrageurs' reading lists to my own. I use these figures to stay close to the intellectual lives of the Japanese traders I discuss in this book and the intersections of their intellectual trajectories and my own. The book concludes with a reflection on the relationship between anthropology and finance and its potentially arbitrageable quality.

In sum, this book is about a particular kind of intellectual excitement that animated a group of Japanese pioneers in derivatives trading.[9] Put another way, this is a study of a kind of utopianism at work in financial markets. Such utopianism has routinely been deemed disastrous to both utopians themselves and to the rest of society (see, e.g., Polanyi [1944] 1957), and in the aftermath of the global financial crisis of 2007 to 2008, it is hard to deny the injustice of the logics of finance. Yet in this book, I insist on the importance of taking financial utopianism seriously. It is only through an active effort to reorient financial market professionals that real market reform will be possible. And this can only happen if financial market professionals are taken seriously as thinking subjects capable of reflecting on and reorienting the place of their expertise in the economy and society. Otherwise, the seemingly universal appeal of finance remains intact. Diversity in the future can be guaranteed only when diversity in the past is kept in view. This book takes the form of an experiment aimed at seeing how far arbitrage can be sustained as a general modality of engagement, not only for Sekai Securities traders but also for myself.

CHAPTER 1

Shakespearean Arbitrage

In June 2005, at an Irish pub in Marunouchi, Tokyo's financial district, Sasaki, the head of a financial derivatives research and development unit at a Japanese megabank, showed me a document stored in his PDA. He had drafted this document for use in training the younger members of his unit. At the beginning of the document, Sasaki asserts, "The source of profit in capitalism is difference [*sai*]." He cites *Venisu no shonin no shihonron* (A theory of capital according to *The Merchant of Venice*), a 1985 book by Katsuhito Iwai (Iwai [1985] 1992), an MIT-trained University of Tokyo economics professor and influential public intellectual. In this book, Iwai interprets the melancholy of Antonio, the play's protagonist, as a symptom of his eventual defeat by the force of money—that is, in Iwai's own terms, by capitalism's exploitation and elimination of difference (*sai*). Sasaki repeated Iwai's contention that in all forms of capitalism, from merchant capitalism to industrial and postindustrial capitalism, the source of profit has always been difference of one kind or another. If profit making in merchant capitalism is based on the difference in the prices of a commodity at two geographical locations, industrial capitalism seeks to exploit the "difference between the value of labor and the value of what that labor produces," while postindustrial capitalism seeks to exploit the difference in the price of information at two temporal locations, the present and the future (Iwai [1985] 1992: 58).[1]

The financial derivatives business is the same, Sasaki argued. The value of a financial derivative product, whether a futures contract (a contract to receive or deliver an asset at a preset price on a preset date) or an options contract (a contract to buy or sell the right to receive or deliver an asset at a preset price on or before a preset date), is defined in terms of—or derives from—the value of its underlying asset, such as a company stock, a stock index, a commodity, or a combination of such assets. Any difference in the market price of a derivatives product and its underlying asset becomes a source of profit. The derivatives business, therefore, is all about the "creation of difference" (*sai no sozo*) between a derivatives product and its underlying asset, which Sasaki quickly paraphrased as the creation of "arbitrage opportunities." In Sasaki's view, arbitrage is the fundamental "principle" (*genri*) of capitalism.

In the late 1980s, Sasaki was part of a group of young traders assembled inside the major Japanese securities firm I call Sekai Securities. Sasaki joined the team in 1988 from a doctoral program in mathematics. The team was originally formed in August 1987, following the government's decision to allow Japanese institutional investors to participate in overseas financial futures markets. The team's founder, Aoki, was the young traders' intellectual leader. Before establishing the team, Aoki had spent four years—from 1981 until 1985—in Sekai's New York branch. While in New York, Aoki learned to trade options. He was acquainted with an American trader who worked for a major U.S. investment bank and who, Aoki recalled proudly in his conversation with me in the fall of 1998, considered him "very promising" (*yubo*) and decided to teach him how to trade options on U.S. Treasury Bond futures. This American trader even allowed Aoki to use his investment bank's computer system to practice trading options. Later, Aoki wrote an introductory book in Japanese on options trading.

Aoki's stay in New York coincided with the time when proprietary trading was a highly profitable activity for U.S. investment banks. Aoki was introduced by his American trader friend to John Meriwether, who was then the head of Salomon Brothers' legendary proprietary trading team, the Government Arbitrage Group, and who later founded the hedge fund Long-Term Capital Management. Meriwether explained to Aoki that "relative value trading" was the primary strategy of U.S. investment banks' proprietary trading teams.[2] When he heard about Meriwether's relative value trading, Aoki thought that arbitrage would become important in Japanese financial markets in the near future.

When Aoki was entrusted by Sekai's management to establish a team devoted to derivatives trading, therefore, his focus was sharply on proprietary trading and arbitrage. In the fall of 1988, the team consisted of four traders, two based in Tokyo, including Sasaki, the other two in Osaka, where futures and options contracts on the Nikkei 225 index had been recently launched. The team also included three system engineers, including Tada, who later became the head of the team, and two administrative assistants. Aoki immediately began to train these young mathematicians and engineers in basic theories and techniques of finance and Wall Street–style proprietary trading, and he instructed them to search for arbitrage opportunities. It was in this context that Aoki introduced the economist Iwai's interpretation of *The Merchant of Venice* to his proprietary trading team. Ultimately, the book would provide a philosophical foundation for the team as a whole. In this sense, Sasaki's handout offers a window into his reading and other intellectual practices associated with his trading career.

ARBITRAGING FICTION AND FINANCE

Before returning to Sasaki's handout and examining its content and background, I turn to Katsuhito Iwai's interpretation of *The Merchant of Venice* and Sekai Securities proprietary traders' response to it.[3] In his book, Iwai seeks to offer a solution to the famous problem of Antonio's weariness, which opens the play: "In sooth, I know not why I am so sad."[4] "What 'sad role' does he have to play?" Iwai asks (Iwai [1985] 1992: 11). In order to understand Antonio's weariness, Iwai argues, it is essential to approach the plot of *The Merchant of Venice* in terms of the dynamic process of capitalism. From this standpoint, Iwai asserts, Antonio's weariness is a symptom not so much of his internal state of mind (p. 10) as of an external cause, the "irreversible" transformation prompted by capitalism (p. 13). By the "irreversible" transformation, Iwai means the ultimate defeat of communal Roman values, which Antonio represents, by the force of money, which Iwai sees as represented by Portia.

The Merchant of Venice has served as an important source of inspiration in a wide range of writings on money and finance, from economic analyses of financial markets (see, e.g., Markowitz 1999) to critiques of capitalism (see, e.g., Maurer 2005c: 136; see also Marx [1867] 1990: 399, 400, 618n30). Numerous efforts also have been made to interpret the play in terms of its economic and financial content. These interpretations have presented divergent configurations of ethnoreligious and economic values as represented by different characters in the play, as well as divergent thematic emphases, from usury (see, e.g., Draper 1935: 39; Pettet [1945] 1969), to exchange (see, e.g., Engle 1986; Newman 1987; Sharp 1986), to the importance of law in economic transactions (see, e.g., Benston 1991; see also Scott 2004; Sokol 1992; Spinosa 1994).[5]

In his influential essay "The Wether and the Ewe: Verbal Usury in *The Merchant of Venice*," Marc Shell uses Shakespeare's play to demonstrate the parallel between financial and literary economies and his more general thesis concerning the "participation of economic form in literature and philosophy, even in the discourse about truth" (Shell [1982] 1993a: 4; see also Osteen and Woodmansee 1999: 15–16).[6] In particular, Shell draws attention to what he terms Shylock's "verbal usury": "As the Jew uses moneys . . . to supplement principal, so he uses puns to exceed the principal meanings of words" (Shell [1982] 1993b: 50). Shell goes on to show how Antonio starts using puns like Shylock and becomes a "usurer" himself (p. 72).

If Shell demonstrates the blurred boundaries between finance and fiction, and money and language, Iwai demonstrates the way money seeks to eliminate difference of all kinds. The focus of Iwai's argument is the idea of difference and his view of capitalism as the repetition of a single form of exchange that "mediates" (*baikai*) and eliminates difference (Iwai [1985] 1992). Antonio's long-distance trade serves as the prototype of this recurring form. Iwai draws attention to Antonio's role as both a man of "ancient Roman honour" (*The Merchant of Venice* III, ii, 294) and a merchant engaged in long-distance trade (Iwai [1985] 1992: 17).[7] Iwai points out that Antonio's dual belonging to the Roman world of communal brotherhood, on the one hand, and to the world of merchant capitalism, on the other, is made possible by the dependence of merchant capitalism on spatial distance between communities engaged in trade (pp. 18–20). Long-distance trade is predicated on the existence and "arbitration" (*chukai*) of a difference in the price of a commodity in two distant locations (pp. 17–18). Iwai's ensuing discussion of *The Merchant of Venice* focuses on how such exploitation of an initial difference in price eventually eliminates that difference and, through an equalization of price, demands a search for further difference elsewhere (pp. 67–68).

Iwai sees a similar exchange relation in the practice of money lending in Venice. In Iwai's view, the confrontation between Antonio and

Shylock stands for the antagonistic and yet "mutually interdependent relationship" between Venice's two separate communities, Christians and Jews (p. 29; cf. Auden 1991: 61). For Christians, who were prohibited from lending money at interest, Jewish money lenders were indispensable (Iwai [1985] 1992: 23–29).[8] To Iwai, the practice of money lending in Venice was like long-distance trade in that both capitalized on the distance between two communities. Iwai also draws attention to how the practice of money lending itself is predicated on the existence of a difference of a sort, that is, "the difference between the present value of money and the future value of money" (p. 25).

In juxtaposing long-distance trade with money lending this way, Iwai highlights not only the parallel between merchants and usurers often pointed out in commentaries on the play (see, e.g., Cohen 1982; Shell [1982] 1993b) but also the process of replicating (or re-creating) difference that is central to the dynamism of the play and to capitalism. In Iwai's terms, this dynamic transformation of capitalism is best depicted in the figure of Portia. He explains that Bassanio's journey to Belmont to win Portia, one cause of which is Antonio's financial debt to Shylock, is itself a replication of long-distance trade (Iwai [1985] 1992: 47–49).[9] In Iwai's analysis, however, Bassanio's quest for Portia ultimately unleashes the full force of money (pp. 54, 59).

For Iwai, Shylock's initial offer not to charge Antonio interest but to lend him money as a "friend" ("Supply your present wants, and take no doit/Of usance for my moneys" [I, iii, 135–136]) anticipates the breakdown of the boundaries between Venice's two communities (pp. 29–30). In the famous trial scene, Shylock demands that the bond be honored, while the Duke of Venice asks for mercy. Portia, who presides over the trial disguised as a legal scholar, plays the "trickster" role to complete the exchange between mercy and law (pp. 34–39).[10] Iwai asserts that "the principle of equivalent exchange or the logic of law [as expressed in Shylock's repeated reference to the bond] was given from the Jewish community to the Christian community whereas 'mercy' was given from the Christian community to the Jewish community. However, as a result of this exchange, each of the two communities thus mediated was deprived of its own distinctive quality and its integrity as a community was lost" (p. 39).[11]

In Iwai's view, Portia is a symbol of money:[12] "The first 'work' of Portia, that is, now freely circulating Money, was to travel secretly from Belmont to Venice and intervene in the trial about the human flesh as a trickster. In that trial, Money, that is, Portia, mediates the difference between the Christian and Jewish communities and accomplishes an exchange of a sort between them" (p. 59). Iwai's point is that Portia's method is long-distance trade (p. 59). In the trial, Iwai points out, Jessica, another symbol of money, ends up receiving part of Shylock's assets (p. 60). Antonio emerges as an embodiment of obsolete "ancient Roman" values as Bassanio, Gratiano, and Lorenzo each unite with Money. Iwai therefore sees the cause of Antonio's weariness in his defeat by capitalism (p. 69).

The Merchant of Venice, according to Iwai, is a story about the mechanism by which money increases itself: "Profits originate from difference between two value systems. Profits are born out of difference" (p. 58). This basic mechanism of profit making applies to all forms of capitalism: merchant, industrial, and postindustrial (p. 58). Here Iwai makes the difference among different kinds of capitalism itself disappear. He also argues that in capitalism the source of profit needs to be sought on an increasingly abstract terrain, because profit making eliminates all obvious differences (pp. 67–68).[13]

In light of the long-standing debate about the play, Iwai's interpretation of it can be disputed point by point. For example, Iwai's understanding of the contrast between Antonio and Shylock as representatives of ancient Roman values and capitalist values, respectively, is perhaps too one-dimensional. Likewise, the antagonism between Jewish and Christian communities in Venice is perhaps exaggerated. Moreover, Iwai's structuralist equation of Portia with Money also problematically eliminates Portia's agency. Finally, Iwai's tendency to reduce the plot to a single theme and procedure repeated over and over may not do justice to the complex and ultimately unresolved quality of the play (see, in particular, Cohen 1982).[14]

Yet Iwai's interpretation of the play inspired Aoki, the founder of the Sekai Securities proprietary trading team, and his traders, including Sasaki, in a particular way. As I have already noted, Iwai's central argument is that profit making in all forms of capitalism lies in the continual search for difference, which Sasaki interpreted as equivalent to the continual search for arbitrage opportunities. Aoki recalled in July 2005 that he had been struck by Iwai's insight that the source of profit in capitalism is difference: "It made the scales fall from my eyes." Aoki was impressed by Iwai's insight about how the working of the principle of arbitrage in Shakespeare's play demonstrated arbitrage as a time-tested principle and strategy, reaching all the way back to the age of merchant capitalism. In this view, the principal means of profit making in capitalism is arbitrage, and all forms of trading are variations of arbitrage. Sasaki told me that his handout reflected this understanding of capitalism that he had "inherited" (*keisho*) from Aoki.

What struck me when Sasaki told me about Iwai's interpretation of the play was his indifference to the reductionist tendency of Iwai's interpretation. Shakespeare's play is widely known in Japan, and Japanese elites such as Aoki and Sasaki, who were educated at the country's highly competitive secondary schools and universities, would be familiar with the play's details. However, neither Aoki nor Sasaki had much to say about those details, or Iwai's choice not to address them. Their attention focused, rather, on Iwai's general observation that the source of profit making in capitalism is difference, which, in the traders' own terms, is equivalent to arbitrage opportunities. How did the economist's engagement with Shakespeare's play generate this effect?

For Aoki and Sasaki, the originality of Iwai's observations lay not so much in his interpretation of each scene of the play as in the overall effect Iwai's argument seems to have generated: it reduces *The Merchant of Venice* to a demonstration of a single economic principle—the identification, exploitation, and elimination of all differences. What Aoki and Sasaki saw was the logic of arbitrage replicating itself across different levels of Iwai's interpretation of *The Merchant of Venice.* Arbitrage as the core principle of capitalism consistently searches for new difference to exploit. As arbitrage eliminates difference, it also eliminates the agents of arbitrage. For example, Antonio and Shylock, practitioners of two different kinds of arbitrage (long-distance trading and money lending) recede to the background as Portia mediates the exchange between the two. In Iwai's interpretation, even this arbitrageur extraordinaire, Portia, ultimately loses her identity as she completes her various arbitraging moves and becomes merely a force of money.

Following this reading, one may add that Iwai also implicitly replicates arbitrage as his own interpretive strategy. Iwai's interpretation itself arbitrages the difference between fiction and finance—it analyzes arbitraging moves in the play as it arbitrages the play itself. The play, and its distinctiveness (or, difference), disappear in Iwai's theory of capitalism. Iwai's interpretive arbitrage strips the play of everything but the principle of arbitrage. One may conclude that Aoki and Sasaki's indifference to the missing details in Iwai's interpretation was an effect of Iwai's own interpretive arbitrage.

ARBITRAGEURS ARBITRAGED

Like Iwai's interpretation of *The Merchant of Venice*, in which characters in the play lose their identity one by one, the trajectories of Sekai traders' professional careers may reveal similar trajectories of capitalism's continual exploitation and elimination of difference, or, in Aoki and Sasaki's terms, *arbitrage*. To anticipate my argument, by the time the reader reaches chapter 6, the principle of arbitrage will seem to have replicated itself across different spheres of life, from derivatives trading to traders' personal lives, as it encounters and eliminates differences one after another. To the extent that Sekai traders have treated arbitrage as the core principle of capitalism and even the core principle of life, they too have found themselves arbitraged.

Arbitrage served, for Aoki and his traders, as one of the most important trading strategies, in both practical and theoretical terms. In 1988, under Aoki's leadership, Sasaki and other traders embarked on arbitrage operations in Japan's newly established stock index futures markets. The Nikkei 225, Japan's representative index, is computed on the basis of 225 stocks selected from those traded at the Tokyo Stock Exchange. The operations typically entailed the simultaneously buying and selling of futures on the Nikkei 225 stock index, traded at the Osaka Stock Exchange, and all the 225 stocks comprising the index at the Tokyo Stock Exchange. This form of arbitrage was relatively simple and profitable. The index futures were consistently overvalued relative to their theoretical "fair" value, and Sekai traders easily locked in profit by simultaneously taking a short (selling) position in the futures market and a long (buying) position in the cash market. Due to its initial success in these operations, the team expanded in the spring of 1989 to include six traders, three system engineers, and two assistants. In 1989, it was reorganized into an independent division with ten traders, three system engineers, and three assistants. The size of the team's index arbitrage position calculated in terms of the size of the maximum position allowed in the cash market also had grown to 30 billion yen ($230 million) by the spring of 1989. After its reorganization into an independent division in May 1989, it exceeded 100 billion yen ($690 million) and, by the end of 1991, it had reached 200 billion yen ($1.3 billion).

However, by 1992, arbitrage opportunities seemed to be disappearing from the Nikkei 225 stock index futures market (see chapter 3; see also H. Miyazaki 2003). Sekai traders then shifted their arbitrage operations to TOPIX, Japan's other major stock index, which is based on the averaged prices of all stocks traded at the Tokyo Stock Exchange. Arbitrage in the TOPIX futures market was always far more complicated than arbitrage in the Nikkei 225 futures market because it would be practically impossible to buy and sell all the stocks traded at the Tokyo Stock Exchange. Arbitrage operations in the TOPIX futures market required a complicated process of virtual replication of the movement of the index with a basket of selected stocks. Sekai traders devoted much time to refining their replication technique for arbitrage in the TOPIX index futures market (and Sasaki's colleague, Ibuka, claimed that the Sekai Securities index arbitrage team had developed the most accurate method of replication). Still, it was far less profitable than arbitrage in the Nikkei 225 futures market.

In Sekai traders' view, they would need to keep fine-tuning their technologies in their search for less self-evident arbitrage opportunities or shift their arbitrage operations to new markets. In this sense, arbitrage contained within itself a propensity for continual redeployment elsewhere. By the mid-1990s, Sekai traders had expanded their arbitrage operations to include other markets, such as the convertible bond markets. This affirms the view shared by theorists from Marx to Keynes, Schumpeter, and Iwai of capitalism as a perpetual movement characterized by expansion and self-destruction (see, e.g., Iwai [1985] 1992: 68, 109; Keynes [1936] 1997; Marx [1867] 1990; Schumpeter [1934] 1983, [1942] 1975).

For Sekai traders, arbitrage also served as a more general interpretive device. Despite their continual search for new arbitrage opportunities in new markets, Sekai's derivatives team struggled to make a profit. Several factors prevented the team from bringing to fruition its initial ambition to be like a Wall Street proprietary trading team. One major factor was the slow and hesitant manner in which the Japanese government deregulated the Japanese financial markets. While the traders were at Sekai, their activities were more or less confined to exchange-traded products and instruments, such as stock index futures and options and stocks traded in the cash market. They also regularly traded convertible bonds, option-like securities issued by a corporation that can be converted to the corporation's shares when certain preset conditions are met. "Over-the-counter" (tailor-made) derivatives, including swaps—contracts to exchange cash flows, such as fixed and non-fixed interest rates or currency exchange rates, at prearranged intervals for a specific duration of time—and structured finance products, such as securitization schemes, were still largely out of their reach. Still, Sekai's derivatives team did experiment briefly with equity swaps, or contracts to exchange an interest rate with a payment based on the movement of a stock index. But the Ministry of Finance informally banned these contracts in 1994, citing their possible infringement of the gambling clause of the Japanese Penal Code. A second factor impeding the team was the financial state of Sekai and other major Japanese securities firms in the 1990s. A series of scandals in the early part of the decade involving these firms' illegal dealings, such as their preferential compensation for losses incurred by certain important clients, weakened them considerably and made it impossible for them to establish a truly global operation in derivatives trading.

By 1998, when I first encountered Aoki and the traders trained under him, they had faced the limitations of their ability to compete with their Euro-American counterparts. Sekai Securities itself eventually entered into a strategic alliance with a U.S. investment bank, and Sekai's derivatives operations were terminated. Tada, then head of the Sekai team, told me that "the Japanese social system as a whole was arbitraged," by which he meant that Sekai and other Japanese financial institutions had been too inefficient to compete with their Euro-American counterparts. Tada subsequently left Sekai to establish an investment fund, where he devised various kinds of new investment schemes. He spoke of these schemes in terms of his own effort to arbitrage Japan's inefficient markets (see also H. Miyazaki 2003, 2005b, 2006b). In these extensions of arbitrage as an interpretive device, Sekai traders alternately became both subjects and objects of arbitrage.

In fact, it was this observation about Sekai arbitrageurs' extensions of arbitrage that prompted Sasaki to tell me in the summer of 2005 about Katsuhito Iwai's interpretation of *The Merchant of Venice* and its significance in his own and other Sekai arbitrageurs' intellectual trajectories. Sasaki suggested that Iwai's interpretation of Shakespeare's play confirmed their own commitment to arbitrage.

It is important to note at this point, however, that Iwai never uses the term "arbitrage" in his interpretation of *The Merchant of Venice*. In Iwai's own terms, the engine of capitalism lies in the continual, and perpetual, search for "difference" in a new market. In Aoki and Sasaki's view, however, Iwai's interpretation of Shakespeare's play confirmed the centrality of arbitrage in capitalism. In this respect, Aoki and Sasaki themselves extended arbitrage to Iwai's interpretation of capitalism, and their reading of Iwai's text can itself be regarded as arbitrage of a sort. The rest of *Arbitraging Japan* can be regarded as an exposition of the significance of this particular reading of Iwai's text on the part of the Sekai traders, and my own extension of it.

ARBITRAGE AS SUBJECT AND METHOD

Arbitrage is a firmly established method by which financial instruments—such as futures, options, and other kinds of derivatives—are priced and traded. Arbitrage is a core category of modern financial economics and a standard trading strategy in investment banks and hedge funds. It is an ostensibly "risk-free" trading strategy that seeks to profit from discrepancies in the prices of economically related assets, such as baskets of stocks and futures contracts on those stocks, by simultaneously buying low and selling high before reversing the trades and unwinding the positions when the prices converge. The idea of "no arbitrage" is central to most pricing methods used in the derivatives business. The fair value of an asset can be calculated in relation to the hypothetical condition of no arbitrage—that is, market efficiency.

Arbitrage is not a new idea. It has long been recognized as a style of trading distinct from speculation, which is based on betting on a particular future price movement. Max Weber distinguishes arbitrage as "a pure example of calculating the numbers" (Weber [1924] 2000: 344) as opposed to speculation, whose "success is dependent upon the onset of the expected change in the general price of the specific good" (p. 345; emphasis removed). Likewise, in his discussion of the role of the "knowledge of the particular circumstances of time and place," Friedrich A. Hayek mentions arbitrage as one of many forms of economic action that "are all performing eminently useful functions based on special knowledge of circumstances of the fleeting moment not known to others" (Hayek [1948] 1980: 80).

In Japan, arbitrage has long existed as a trading strategy. In its technical use, arbitrage is usually translated as *saitei* (also meaning "arbitration") or *saiteitorihiki* ("arbitrage transactions"), but it is also known more informally as *sayatori* (literally, "the grabbing of a difference"). *Nihon kokugo daijiten,* the most comprehensive dictionary of the Japanese language, attributes the original use of the term *saya* (apparently derived from *sai,* or "difference") to Edo-period rice trading. *Saya* referred to the difference, exploited by some traders, between the price of a *choaimai,* or "on-the-book rice" contract—a contract to be settled without physical delivery—and the price of rice in the *shomai,* or "real rice" market, at the Dojima Rice Exchange in Osaka. As Ulrike Schaede has clarified in her study of the Dojima Rice Exchange, *choaimai* trading was essentially trading in rice bill (*kome gitte*) futures, while *shomai* trading was forward trading (Schaede 1991: 351, 354, 361); in this context, *sayatori* was arbitrage between futures and forward contracts.[15]

Arbitrage has become a significant and powerful category since it emerged as a core idea in modern financial economics (see, e.g., Bernstein [1992] 1993; P. Harrison 1997; MacKenzie 2006). The idea of arbitrage has played a major role in the development of contemporary financial theory. Most theories of asset valuation take for granted that arbitrageurs swiftly discover and profit from mispriced assets and, in so doing, keep financial markets efficient. In financial economics, therefore, the value of derivatives products, such as options, is usually computed by assuming a hypothetical condition in which there are no arbitrage opportunities between economically related securities because arbitrageurs have already seized all such opportunities (see, e.g., Hull 1997: 12–13; Neftci 2000: 13; Ross 2005). This computation, in turn, helps arbitrageurs to spot and exploit arbitrage opportunities, because any variability in asset price from one market to another suggests that the assets have not yet been arbitraged. As one standard textbook observes, "The very existence of arbitrageurs means that, in practice, only very small arbitrage opportunities are observed in the prices that are quoted in most financial markets" (Hull 1997: 12). Arbitrage is ironically so important that it is absent. As Philip H. Dybvig and Stephen A. Ross have noted, "Most of modern finance is based on either the intuitive or the actual theory of the absence of arbitrage. In fact, it is possible to view absence of arbitrage as the one concept that unifies all of finance" (Dybvig and Ross 1987: 104). The condition of "no arbitrage" is arbitrage's own starting point, as well as its endpoint.

Arbitrage is also widely deployed by professional traders worldwide. Many investment banks' proprietary trading teams, hedge funds, and other significant market players in derivatives markets have adopted arbitrage or arbitrage-like relative value trading as their primary trading strategy. To the extent that the idea of no arbitrage lies behind almost all asset valuation models, investment bankers' over-the-counter derivatives business also follows the logic of arbitrage.

Arbitrage has also been linked to a number of recent financial crises and scandals, including the 1998 failure of the Connecticut-based hedge fund Long-Term Capital Management (LTCM) (see, e.g., Lewis 1999; Lowenstein 2000; Soros 1998; and especially MacKenzie 2006 for the details of LTCM's arbitrage operations; see Boesky 1985; Endlich [1999] 2000: 109–119; Kestenbaum 1999; United States Congress 1987 for other cases of arbitrage-related crises and scandals). Additionally, the subprime mortgage–related crisis of 2007–2008 has been attributed to a practice known as "ratings arbitrage" (see, e.g., Hull and White 2010 and Nadauld and Sherlund 2009 for a theoretical formulation of the concept). In a 2009 op-ed article in the *New York Times,* Joe Nocera writes:

> When you start asking around about how A.I.G. made money during the housing bubble, you hear the same two phrases again and again: "regulatory arbitrage" and "ratings arbitrage." The word "arbitrage" usually means taking advantage of a price differential between two securities—a bond and stock of the same company, for instance—that are related in some way. When the word is used to describe A.I.G.'s actions, however, it means something entirely different. It means taking advantage of a loophole in the rules. A less polite but perhaps more accurate term would be "scam." (Nocera 2009)

Such extension—or overextension—of the category and practice of arbitrage, and the associated ambiguity of the category, is the central theoretical, methodological, and even ethical problem my ethnographic inquiry seeks to confront. Arbitrage can be extended to various markets and ostensibly mispriced assets, goods, and services; various forms of academic theoretical innovation; and various kinds of transactions.

The extensibility of arbitrage also presents its own challenge to an analysis of arbitrage. Arbitrage is not only a theoretical construct of financial economics and a practical trading strategy but also an interpretive framework that is widely deployable to various phenomena, economic and otherwise. For example, arbitrage has sometimes been deployed explicitly as an analytical term in accounts of the development of financial theories and practices, as in Paul Harrison's description of the history of financial economics as a process of "intellectual arbitrage" (P. Harrison 1997). According to Harrison, neoclassical economists arbitraged the field of financial economics: "[The] success [of neoclassical economics in finance] is the success of intellectual arbitrage, and it cannot last because its own success eliminates the reasons for that success, erasing the opportunity" (p. 173). Harrison notes: "The successful application of economic theory in finance must be attributed to the notion of arbitrage. Not only could something 'scientific' be said about speculative market prices, but also the economics theory seemed able to explain reality. This made finance all the more palatable to economists. Arbitrage was the theoretical force behind each of the major economic innovations in finance" (p. 180). Harrison regards arbitrage as "the fundamental truth" and "an engine for innovation" (p. 185).[16]

Arbitrage is not an entirely foreign topic to anthropology, either. In his celebrated study of a Moroccan bazaar (*suq*) and its economy of information, in which "trade goes on, at great pace and some efficiency, in a moral climate that seems almost designed to prevent it" (Geertz 1979: 212), Clifford Geertz describes activities of a category of bazaar traders known as *sebaibis,* which he translates as "arbitrageurs":

> Just which markets a given sebaibi operates in, as well as what he buys and sells in them, depend on his personal contacts and his familiarity with local situations, products, in turn, of his particular background and experience. His direct and detailed knowledge of diverse bazaar environments, or rather of a definite, limited set of them, and his ability to move effectively among them capturing the profit of price discrepancies are the basis of his living. . . .
>
> Unlike other sorts of buyer-sellers, sebaibis deal in a variety of goods rather than focusing on one or two. . . . Sebaibis (who almost never hold goods for more than a few days) live by suq-to-suq trading, jobbing an income out of a sort of commercial cosmopolitanism. (pp. 188–189)

Geertz draws attention to the way "the sebaibi connects suqs laterally" (p. 190) and contributes to the efficient working of the bazaar.[17]

I examine arbitrage's extensibility by extending it to a point at which it is no longer extensible. What follows is an ethnographic analysis of arbitrage as a *modality of engagement* in a historically specific location and time. My investigation focuses on a group of Japanese traders engaged in arbitrage operations of many different kinds, using futures, options, and other derivatives. My initial analytical focus is on the practice of arbitrage and its associated activities. These include the formulation of trading plans, the execution of trading orders, the drafting of various documents associated with risk management and regulatory changes, the development of trading and risk management systems, collaborative work with American financial economists, the translation of English-language texts concerning financial economics and trading strategies, and the coordination with exchanges and regulatory authorities.

The pioneering Japanese derivatives traders whose career trajectories I examine in this book encountered the idea of arbitrage and stretched (and sometimes overstretched) the category to various objects. Tada's deployment of arbitrage with which I opened this book is one of numerous examples of such extension. Arbitrage has regularly served for Tada and other traders as a framework not only for investment decisions they make in the market but also for choices they make in their personal lives. Ultimately, arbitrage surfaced as more than just a trading strategy. For many of these Japanese traders, arbitrage became a principle of capitalism, of life, and even of mind. Arbitrage as a market positionality afforded them a distinctive general framework for approaching the world. This extensibility resides in arbitrage's ambiguity, lateral and relativistic perspective, and practical orientation toward its own endpoint. Seeing the parallel between market action and other facets of social life itself is a cause and effect of these traders' engagements with the extensible logics of arbitrage.

I examine various kinds of thought and imagination inspired by the technical, aesthetic, and ethical features of arbitrage. In extending from external objects to internal matters, arbitrage has posed epistemological and ontological problems that have shaken the integrity of the category itself. My particular focus is on the ambiguity, instability, and indeterminacy of the category revealed in its extensions, not only for the Japanese traders who participated but also for my study itself. The latter point is important because it serves as a reminder of arbitrage's notably slippery status as a concept, a strategy, and a modality.[18]

AN AUTOBIOGRAPHICAL BIBLIOGRAPHY

Sasaki's handout ends with a section on further readings. He recommends some of the best-known texts in financial economics, including Fischer Black and Myron Scholes's canonical 1973 paper "The Pricing of Options and Corporate Liabilities" (Black and Scholes 1973), which introduced what would become the "Black-Scholes formula," the most widely used formula for pricing options contracts, and J. Michael Harrison and David M. Kreps's 1979 paper "Martingales and Arbitrage in Multiperiod Securities Markets," which replicates Black and Scholes's thesis using stochastic processes known as martingales (Harrison and Kreps 1979; see also Harrison and Pliska 1981). Sasaki also recommends Ioannis Karatzas and Steven E. Shreve's introductory textbook on stochastic calculus, *Brownian Motion and Stochastic Calculus* (Karatzas and Shreve 1988), as essential reading for appreciating the full significance of Harrison and Kreps's contribution to the development of financial economics.

Sasaki's handout is implicitly autobiographical. Sasaki joined Sekai Securities in 1988, when he was a second-year doctoral student in mathematical physics. He told me in June 2000 that he had not been strongly motivated to become an academic, so he began to visit manufacturing companies to consider other career options, but he did not find their laboratories particularly interesting. However, when he visited securities firms, he became interested in options trading after learning that it demanded a knowledge of partial differential equations, which he routinely handled as a student in mathematical physics. Sasaki expressed his interest in options trading at his interview at Sekai Securities and was assigned to the firm's newly established derivatives team. He was immediately put in charge of the team's launching of index arbitrage operations.

The bibliography included in Sasaki's handout listed the same academic works that had played the most important roles in this mathematician turned trader's own intellectual trajectory. For example, in his previous conversations with me, Sasaki had told me about the significance of Harrison and Kreps's 1979 paper in his own professional career. In Sasaki's view, Harrison and Kreps's work recast Black and Scholes's thesis in what he thought were mathematically more rigorous terms (cf. MacKenzie 2003a: 858). Sasaki had expressed to me his regret that he had not known of Harrison and Kreps's work until 1993, as previously his knowledge of financial economics had been based on a somewhat superficial understanding of Black and Scholes's paper. Sasaki had heard from his colleagues in Sekai Securities' research wing that in order to understand financial economics, one needed to have a sure grasp of stochastic processes, and in 1993, he decided to devote some time to updating his knowledge of stochastic calculus. Sasaki read Harrison and Kreps's paper and went on to carefully study Karatzas and Shreve's textbook on stochastic calculus (Karatzas and Shreve 1988). Sasaki told me that, for four months, he spent every weekend reading the textbook.

In reflecting Sasaki's own intellectual trajectory, the handout may be seen as what I term a bibliographical autobiography. Like all autobiographies, Sasaki's also had a particular vision for the future (see, e.g., Ochs and Capps 1996). In preparing the handout, Sasaki had another goal: he wanted to take steps toward an academic publication. He told me:

> I don't think that I will be able to retire early like foreigners. I am already in my mid-forties, and I am in this situation. I don't know how I will be able to manage to work like this until I turn fifty or fifty-five. I feel I need to transmit [*hasshin*] something to the world. Perhaps I will be able to write a working paper. How about that? I am busy with various things at the moment but I will put some thought to it. [I will be able to write something] perhaps by the time I turn sixty. After that, I will spend the rest of my life reading mathematical papers. (June 2005)

Over the previous three years, Sasaki had actively sought opportunities to contribute to the knowledge of financial economics. He had acquainted himself with a finance economics professor through the professor's informal seminar. The professor, who was editing a dictionary of key words in financial economics, had commissioned Sasaki to contribute several entries. Sasaki also had participated in the translation of an introductory textbook in mathematics for finance. This was a collaborative project with two other early members of Aoki's derivatives team, both of whom had obtained doctoral degrees in economics after leaving Sekai Securities. Sasaki's next goal was to submit a paper to an academic journal like *Stochastic Processes and Their Applications*. In addition, Sasaki assembled young people from graduate programs in mathematics and encouraged them to write academic papers. In all these academically oriented activities, Sasaki said, he had sought to leave his footprint (*sokuseki wo nokosu*) on society.

Sasaki's bibliographical autobiography and his dream of leaving an imprint on history may be regarded as his response to the paradox of the arbitrageur's self-canceling identity. In Sasaki's handout and dream, arbitrage remained the subject of his scholarly investigation, but he also managed to turn arbitrage—the method that he and his colleagues had used in their various investment activities—into a subject of pure contemplation. In other words, Sasaki's bibliographic referencing served as a device to offset arbitrage's propensity to eliminate difference while enabling him to stay focused on arbitrage itself as a subject, *not* as a method (cf. H. Miyazaki 2004b, 2005a).

As arbitrage demands continuous extension to new markets and new economic terrains, it also invites extension as an interpretive framework in arbitrageurs' career strategies, personal lives, and general intellectual endeavors. In order to demonstrate this point, I opened this chapter with a mundane example of the use to which the idea of arbitrage is put. Sasaki's handout explains the basic mathematical procedures entailed in the pricing of financial derivatives in terms of the notion of arbitrage. I have sought to demonstrate that the handout's bibliography in turn brings to light the trader's own intellectual trajectory and personal dream, paying particular attention to Sasaki's reference to Iwai's interpretation of *The Merchant of Venice* in terms of the idea of the identification, creation, and exploitation of difference as the essence of capitalism. I have drawn attention to Sasaki's own extension of arbitrage to his interpretation of Iwai's book, which does not itself mention the idea of arbitrage.

Sasaki's extension of arbitrage in turn has implications for my own task of writing about the trajectories of Sekai arbitrageurs' use of arbitrage as a trading strategy, a theoretical construct, and a modality of life. The challenge lies in how and when such extensions can be detected. Sasaki's bibliographical reference to what he saw as Iwai's interpretive arbitrage, which brings to light Sasaki's own intellectual trajectory and dream for the future, serves as a guide. Like Sasaki's bibliographical autobiography, my account of Sekai traders' arbitrage operations will take the form of bibliographical biography.[19]

My use of bibliographical biography as a mode of ethnographic account gestures toward three goals. First, in examining the books, academic papers, and various work documents that traders read, write, and cite, I seek to take their thinking seriously as a window into their practical and theoretical engagement with the market, and with capitalism more generally. Second, in identifying a variety of sources of intellectual inspiration, I seek to bring into view the loosely structured way that thinking takes place in the vicinity of professional work and practice. Third, in drawing attention to the way ideas travel, I seek to identify the intersections of Sekai traders' professional and personal dreams. Sasaki's handout again serves as a model here: if Iwai's analysis ultimately foregrounds the perpetual movement of capitalism, Sasaki's handout points to both the endlessness of arbitrage and the endpoint of arbitrage, where another dream takes off.

These dreams would not exist without a firm commitment to theories and techniques of finance. But they are also the substance of the market; without these dreams Soros is not Soros, and Sasaki is not Sasaki. That is, without these dreams traders are reduced to interests and motivations, which they would quickly lose. These dreams appear in articulation with but move in a different trajectory from theories and techniques of finance. In this way the virtuality of finance theory (such as arbitrage) generates and is supported by a second order of virtuality (such as personal dreams). Ultimately, a defining feature of both orders of virtuality is their ambiguous openness to the future. Rather than understanding the market as a collection of interests and motivations, I seek to recapture the possibility of seeing these orders of virtuality as parallel, coconstituting, and even arbitrageable. In this sense, the market is an economy of dreams.

CHAPTER 2

Between Arbitrage and Speculation

In May 1990, Aoki and Sasaki published a paper on the economic function of stock index arbitrage in a securities industry journal. The goal of the paper was to defend the practice of arbitrage using the Nikkei 225 stock index futures contracts, in other words, arbitrage between a futures contract on the Nikkei 225 and the underlying "basket" of 225 stocks that were used to compute the value of the index. This form of arbitrage became popular among proprietary trading teams of Euro-American investment banks and major Japanese securities firms beginning in the late 1980s. In these traders' view, the Japanese stock index future was regularly "overvalued" relative to its theoretical value and therefore presented numerous arbitrage opportunities. In more concrete terms, this meant that the "basis," or difference in the values of the index future and the index itself, was significantly larger than the theoretically calculated difference between the two (see, e.g., Adachi and Kurasawa 1993; Brenner, Subrahmanyam, and Uno 1991a, 1991b). The relationship between the theoretical, "arbitrage-free," price of a futures contract is calculated on the basis of the present value of the index and transaction costs and taxes associated with the execution of arbitrage.

The execution of index arbitrage using the Nikkei 225 futures was fairly straightforward. The Nikkei 225 index is a relatively simple stock index calculated on the basis of a selection of 225 stocks traded at the Tokyo Stock Exchange. Futures contracts lock in the price of an asset at a preset future date, but unlike many futures contracts on commodities, such as silver, the futures contracts on the Nikkei 225 index do not entail the physical delivery of their underlying asset. Rather, index futures contracts are always settled in cash. Futures contracts with five different settlement dates (for example, March, June, September, December, and March of the following year) are traded at any time. At the settlement date (typically the second Friday of March, June, September, or December), the special value of the index, known as the "special quotation," is calculated on the basis of the value of that Nikkei 225 index at the opening of the day. This "special quotation" is solely for settlement purposes, so that the difference between the contract price of the futures contract and the settlement price of the index may be calculated.[1] This means that at the settlement date of the futures contract, the value of the futures contract and the value of the index are made to converge.

In the late 1980s and the early 1990s, a typical index arbitrage operation using the Nikkei 225 index futures would take the form of so-called cash-and-carry arbitrage (*kai saitei* in Japanese; literally, "buying arbitrage"). This entailed simultaneously selling a Nikkei 225 index futures contract and buying a basket of all 225 underlying stocks at the particular moment at which the value of the futures contract exceeded its fair value. In arbitrageurs' own view, at least in theory, arbitrageurs would make virtually risk-free profit by simultaneously buying back the futures contract and selling the underlying basket of stocks at the settlement date.

Such index arbitrage was a lucrative form of investment for market participants who had both the capital and the technology to execute such orders (see, e.g., Dattel 1994: 192–193; M. Miller 1997: 29–34). As Philippe Avril, head of the currency options division of Indo-Suez Bank's Tokyo branch from 1986 until 1990, recalls in his 2000 Japanese-language book: "Following its launching at the Osaka Stock Exchange, the Nikkei Index futures contracts quickly became popular [among foreign traders] because of their regular mispricing. Foreign traders immediately noticed that the basis, or the difference between futures and [their underling stock index], significantly exceeds the theoretical value quite regularly. This led each investment bank to create a special division devoted to so-called cash-and-carry arbitrage" (Avril 2000: 28).

Stock index arbitrage became a target of tighter regulatory control after the spring of 1990, as index arbitrage–related trades were reported

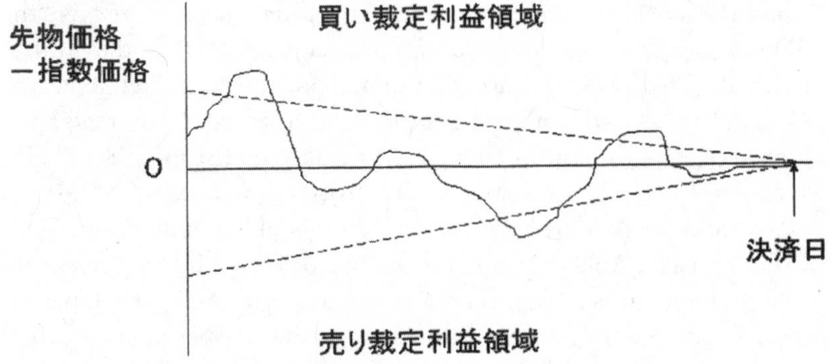

FIGURE 1. Schematic image of Nikkei 225 index arbitrage, created by Tada (December 2011). The image shows a hypothetical movement in the difference between the price of a Nikkei 225 futures contract and the value of the Nikkei 225 index and their conversion at the settlement date of the contract. The area above the horizontal line indicates the area for "cash-and-carry" arbitrage, in which the price of the futures contract exceeds its fair value. The area below the horizontal line indicates the area for "reverse cash-and-carry" arbitrage, in which the price of the futures contract is lower than its fair value.

to regulatory authorities and more information about these positions was disclosed publicly. This form of arbitrage emerged as a particular target of public criticism following a series of stock market crashes in early 1990. At the end of the Tokyo Stock Exchange's closing trading session on December 29, 1989, the Nikkei 225 index had climbed to an all-time high of 38,915.87 yen (see, e.g., Kobayashi 1993: 277; Uchida 1995: 195). In what would turn out to be the beginning of the dramatic collapse of Japan's stock market bubble, the Nikkei index then fell sharply in early 1990. The index fell 1,161.19 yen on February 21 and 1,560.10 yen on February 26. On April 2, 1990, the index further slid to 28,002.07 yen, losing 1978.38 yen or 6.6 percent of its value. The mainstream Japanese media immediately blamed the market's sudden downturn on the index arbitrage operations of foreign investment banks and major Japanese securities firms.[2]

According to media reports following the stock market crashes of 1990, investors rushed to sell their stock portfolios, fearing arbitrageurs' imminent moves to dissolve their long positions in the cash market as the settlement date of a futures contract approached. In other words, index arbitrage induced a massive volume of selling orders, which in turn drove the market to crash. In these media reports, the trading of stock index futures was regarded as "the culprit" (*akudama*) behind the stock market crashes" and was often characterized as "the tail wagging the dog" (*inu no shippo*), suggesting that the futures market dictated the direction of its underlying stock market. A heated public debate ensued concerning the legitimacy of index arbitrage operations (see, e.g., Kunimura 1990; Y. Miyazaki 1992: 179–211; see also M. Miller 1997: 29–34; Tokyo Shoken Torihikijo 2002: 665–666).[3]

Aoki and Sasaki's article responded to this public indictment. Since the fall of 1988, Aoki's team had been one of a handful of proprietary trading teams taking large index arbitrage positions in the Japanese markets, and Sasaki had been in charge of those operations. In their joint article, Aoki and Sasaki sought to refute critics' claims point by point. First, Aoki and Sasaki examined the movements of the Nikkei 225 index on the days of February 26, 1990, and April 2, 1990, when the stock market crashed. In their observation, on both days, the index futures fell so dramatically in the morning trading session that futures ceased to serve as effective hedging tools. This prompted general investors to start selling their stocks in the cash market and drove the index down. Aoki and Sasaki pointed out that, in fact, arbitrageurs prevented the index from falling further in the afternoon session of each day by engaging in cash-and-carry arbitrage between the Nikkei 225 futures contract traded at the Singapore Mercantile Exchange (SIMEX) and its underlying basket of stocks traded at the Tokyo Stock Exchange.

Aoki and Sasaki also disputed the claim that index arbitrage–related positions in the cash market caused investors to rush to sell their portfolios. In their view, there was no necessary correlation between cash-and-carry arbitrage and stock market crashes. They reminded the reader of a similar situation in 1989, in which index arbitrage–related positions in the cash market attracted much media attention but the stock market did not crash. They also added that arbitrageurs often rolled over their positions instead of dissolving their positions to cash in their profit. In fact, Sekai arbitrageurs' self-imposed policy at that time was to roll over their arbitrage positions as long as the difference between the futures contract that had reached its settlement date and the futures contract with a settlement date three months later did not exceed 130 yen.

At the end of their article, Aoki and Sasaki discussed three different types of players in futures markets—hedgers, speculators, and arbitrageurs. According to Aoki and Sasaki, hedgers are investors who hold a portfolio of stocks and use futures contracts to hedge the risk of price fluctuations in the cash market, while speculators are willing to bet on their prediction regarding the direction of the market. For Aoki and Sasaki, arbitrageurs play a dynamic and integrative role in the market by exploiting the discrepancy between the value of the futures contract and the value of its underlying assets. In other words, arbitrageurs facilitate a closer linkage between the futures markets and the cash markets and thereby enable futures contracts to serve as effective risk management tools. This is a standard description of the composition of the futures market used in textbooks of financial economics, such as John C. Hull's widely used *Options, Futures, and Other Derivatives,* which many Sekai traders trained under Aoki regarded as their "bible" (*baiburu*) and meticulously studied.

In practical terms, however, a clear distinction between arbitrage and speculation cannot be easily sustained. The category of arbitrage remained elusive for Sekai Securities arbitrageurs themselves, and in actual arbitrage operations, the difference between arbitrage and speculation was often blurred. Aoki, Sasaki, and other Sekai traders often articulated this blurring in terms of two essential definitions of arbitrage regularly found in financial economics textbooks: the idea of arbitrage as "risk-free" trading, and the idea of arbitrage as market efficiency–generating trading. More importantly, such ambiguity defined arbitrage and shaped the particular kind of commitment arbitrageurs had to the category of arbitrage itself.

ARBITRAGE VERSUS SPECULATION

Given the centrality of arbitrage to both financial economics and financial markets, it is not surprising that arbitrage has recently surfaced as a focus of intense debate in the social studies of finance (see Beunza, Hardie, and MacKenzie 2006; Beunza and Stark 2004, 2005; Hardie 2004; MacKenzie 2001, 2003a, 2003b, 2006, 2009; MacKenzie and Millo 2003; see also H. Miyazaki 2003, 2005b, 2007, 2010b). In fact, it is arbitrage's prominence in both theory and practice that has made it such an attractive subject for these scholars. Donald MacKenzie has extended Michel Callon's thesis concerning the place of economic theories in the market to analyze what MacKenzie terms the "performativity of finance theory" (MacKenzie 2001: 130) in his "sociology of arbitrage." MacKenzie asserts, "Finance theory itself has played an important role in its assumptions becoming more realistic" (p. 133). The convergence between finance theory and the market, according to MacKenzie, takes place in particular through arbitrage (see MacKenzie

2001, 2003a, 2003b; MacKenzie and Millo 2003): "Finance theory is itself drawn on by modern arbitrageurs, so arbitrage is a key issue for the 'performativity' of economics: the thesis that economics creates the phenomena it describes, rather than describing an already existing 'economy.' . . . To the extent that arbitrageurs can eliminate the price discrepancies that finance theory helps them to identify, they thereby render the theory performative: price patterns in the markets become as described by the theory" (MacKenzie 2003b: 350–351).

MacKenzie's project has focused on investigating empirically the extent to which arbitrage generates this effect (see MacKenzie 2003a, 2003b, 2006; MacKenzie and Millo 2003). Ultimately, he argues that arbitrage operations are social and even sociological, in that they are always conscious of other arbitrageurs and are often constrained by the capital available to them. He suggests that, for this reason, the concept of arbitrage should serve as an important linkage between financial economics and economic sociology (see MacKenzie 2003a, 2003b, 2006; see also Beunza, Hardie, and MacKenzie 2006: 741).

From a somewhat different sociological perspective, Daniel Beunza and David Stark also focus on arbitrage in their study of a Wall Street trading room. In their view, arbitrage is "the trading strategy that best represents the distinctive combination of connectivity, knowledge and computing that we regard as the defining feature of the quantitative revolution in finance" (Beunza and Stark 2004: 370). If MacKenzie has focused on evaluating the effectiveness of the concept of arbitrage in linking financial economics to financial markets, Beunza and Stark insist on the importance of a more microsociological approach. This approach is closer to the so-called laboratory studies originally developed by Karin Knorr-Cetina, Bruno Latour and Steve Woolgar, Michael Lynch, and others in their work on scientific laboratories (see, e.g., Knorr-Cetina 1981; Latour 1987; Latour and Woolgar [1979] 1986; Lynch 1985) and recently applied by Knorr-Cetina and Urs Bruegger and others to the study of financial markets (see, e.g., Knorr-Cetina and Bruegger 2000, 2002). According to Beunza and Stark, arbitrage consists of "an art of association": "Arbitrage constitutes a distinctive trading strategy that operates by making associations among securities. . . . The peculiar valuation that takes place in arbitrage is based on an operation that makes something the measure of something else, associating securities to each other" (Beunza and Stark 2004: 374).

Approaching the trading room as a laboratory, Beunza and Stark demonstrate how the arrangement of computers and desks enables particular forms of cognition, interpretation, and innovation. In particular, the spatial arrangement of the trading room enables arbitrage's central procedure of association across different kinds of assets. The placement of trading desks specializing in different kinds of arbitrage operations, customized according to their respective "principle of valuation" and equipped with different calculative devices and mathematical formulas, facilitates information sharing, cooperation, and coordination across the trading desks. This has created an "ecology of diverse evaluative principles" (Beunza and Stark 2004: 374).

The starting premise of all these projects is that actual arbitrage operations are different from the textbook definitions of arbitrage, such as the one in John C. Hull's widely referenced financial economics textbook: "Arbitrage involves locking in a riskless profit by entering simultaneously into transactions in two or more markets" (Hull 1997: 12).[4] After quoting Hull's definition, Beunza and Stark point out that actual arbitrage operations are not so simple: "Reducing arbitrage to an unproblematic operation that links the obvious (gold in London, gold in New York), as textbook treatments do, is doubly misleading, for modern arbitrage is neither obvious nor unproblematic. It provides profit opportunities by associating the unexpected, and it entails real exposure to substantial losses" (Beunza and Stark 2004: 374).

Likewise, MacKenzie points out that almost no arbitrage is risk-free: "In finance theory, arbitrage is conceived as involving no risk and demanding no capital. . . . Much 'real-world' arbitrage involves risk and demands capital" (MacKenzie 2003b: 353; see also Beunza, Hardie, and MacKenzie 2006: 724). What interests me about both of these projects is their failure to examine a standard typology underlying this textbook definition of arbitrage. In the textbook mentioned above, Hull situates arbitrageurs as one of three types of participants in the derivatives markets:

> Traders of derivatives can be categorized as hedgers, speculators, or arbitrageurs. . . . Hedgers are interested in reducing a risk that they already face. . . . Whereas hedgers want to eliminate an exposure to movements in the price of an asset, speculators wish to take a position in the market. Either they are betting that a price will go up or they are betting that it will go down. . . . Arbitrageurs are a third important group of participants in derivatives markets. (Hull 1997: 10–12)

In Hull's typology, the three types of market participants are distinguished from one another by their different approaches to risk. Hedgers seek to reduce the risk they confront. Speculators actively take risks.

Arbitrageurs engage in risk-free trading.[5] The three types of market participants also correspond to three different temporal locations in the market. Hedgers enter derivatives markets in order to reduce their exposure to a "risk that they already face"; speculators bet on the future direction of the market; arbitrageurs take positions in more than two economically related markets simultaneously. There is a long genealogy of such typology in writings on financial markets.[6]

The work of Beunza and Stark and of MacKenzie does not challenge this typology. On the contrary, it solidifies it by presenting arbitrage as something unique and different from other forms of trading (see Hardie 2004: 240). In Beunza and Stark's work, arbitrage is regarded as "an art of association": "Arbitrage constitutes a distinctive trading strategy that operates by making associations among securities" (Beunza and Stark 2004: 374). In MacKenzie's work, arbitrage becomes an important linkage between financial economics and financial markets, and potentially even between financial economics and economic sociology.

Starting from the same preoccupation as Beunza, Stark, and MacKenzie with the difference between the "theory" and "practice" of arbitrage, Iain Hardie instead proposes a narrower definition of arbitrage, which he maintains is "closer to the reality of the financial markets" (p. 240). In Hardie's view, only those operations that are truly and objectively "guaranteed" (p. 245) to produce a risk-free profit should fall under the analytical category of arbitrage. His larger point is that the typological treatment of arbitrageurs has prevented a "broader consideration of investor activity" (p. 240). Hardie argues, "The bulk of what are termed arbitrageurs do not represent a separate investor type, to be contrasted analytically from the bulk of investors who are 'noise traders' or irrational. . . . The vast majority of investors share similar approaches and rationality" (p. 240).

Despite the commitment of all of these projects to understanding the practice of arbitrage, what is lacking in each, ironically, is attention to the practical uses by market participants themselves of the textbook description of arbitrage and the accompanying typology of market participants. In what follows, therefore, I put the "theory" versus "practice" question aside and examine how market participants use the textbook typology of market participants. In particular, I examine arbitrageurs' own use of the typology generally and of the category of arbitrage specifically. As Hardie implies, arbitrageurs' own use of the category is also "inconsistent" (Hardie 2004: 239–243).

The inconsistent uses to which the category of arbitrage is put raises ethical issues. I argue that this inconsistency is symptomatic of a particular kind of epistemological stance that arbitrageurs strive to maintain, a particular kind of identity that they seek to cultivate, and most importantly, a particular kind of ethical commitment to ambiguity that the category demands. I examine arbitrageurs' own divergent, yet uniformly ambiguous, efforts to differentiate themselves from other market participants, such as "speculators." Here I seek to demonstrate that the textbook typology of market participants is generative not only of different approaches to the market but also of different modalities of engagement with the typology itself.

RISK-FREE ARBITRAGE

If financial economics textbooks often define arbitrage as a risk-free operation, realist descriptions of arbitrage posit it as a fundamentally risky operation. This realist description of arbitrage has been developed in the work of social studies of finance scholars, including Daniel Beunza, David Stark, Donald MacKenzie, and others, as well as by behavioral finance scholars, such as Andrei Shleifer and Robert W. Vishny (Shleifer and Vishny 1997).

Sekai Securities arbitrageurs took it as common sense that actual arbitrage operations are risky and do not follow the textbook version of arbitrage. No Sekai trader actually believed that his arbitrage operations were risk-free. Sekai arbitrageurs' understanding of their own index arbitrage operations in the late 1980s and early 1990s was a case in point. From one point of view, the arbitrage between the futures contract on the Nikkei 225, traded at the Osaka Stock Exchange, and its underlying basket of stocks, traded at the Tokyo Stock Exchange—two economically related assets in two different geographical locales—seems to epitomize the textbook definition of arbitrage.

Sekai arbitrageurs pointed out to me that in actual arbitrage operations they needed to take various kinds of risks for different reasons. First, they complained that management at Sekai did not understand arbitrage and regularly interfered with their activities. Like most other Japanese securities firms at the time, Sekai derived most of its revenue from commissions the firm received from its clients. Sekai's most important clients were institutional investors, such as banks and insurance companies, whose shares were included in the Nikkei 225 index, and they did not like the fluctuation of the price of their shares caused by Sekai's index arbitrage operations. Consequently, according to Sekai traders, Sekai's management did not allow its arbitrage team to freely buy and sell all of the 225 stocks. It did not value proprietary trading and sided with the firm's sales forces, who earned a commission when there was a conflict between the proprietary trading team and the firm's sales forces and their clients. As a result, Sekai arbitrageurs often avoided trading those company shares and instead replicated a basket of stocks whose movement would only roughly track the index. In the arbitrageurs' view, management's interference created a situation in which they needed to take unnecessary risks.

Second, the traders in Aoki's team were often forced to close their positions prematurely because of momentary nominal loss caused by an unexpected movement in the market, even if they believed that eventually they would regain their loss. In trading futures on the Nikkei 225 index, as members of the Osaka Stock Exchange, securities firms are required to deposit a "margin"—a certain percentage of the value of a futures contract—with the exchange. This margin is adjusted according to the daily fluctuation of the price of the contract. Because at the settlement date the value of the index future and the value of the index are made to converge, index arbitrage operations using futures on the Nikkei 225 index are theoretically risk-free. However, this is only the case if one holds one's arbitraging position until the settlement date of the futures contract.

Third, and perhaps most significant, Sekai arbitrageurs did not always trade futures and their underlying stocks simultaneously. This was partly because various technological constraints prevented them from making timely executions and partly because, in their view, success in index arbitrage often depended on successful "speculation" on the timing of the trades (see also Avril 2000: 29–30).

Yet, despite their appreciation of the speculative nature of arbitrage, Sekai arbitrageurs still held onto the textbook distinction between arbitrage and speculation. Although they all agreed that they would need to take risks in their arbitrage operations, they blamed the specific institutional and technological obstacles they faced within their firm for causing their arbitrage operations to deviate from the textbook version of arbitrage. From their point of view, the speculative trades they needed to make did not make their operations simply speculative. In their conceptualization, those speculative trades were subsumed under the rubric of risk-free arbitrage.

Tada, who oversaw Sekai's arbitrage operations in the mid- and late 1990s, told me in 2000 that, in his view, arbitrage had served as a kind of "framework" (*wakugumi*). He said that he had encouraged his traders to pursue every kind of mispricing as a potential arbitrage opportunity, including that between individual stocks within the "framework" of index arbitrage operations. This meant that his traders would search for individual stocks that were undervalued relative to other related stocks, while simultaneously holding arbitrage positions in the index futures contract and its underlying basket of stocks. Technically, Tada admitted to me, such trades in individual stocks would count as speculation, but in his view, those trades were made within the "framework" of arbitrage.

Tada also said that the "framework" of arbitrage could easily fall apart if the speculative aspect of trading was stretched too far. He mentioned the much-discussed case of Long-Term Capital Management (LTCM) as an example. According to Tada, the hedge fund's trading strategy was based on arbitrage and was not inherently wrong; LTCM simply became overconfident and increased its leverage too much, and hence its arbitrage became nothing but speculation. Underlying Tada's understanding of the failure of LTCM's arbitrage was an assumption that an arbitrage operation could remain risk-free as long as one kept one's positions within the limits of the capital at one's disposal. In other words, too much arbitrage becomes speculation.[7]

In all of these reflections on the ambiguous and delicate distinction between arbitrage and speculation, therefore, Sekai arbitrageurs upheld the textbook distinction between risk-free arbitrage and risky speculation, which in fact helped them to articulate their own ambiguous sense of the difference between the two. An examination of the traders' understanding of the relationship between arbitrage and market efficiency makes this point clearer.

EFFICIENCY AS CAUSE AND EFFECT

The efficient-market hypothesis, that is, the assumption that financial markets can be regarded as efficient because "prices always 'fully reflect' available information" (Fama 1970: 383), is a controversial proposition (see, e.g., Henwood [1997] 1998: 161–183; MacKenzie 2006: 65–67, 94–98; Shiller [2000] 2001: 171–190). According to Donald MacKenzie, however, the efficient-market hypothesis has played a significant role in financial markets. He notes that financial economics and its underlying assumptions, especially the assumption regarding market efficiency, have served as resources of justification and legitimacy in the financial markets (MacKenzie 2006: 251–252): "To say of a financial market that it is 'efficient'—that its prices incorporate, nearly instantaneously, all available price-relevant information—is to say something commendatory about it, and that has been what orthodox financial economics has said about the central capital markets of the advanced industrial world" (p. 251). MacKenzie goes on to suggest that the efficient-market hypothesis often enables arbitrageurs to discover arbitrage opportunities: "The [efficient-market] hypothesis provided a systematic framework within which researchers identified 'anomalies': market phenomena at variance with the hypothesis. Most of those researchers had an efficient-market viewpoint. . . . Once anomalies were identified, they were often made the object of trading strategies that, in general, seem to have had the effect of reducing their size or even of eliminating them" (pp. 255–256). On the basis of this observation, MacKenzie remarks: "Practical action informed by efficient-market theory thus had the effect, at least sometimes, of making markets more consistent with their portrayal by the theory" (p. 256).

As I discussed at the beginning of this chapter, the idea of market efficiency, and of the active role arbitrageurs play in achieving it, also served as a key concept for Sekai arbitrageurs in their efforts to legitimize their arbitrage operations in the early 1990s, when index arbitrage operations became a regulatory target of the Japanese government's Ministry of Finance (see, e.g., M. Miller 1997: 29–34). Recall that in their response to the media criticism of the negative impact of arbitrage on the cash market, Aoki and Sasaki reproduced the textbook description of arbitrage's economic function and asserted that arbitrage performed the important economic function of linking the cash and futures markets so that investors might use the futures markets for hedging. Here the textbook definition of arbitrage served for arbitrageurs as a source of legitimacy (H. Miyazaki 2005b: 171–172).

However, for Sekai traders, the efficiency-generating component of arbitrage was more than a rhetorical source of legitimacy. It was also a marker of their unique epistemological stance. One manifestation of this stance was found in their view of prediction, in which, unlike speculators, arbitrageurs should not be interested in claiming any specific knowledge of future price movements. Arbitrage was predicated precisely on the impossibility of such knowledge. In place of prediction, arbitrageurs focused rather on detecting what they called "anomalies" (*yugami,* literally "distortions"), or signs of market inefficiency. For example, Koyama, a chemical engineer turned options trader, told me that he always tried to make profits in the way the market returns to equilibrium. He said, "I do not care about whether the market goes up or down tomorrow, but I can tell when someone throws a stone into a pond. I can statistically deal with the way the waves disappear" (February 2000). Underlying Koyama's focus on present anomalies was his distrust in his own capacity to predict the future direction of the market.

Sekai arbitrageurs' distrust of their own capacity to predict price movements also resonated with their collective commitment to discipline and rationality (see also H. Miyazaki 2006b). Tanaka, who joined Sekai Securities after studying econometrics at college, was part of Sekai's stock index arbitrage team in the early 1990s and later became a convertible bond trader at a European investment bank. For him, arbitrage demanded a commitment to trading within the limits of rational calculation. Tanaka told me in May 2000, "Speculation just does not suit my inclination. . . . Arbitrage demands a mechanical response, which in turn requires discipline. It is a craft. . . . I am not interested in speculation because I do not trust my own opinion [about the market]."

Many of the traders who had been assigned to Sekai's index arbitrage operations in the late 1980s and early 1990s mentioned a similar analogy to "craftsmanship" (*shokuningei*). Arbitrage was not so much about the correctness of one's knowledge about the market as one's ability to respond in a disciplined manner to anomalies. Tanaka noted that "arbitrage is like table tennis—you just respond to what comes to you, although you can be a little creative by adding some spin, etc. If you try to do too much, the ball will go beyond the lines" (July 2000). Here arbitrageurs were willing to subject themselves to what they regarded as objective and rational rules (see H. Miyazaki 2006b). In their view, the market as a collectivity of rational actors needed to be met with an equally rational approach.

As should be clear by now, these arbitrageurs' distrust of their own predictive capacity coexisted with a faith-like commitment to the market's general inclination toward equilibrium and a state of efficiency, and ultimately their belief in the market's underlying rationality. The traders held a deep utopian conviction that they were contributing to society by making it more efficient. In other words, despite their skepticism about the efficacy of their own prediction, they saw themselves as agents of a wider market efficiency. Tanaka told me, "There is something meaningless [*munashii*] about speculation. At least arbitrage contributes to society by driving the market to efficiency" (July 2000). At the same time, Tanaka admitted to himself, "It is true that what I do now can be called speculation. Yesterday's volatility was 40 percent.[8] Today's is 39 percent. Is this really true? I don't know" (July 2000).

Underlying this coexistence of belief and doubt was a circularity central to arbitrageurs' conception of their own agency. To the extent that arbitrageurs sought to eliminate what they saw as market anomalies, they believed that their own arbitrage work would eventually rid the market of arbitrage opportunities both for themselves and for other arbitrageurs. In reality, of course, more arbitrage opportunities would become available elsewhere, or in the same market in the future. Nevertheless, the traders held onto the belief that, by their own acts, they would eliminate the reason for their own existence. I call this phenomenon the "self-closing propensity" of arbitrage, and I examine Sekai arbitrageurs' various visions of an endpoint to arbitrage and what might come after arbitrage in the chapters that follow (see also H. Miyazaki 2003, 2006b, 2009b).

In these arbitrageurs' view, the propensity toward market efficiency was a given fact about the market independent of their own specific choices or intentions. Even if they themselves did not engage in stock index arbitrage, other market participants would quickly take advantage of arbitrage opportunities. As Koyama once told me of Sekai's early stock index arbitrage operations, "If we did not do it, someone else would have" (March 2000). Underlying this view was an assumption that arbitrageurs are an intrinsic part of the market's internal price adjustment mechanism. Sekai arbitrageurs therefore reasoned that the market had become more efficient when their arbitrage operations became less profitable. In this circular, and somewhat paradoxical, logic, they were at once active agents and substitutable elements of market efficiency.

This circularity is critical to arbitrage and its extensibility. In their conceptualization of arbitrage, Sekai arbitrageurs sought to sustain this double vision of the market as self-correcting and arbitrageurs themselves as agents of that market force. It is easy to see that this leaves little space for responsibility for their own actions. Ultimately, arbitrageurs are nothing but utopians, in the sense of the term in which Karl Polanyi once described the view of a self-correcting market (Polanyi

[1944] 1957: 3). In other words, arbitrage simultaneously presupposes and is oriented towards an admittedly unrealistic vision of market efficiency. However, it is important to note that sustaining this vision itself demands a rather complex maneuver on the part of arbitrageurs, and it is in the intellectual labor they perform and its unexpected consequences that their sense of social responsibility resides.

AN ECONOMY OF BELIEF AND DOUBT

The ambiguity of these arbitrageurs' conception of their own agency resonates with the ambiguity that permeated their understanding of the difference between arbitrage and speculation. First, they insisted that arbitrage was at once risk-free and risky. In articulating this, Sekai arbitrageurs adhered to the textbook distinction between arbitrage and speculation but alluded to the real possibility that their arbitrage operations could easily become speculation.

Second, arbitrageurs presented themselves as at once occupying a specific market positionality and being part of a more general market mechanism. Here again, the circular logic in the textbook definition of arbitrage—that market efficiency or the condition of no arbitrage can be assumed because of the presence of arbitrageurs—allowed the Sekai arbitrageurs to keep this ambiguity in view.

Third, arbitrage was at once particular and universal. For Aoki, who had introduced the concept of arbitrage to his team, arbitrage stood for rationality, as manifested in the mathematics and the technology entailed in arbitrage operations. When Aoki introduced the notion of arbitrage to the Japanese securities firm, he presented it as a more rational and more scientific alternative to an approach to the market characterized by "intuition, guts, and charts" (*kan to dokyo to chato*). In Aoki's view, therefore, speculation and arbitrage represented very different modalities of engagement with the market: the first was based on one's belief in oneself, and the second was based on the limits of such belief. Aoki's traders, such as Sasaki, also were persuaded that arbitrage was the fundamental principle of capitalism. The slipperiness of their nonbelief in belief can be illustrated by Aoki's own slippage, which his traders repeatedly mentioned to me. Even Aoki sometimes insisted that speculators were engaged in nothing but arbitrage, albeit unconsciously, although he usually later retracted the statement. In this reasoning, the categorical differentiation between arbitrage and speculation again collapsed, albeit in a reverse fashion to the way arbitrage became speculation. Despite his traders' strong commitment to the category of arbitrage, however, Aoki repeatedly insisted to me that arbitrage was simply a theoretical construct based on the efficient-market hypothesis. He told me in August 2001, "[The efficient-market hypothesis] is nothing but a hypothesis. As long as you stick with it, it would be upheld." Aoki made this comment to me as he elaborated on his general philosophy about the importance of not believing in one idea: "People tend to have faith in something. You should not have faith in anything."

This combination of belief and doubt was central to the Sekai arbitrageurs' understanding of arbitrage. They shared a commitment to resisting speculation as a mode of engagement with the market. Yet they were also willing to entertain moments of doubt about this distinction. Perhaps their arbitrage operations were nothing but speculation. Alternatively, everything that takes place in the market could be seen as arbitrage.

There was a consistent doubleness to arbitrageurs' apprehension of their arbitrage operations. The arbitrageurs saw themselves as engaged in risky speculation while remaining within the framework of risk-free arbitrage. They saw themselves as contributing to society by realizing market efficiency while also seeing themselves simply as part of the general market dynamism and the market's tendency toward efficiency. This persistent perspective on the doubleness of their positionality was generative of what I view as an ethical commitment to embracing ambiguity and the unknowability of the market. As either a "framework" or an object of "belief," the category of arbitrage demanded the embrace of its ambiguity, the resulting mixture of belief and doubt, and the work required to maintain such ambiguity.

For the Sekai arbitrageurs, then, what distinguished arbitrage from other modalities of engagement with the market was this combination of belief and doubt and its resulting ambiguity. This ambiguity derived from the arbitrageurs' particular perspective on the textbook typology of market participants. More precisely, the textbook distinction between arbitrage and speculation allowed arbitrageurs to articulate the ambiguity of arbitrage and the combination of belief in and doubt about it.

Despite their appreciation for the fuzziness of the distinction between arbitrage and speculation, Sekai traders still held onto the distinctiveness of the category of arbitrage, which they insistently extended to various investments and other facets of life. This was because, for them, arbitrage was more than a regulatory category or a trading practice; it served as an object of a particular ethical commitment and attachment. Their commitment to arbitrage revolved around not so much the difference between theory and practice as the ambiguity of the category itself. Arbitrageurs often see market efficiency when they are unable to detect arbitrage opportunities. That is, arbitrage is seen as exploiting inefficient markets and contributing to market efficiency, but the idea of an efficient market itself enables arbitrage opportunities to be apprehended as arbitrage opportunities (MacKenzie 2006).

ARBITRAGE AS AN IDEAL TYPE

Categories such as hedgers, speculators, and arbitrageurs are what we might call ideal types. All market participants necessarily engage in at least two of the trading strategies these categories represent. Sekai traders both hedged their positions and speculated in the context of their arbitrage operations. For traders, this did not mean that the category of arbitrage should be abandoned. On the contrary, from the traders' point of view, they were arbitrageurs, not hedgers or speculators. In other words, the category of arbitrage was an important marker of a particular epistemological stance, identity, and ethical commitment and had some important practical functions and implications for its users. Arbitrage's logical circularity and semantic fluidity ironically affords the category a particular kind of productivity.

In considering the interplay of categories of economic analysis, such as speculators and arbitrageurs, one might recall two classic works on ideal types in sociology and anthropology, respectively: the work of Max Weber and Edmund Leach. In *Economy and Society* and other writings, Weber famously discusses the uses of ideal types, such as *homo economicus,* in economic theory (see Swedberg 2005: 74, 119): "The concepts and 'laws' of pure economic theory are examples of this kind of ideal type. They state what course a given type of human action would take if it were strictly rational, unaffected by errors or emotional factors and if, furthermore, it were completely and unequivocally directed to a single end, the maximization of economic advantage. In reality, action takes exactly this course only in unusual cases, as sometimes on the stock exchange; and even then there is usually only an approximation to the ideal type" (Weber [1922] 1978: 9). Weber's broader discussion focuses on the utility of such concepts as categories of social scientific analysis, and it is anchored in the general question of how models relate to realities (see also Parsons 1937). This question, which permeates the sociology of financial markets, does not necessarily shed much light on economic actors' own uses of these ideal types.

My discussion of the relationship between arbitrage and speculation is closer to the anthropologist Edmund Leach's discussion of "as if" descriptions in *Political Systems of Highland Burma* (see also Comaroff and Comaroff 1992: 22–25; Riles 2010). In that work, Leach identifies three contrasting forms of political organization among Kachins—*gumsa, gumlao,* and Shan—according to their respective emphasis on the principles of equality and hierarchy: "In this book my descriptions of *gumsa, gumlao* and Shan patterns of organisation are largely *as if* descriptions—they relate to ideal models rather than real societies, and what I have been trying to do is to present a convincing model of what happens when such *as if* systems interact" (Leach [1954] 1970: 285; original emphases). Note Leach's attention to interaction. What concerns Leach is not so much the empirical reality of those ideal systems as the dynamism between them. In other words, Leach deploys "as if" constructs to generate a dynamic model of social action.[9]

According to Leach, this deployment of ideal types reflects an indigenous model of society: "My claim is that Kachins and Shans actually think of their own society in this sort of way. Kachins *themselves* tend to think of the difference between *gumsa* and *gumlao* and the difference between *gumsa* and Shan as being differences of the same general kind. Further they recognize that these differences are not absolute—individuals may change from one category into another (Leach [1954] 1970: 285–286; original emphases).

Sekai arbitrageurs' use of the distinction between arbitrage and speculation resonates with the use of ideal types among Kachins and Shans as described by Leach. In both cases, the use of a typology generates an effect of dynamic oscillation between ideal types. Like the Kachins and Shans in Leach's work, Sekai arbitrageurs were well aware of the fact that hedgers, speculators, and arbitrageurs are "as if" categories. In their opinion, the difference between speculators and arbitrageurs was particularly fuzzy. These self-designated arbitrageurs often referred to the possibility that the very distinction on which their identity was founded might not stand. Yet they also insisted on their identification with and commitment to the category of arbitrage. More precisely, they identified themselves with the category's ambiguity. Instead of doing away with the distinction between arbitrage and speculation, they traded as if they were arbitrageurs, not speculators.

The textbook typology helped the arbitrageurs to keep this "as if" stance in view.

The "as if" quality of arbitrage points to the asymmetrical relationship between arbitrage and speculation. In arbitrageurs' view, arbitrage easily collapsed into speculation. It was as though speculation was a default position, whereas arbitrage was a delicate achievement. What concerns me, therefore, is not so much the relationship between the theory of arbitrage and actual arbitrage operations, as has been the focus of the sociology of financial markets, but rather the elusive quality of the category of arbitrage. What is striking about the "as if" contrast between arbitrage and speculation is its capacity to point to the *work* the category demands of its users in order to sustain its own ambiguity and associated productivity.

ARBITRAGE AND AMBIGUITY

In the final chapter of his book *An Engine, Not a Camera: How Financial Models Shape Markets,* Donald MacKenzie discusses what he terms the "ambivalence of finance theory" (MacKenzie 2006: 247). He refers to financial economists' "capacity both to be committed to a model and, simultaneously, to doubt the extent of its empirical validity." He continues: "Finance theorists believed that markets were made efficient by the actions of arbitrageurs and other knowledgeable investors, so there was no contradiction in those theorists seeking to take these actions themselves. Nevertheless, that they did so shows that they did not construe market efficiency as an already-achieved fact. Rather, the achievement of efficiency was a process—perhaps an endless process—in which they could themselves sometimes take part and from which they could profit" (p. 248).

MacKenzie's attention to the ambivalence of financial economists with regard to their own theoretical constructs reverberates with my ethnographic observations about Japanese arbitrageurs' sense of ambiguity concerning their own arbitrage operations and the theoretical assumptions underlying those operations. However, what primarily concerns financial economists (and MacKenzie) is different from what concerned the arbitrageurs I studied. For the latter, the mixed sense of belief and doubt that arbitrage entailed did not have much to do with the relationship between theory and practice or the empirical validity of theoretical assumptions associated with arbitrage, such as the efficient-market hypothesis. They were well aware of the discrepancy between theory and practice. Rather, the arbitrageurs' sense of the ambiguity of the category of arbitrage and its resulting simultaneous presence and absence was a defining feature of their own identity in contrast with speculators, who in their view tended to believe too much in themselves and their opinions. In this way, Sekai arbitrageurs were capable of selectively appropriating, and also being constrained by, the textbook typology of traders. Attention to the way arbitrage appears and disappears on arbitrageurs' own epistemological and ontological horizon points to the centrality of what I call an economy of belief and doubt and of ambiguity in financial trading. From arbitrageurs' own point of view, in other words, the category of arbitrage was elusive and even precarious, and it demanded both ethical commitment and deep skepticism. The arbitrageurs were not pulled to the two directions (of arbitrage and speculation), nor were they ambivalent about their position between these two ideal types. The ethical commitment to the category was possible despite its doubtful status precisely because the category stood for ambiguity. Their belief was a belief in ambiguity itself.

The sociological debate about arbitrage has revolved around the tension between the textbook definition of arbitrage and actual arbitrage operations and has sought to redefine the category in terms of the latter. If MacKenzie's work examines the sociologically conditioned recursive relationship between arbitraging practices and their underlying theoretical assumptions, Beunza and Stark define arbitrage in terms of its associational logic. In contrast to these works that have, in my view, unintentionally solidified the category of arbitrage, Hardie has sought to dissolve the typology of traders itself by adopting an intentionally narrow definition of arbitrage.

What seems to be missing on both sides of this debate is attention to the way the category of arbitrage, and the typology of traders, functions in the financial markets. In the case of Sekai traders, the category of arbitrage generated a particular kind of ambiguous engagement with the practice of arbitrage and the textbook typology of speculators and arbitrageurs more generally. It is my contention that in its rush to reintroduce realism, or to make financial categories "more precise" (Hardie 2004: 243), the sociology of arbitrage has inadvertently erased the dynamism of belief and doubt in the market that is such a central aspect of market practice. In this chapter, I have drawn attention to the fundamentally ambiguous nature of the category of arbitrage and have sought to recapture that ambiguity. The Sekai arbitrageurs' own embrace of the ambiguity of arbitrage suggests that the real challenge for the sociology of arbitrage resides in whether sociologists may be able to sustain an equally dynamic relationship between belief in and doubt about their own analytical category of arbitrage.[10]

It is such ambiguity that allows the category of arbitrage to be stretched to various objects of arbitrage. Ambiguity allows associational reasoning. Arbitrage's relativistic stance in turn requires its further extensions. In the trajectories of the Sekai derivatives team's operations and business ventures, the object of arbitrage shifted from the Nikkei 225 stock index to TOPIX, convertible bonds, and other assets. Arbitrage sensibility has been extended further to newer forms of business, including securitization and mergers and acquisitions. Each time the category of arbitrage is extended, the category has become more ambiguous. For my interlocutor-traders, arbitrage soon became more than a trading strategy and a theoretical construct. Ultimately, it became an ethical commitment to a certain relativistic perspective on everything.

My attention to ambiguity here is different from the long-standing attention to the positive and negative functions of ambiguity in organizational sociology and management studies (see, e.g., March and Olson 1979; see also March 2010). My focus is on the tricky problem of how to capture both ambiguity and its absence in arbitrageurs' reflexive work. In other words, using arbitrage as a modality of ethnographic engagement calls for a certain attentiveness to the way it evaporates as it is explicitly put to use. The overall structure of the book is meant to capture this precariousness, which is inherent in the practice of arbitrage. My goal is to retain and replicate arbitrageurs' consistent sense of the simultaneous presence and absence of arbitrage itself in my own analysis.

BETTING ON THE WILL NOT TO BET

There is certainly an element of faith in arbitrage and its underlying assumptions, such as the assumption that the prices of two economically equivalent assets and commodities will converge. Even if the price difference between such assets or commodities widens unexpectedly, arbitrageurs believe they need only wait for the eventual convergence of prices, as long as they have access to sufficient funds to finance their trading positions.

These are all theoretical assumptions and fictions. They may even be false. But arbitrageurs take these assumptions as the basis of their market action. In speculation, traders bet on their own judgments, opinions, and predictions; they bet on themselves. They are consistent in this. In contrast, arbitrageurs are skeptical of their own judgments, opinions, and predictions. They entertain a much more relativistic view of the market. In other words, if arbitrageurs bet at all, they bet not on themselves but on this relativistic market positionality. They bet on their *will not to bet.*

Here I am not simply repeating the truism that there is nothing certain and predetermined in the world, and that every action can be regarded as an act of wagering. In contrast to this view, arbitrage entails a will to embrace the world's uncertainty, indeterminacy, and ultimate unknowability and to maintain a relativistic perspective.

In order to appreciate further arbitrageurs' willingness to embrace ambiguity, uncertainty, and unknowability, I return to the article that Aoki and Sasaki coauthored in 1990, this time to examine another important purpose that the paper served: the training of Sasaki in rational thinking. In this book, *rationality,* like *trust* and *risk,* is not my analytical term (cf. Beck 1992; Ewald 1991; Weber [1930] 1992; Yamagishi, Cook, and Watabe 1998). Rather, as in other work on the Japanese fascination with rationalization (*gorika*) in a wide range of social spheres at various points in the twentieth century, these are concepts the actors themselves deployed to analyze their present and reorient their knowledge for the future (see, e.g., Hein 2004; Kelly 1986; Tsutsui 1998).[11]

Upon joining Aoki's team from a doctoral program in mathematical physics in the summer of 1988, Sasaki was assigned to the team's index arbitrage operations. When the Osaka Stock Exchange approached Aoki and asked him to write an article on the economic function of Nikkei 225 stock index arbitrage in order to defend stock index arbitrage operations and index futures trading, more generally, in the midst of the increasingly heightening critique of arbitrage and futures trading, Aoki instructed Sasaki to gather market data to defend their operations in economic terms. Sasaki prepared a number of charts describing the relationship between the value fluctuation of the stock index future and that of the index at the time of the two crashes mentioned at the beginning of this chapter. Sasaki prepared the first draft of their joint article, and Aoki returned Sasaki's draft with numerous comments written in red ink. Sasaki recalled in August 2001 that the draft he had prepared had gone through several rigorous revisions, and he suspected that the final version contained no more than half of his own original text.

Such rigorous editing of young traders' drafts was Aoki's standard method of training in logical reasoning and rational thinking. This particular brand of logicality and rationality was anchored in Aoki's view of the world of the Japanese securities firm as *iikagen* ("careless," and by implication "arbitrary" and "unprincipled") and *higori* ("irrational"). Aoki told me in August 2001, "There are various irrational aspects of the securities firm. Wherever you are, you should not do careless work. You need to choose the kind of profession that demands that of yourself thoroughly. . . . You first need to think clearly and logically, which all depends on to what extent you can refine your own text." Clear and logical thinking was Aoki's response to what he saw as the Japanese firm's irrational world dominated by sales forces that would be willing to bend any rules for the sake of profit. In his view, the firm's sales forces were preoccupied with market share and were not thinking rationally about the overall economic and social roles firms such as Sekai needed to play.

Aoki's commitment to logicality and rationality through rigorous editing of young traders' texts parallels his project of establishing a Wall Street–style proprietary trading team inside the Japanese securities firm. According to Aoki, most Japanese traders focused on selecting stocks that they believed would go up. For Aoki, this "faith" (*shinko*) in perpetual growth (*migikataatari,* literally meaning "with the right shoulder up") was irrational. Arbitrage or relative value trading was based on a more relativistic form of engagement with the market and was not based on such irrational belief. Aoki sought to institute a "scientific" (*kagakuteki*) approach to the market because "humans would not be able to reach God's level" (October 1998), meaning that humans would not be able to master, or even know, the market. He told me in 1998 that he wanted to teach his young traders how to "interact with" (*tsukiau*) the market. Under Aoki's leadership, the education of young traders took for granted the uncertainty, indeterminacy, and unknowability of the market. In internal papers written under Aoki's supervision, there were frequent references to the nature of the market as something uncontrollable.[12] In other words, Aoki's team embodied a series of his own personal ambitions: Aoki sought to rationalize Sekai's approach to the market. Moreover, this project of rationalization was explicitly linked to another, broader, project of rationalization in the market.

Aoki and Sasaki's joint article was one of many that Aoki's team drafted in the context of the industry-wide debate about the future of Japan's derivatives markets in the early 1990s. Some of these articles were written in response to the Osaka Stock Exchange's questionnaire to market participants. Others were submitted to the Ministry of Finance. All stressed that the trading of futures and options was not the cause of the stock market's downturn.[13] They noted that some industry insiders used stock index arbitrage operations as a "scapegoat," and they pointed out that such criticism was a manifestation of Japanese investors' ignorance of the problem of risk and the importance of risk management, on the one hand, and a manifestation of their long-standing faith in the linear growth of the market, on the other.[14]

In these articles, Aoki and his traders also emphasized the importance of a shift to the market mechanism in the Japanese economy. Aoki often cited the argument put forward by Shoichi Royama, then professor of economics at Osaka University and one of the most vocal proponents of financial deregulation at the time. Following the Ministry of Finance's announcement of further regulatory measures aiming to reduce the trading volume of the Nikkei 225 index futures, Royama noted in an interview published in *Nihon Keizai Shinbun* (see also Royama 1997: 179–180), "Proponents of the argument that futures are the culprit criticize arbitrage operations using the difference between futures and cash markets for distorting the price formation process in the cash market. This is entirely untrue. I believe that arbitrage is one of the most important elements in the management of the market economy. . . . Denying arbitrage means denying the market economy."[15] Aoki particularly liked citing Royama's idea of index futures as "international public property" (*kokusai kokyozai*), and Royama's insistence that the market should decide on how index futures should be used.[16] In Aoki's and his traders' opinion, the futures market would promote free competition, which in turn would lead to rationalization and efficiency. Underlying this perspective was an assumption that the Japanese financial markets were irrational and inefficient.

For Aoki, the problem of rationality, in the sense of logicality, lay at the heart of his effort to educate his young traders in the logic of arbitrage. In his view, arbitrage presupposes the fundamental rationality of market action. Central to the idea of arbitrage as the basis of the pricing of derivatives products is the idea that market participants must act rationally, in the sense that they seize arbitrage opportunities when they find them. Without this assumption, arbitrage is impossible. At the same time, arbitrage opportunities only exist when market action is not entirely rational. This paradox in turn entails a peculiar notion of the agency of arbitrageurs. Arbitrageurs are simultaneously individual rational actors and substitutable elements of the general market mechanism. There is a kind of doubleness and ambiguity to these arbitrageurs' commitment to rationality.

In his effort to train Sasaki in logical reasoning, Aoki sought to instill in him a view of the market as fundamentally unknowable. For Aoki, arbitrage, and the kind of rationality it entails, constituted a solution to the epistemological problems presented by the view of the market as unknowable. But this perspective on the market, and the more general view of knowledge that accompanies it, in turn demanded that arbitrageurs develop skepticism about arbitrage itself. This simultaneous faith in and skepticism about arbitrage defined arbitrage in contrast to speculation. The difference between arbitrage and speculation, then, had less to do with their respective economic functions and approaches to risk, as argued in Aoki and Sasaki's paper, than with the delicate vision of two opposing perspectives maintained in their attitude toward belief and doubt in the possibility of achieving market efficiency, rational action, and knowledge itself within their particular market strategy and positionality.

Belief or faith is frequently invoked in the current debate about the global financial crisis. For example, Joseph Stiglitz has pointed to the shaking of "economic beliefs" as a result of the financial crisis. Stiglitz declares, "When the world economy went into freefall in 2008, so too did our beliefs. Long-standing views about economics, about America, and about our heroes have also been in freefall" (Stiglitz 2010: xvi). In his view, the financial crisis "has uncovered fundamental flaws in the capitalist system, or at least the peculiar version of capitalism that emerged in the latter part of the twentieth century in the United States. . . . It is not just a matter of flawed individuals or specific mistakes, nor is it a matter of fixing a few minor problems or tweaking a few policies" (p. xxi). In deploying belief as an analytical framework, Stiglitz draws attention to the need to think broadly about the way we approach financial markets and the economy more generally. Implicit in his argument is the possibility of defining a new set of more humanistic (and more "balanced") values—that is, new objects of belief (see, e.g., p. 17).[17]

It is commonplace to observe that the entire world of money and finance rests on faith (see, e.g., Henwood 1998: 151; Soros 2009:

74–75; Taylor 2004: 286). Marieke de Goede has complicated this observation by noting that "the creation and maintenance of faith in modern currencies is a much more tenuous and unstable project than is generally conceded" (de Goede 2005: xxiv). Underlying her argument is the recognition that faith requires continuous work (see also H. Miyazaki 2000, 2004b). De Goede's analytical attention focuses on instances of the failure of such work as points of critical intervention (see de Goede 2005: xxvi, 150–151).

What still seems lacking in all these references to the role of faith in money and finance, and perhaps in the economy more generally, however, is a nuanced understanding of the different kinds of belief or faith at work in the market. In this book, I draw attention to an ambiguous and subjunctive form of faith entailed in arbitrage. Like de Goede, I also examine the work Sekai Securities arbitrageurs have done to sustain such faith in arbitrage.

Some attention has recently been paid to financial market professionals' reflexive and somewhat murky embrace of the impossibility of achieving certain knowledge of the market at the margins of their quantitative and technocratic modes of analysis (see, e.g., Holmes 2009; Holmes and Marcus 2005; Maurer 2005a, 2005c, 2006b; Miyazaki and Riles 2005; Riles 2004b, 2010, 2011; Thrift 2005; Zaloom 2006). Sekai Securities arbitrageurs' ambiguous faith in arbitrage highlights the need for more sustained ethnographic attention to the central role conceptual ambiguity plays in both finance and its critical accounts.[18] In other words, arbitrageurs' faith invites a more nuanced use of belief and doubt in the critique of capitalism, and the critical study of financial markets, more specifically. The case of Sekai Securities arbitrageurs hints at the possibility that it is not so much financial market professionals' blind faith in finance, as their much murkier and more ambiguous commitment to theories and techniques of finance, that shapes financial markets.

In this light, there is something misleading about Stiglitz's and other critics' indictment of our past collective speculative faith in money and finance. If there is a lesson to be learned from the relatively small Japanese experiment with theories and techniques of finance that I am chronicling in this book, it is the possibility to see the role played by ambiguity, faith, and self-doubt in financial markets. In this recognition of their ambiguous faith in themselves, finance, and capitalism, economic actors appear not as simple decision makers to be regulated, but as thinking subjects.

In order to recapture such doubleness and the resulting ambiguity entailed in the idea of arbitrage both methodologically and ethnographically, I investigate further in the chapters that follow to what extent, and in what way, arbitrage can be sustainable as a framework for my own account of Sekai arbitrageurs' professional and personal intellectual trajectories. In the next two chapters, I investigate the dynamism of arbitrage's extensibility by examining the trajectory of Aoki's and his successor Tada's dream of creating a Japanese proprietary trading team in the Japanese firm over the course of the operation of Sekai's proprietary trading team from 1987 until 1998 and their shared dream's various unintended consequences. Aoki's stance on the market and his effort to train young traders as part of the Japanese firm's overall emphasis on learning generated unexpected outcomes in terms of the traders' experience of arbitrage. I wish to bring into focus the affinity and tension between certain institutional properties of the Japanese securities firm, such as its characteristic incentive structure, and certain properties of theories and techniques of arbitrage, before examining the way arbitrage later began to fall apart as a framework for Sekai arbitrageurs themselves as well as for my own analysis.

CHAPTER 3

Trading on the Limits of Learning

Discipline is a universally popular subject in the financial trading profession.[1] For Sekai Securities traders trained under Aoki, the topic of discipline was tightly linked with the Wall Street securities analyst Jack D. Schwager's popular book *Market Wizards: Interviews with Top Traders*. *Market Wizards* assembles Schwager's interviews with seventeen U.S.-based traders. Schwager's book occupied a particularly important place on the Sekai proprietary trading team's reading list. Among many other lessons for novice traders, Schwager draws particular attention to the importance of discipline, the "word most frequently mentioned" in the interviews he conducted: "Each trader had found a methodology that worked for him and remained true to that approach" (Schwager [1989] 1993: 439).[2]

Sekai traders debated among themselves, and liked discussing with me, the nature of "discipline" (*dishipurin*). They approached the problem of discipline in terms of the question of how to lose in the market. Sekai traders often pointed out to me that bad traders easily diverted from rules they set for themselves, especially rules as to the timing of "loss cutting"—that is, when to unwind a trading position in order to avoid further losses—and they regularly attributed their trading losses to their own lack of discipline to "stick to rules."

This formulation of discipline has a distinctive temporal dimension. A commitment to discipline assumes that undisciplined persons are almost always prone to diverge from their initial intentions as their action unfolds. Only through discipline would one be able to stick to the rule one sets for oneself. Discipline, in other words, is a hold put on one's agency. As theorists of rational action have shown, such limitation of one's own agency could also be a source of moral empowerment (see, e.g., Elster 2000; Rubenfeld 2001). In this sense, traders' regular reference to the importance of discipline itself constitutes what Webb Keane has termed a "modality" of ethics that affords a moment of "self-distancing," or "objectification" (Keane 2010: 81–82).

Sekai traders' preoccupation with discipline also reflects the centrality of Schwager's book to Aoki's team. *Market Wizards,* first published in 1989, was introduced to Sekai's proprietary trading team by Kimura, a young trader who had spent a couple of years in the late 1980s in Sekai's Chicago office learning to trade futures and options. Kimura was part of Sekai's then rapidly growing futures trading operation in Chicago, a global center of derivatives trading. Sekai Securities set up the Chicago office in 1987, after the ban on financial futures trading previously imposed on Japanese institutional investors was lifted. Sekai was one of the first Japanese securities firms to participate in Chicago's futures market. The firm made an arrangement with a leading local futures commission merchant to have a booth dedicated to large orders from Japanese banks, life insurance firms, and other institutional investors before formally becoming a clearing member of the Chicago Board of Trade in 1988.[3] Sekai's fee revenue quickly rose from approximately $60,000 in 1987 to over $150,000 by the beginning of 1988. The size of Sekai's Chicago office, which started with two staff members, also increased to include more than ten employees by 1988. Many of Sekai's derivatives traders were sent by Aoki to Chicago as trainees to learn about the U.S. derivatives markets. In Tokyo, these traders were called "returnees from Chicago" (*Shikago gaeri*), which connoted both respect and envy. Kimura was one of these returnees, and *Market Wizards* (and its lesson on discipline) was his main souvenir. Aoki and the traders under him meticulously studied Schwager's book.

Market Wizards therefore was not simply an authoritative source of information about American trading techniques and philosophies but also a symbol of Sekai's success in the Chicago derivatives markets during the late 1980s. In this sense, the theme of discipline was inseparable from the initial ambition of Aoki and other Sekai traders to "catch up with and overtake" (*oitsuke oikose*) their Euro-American counterparts. In other words, discipline was something Japanese traders ought to learn from Euro-American traders.

LEARNING VERSUS "INCENTIVE"

"Trading is like walking on a tightrope," Tada told me in the trading room of Sekai Securities in November 1998. A former steel plant engineer, Tada had succeeded Aoki as head of Sekai's proprietary trading team in 1995. He explained what he meant by the analogy: "When you see someone walking on a tightrope in a circus performance, it looks magical. However, there is no magic. In fact, you can learn all there is to learn about how people do it. Yet that does not mean that you can do it yourself." That trading demands tacit knowledge rather than explicit and formal knowledge is perhaps not surprising (see Lave and Wenger 1991), but Tada's analogy reflected his broader belief that the once-celebrated Japanese institutional commitment to learning had failed. Tada told me: "Foreigners always said there is nothing called 'education' [*kyoiku*] in the world of trading. You have to climb up the ladder on your own. But we had a Japanese idea that we could educate or train ourselves. It was a beautiful idea, and the firm invested in it. But it was impossible" (November 1998).

An emphasis on learning (and education) has long been a defining feature of Japanese society. Japanese have been regarded as avid learners. In the popular representation, the collective Japanese commitment to learning has manifested itself as a zeal for borrowing, adjusting, refining, and ultimately innovating on foreign knowledge and technology. Japan's rapid postwar economic development has been attributed to the collective Japanese aspiration to learn. According to Ezra Vogel, "If any single factor explains Japanese success, it is the group-directed quest for knowledge" (Vogel 1979: 27). The construction of the Japanese self vis-à-vis foreigners entailed in the process of learning has had elements of nationalism. For example, Thomas Rohlen notes that the Japanese interest in foreign knowledge and technology has been grounded in a desire to exceed foreigners and prove "Japan's competence" (Rohlen 1992: 326). Therefore, "learning" (*gakushu*) entailed a specific directionality as well as a hierarchical relationship. In the process of acquiring "superior" foreign knowledge and technology, Japanese learners expected to surpass their foreign counterparts by refining that knowledge and technology (see, e.g., Westney 1987).

Scholars have also noted that the Japanese capacity to learn is grounded in each individual's pursuit of perfection, refinement, and ultimately self-realization, which is reminiscent of the Confucian notion of learning (Rohlen and Letendre 1996: 9; Smith 1983). Of course, as

William W. Kelly (1998) argues, the notion that learning is a distinctively Japanese practice grounded in Confucianism is an ideological construction, and it is difficult to pin down precise cultural differences in learning practices. Nevertheless, learning became an emblem of Japanese economic institutions and served as a marker of "Japaneseness" throughout Japan's high-growth period.[4]

For Tada, the appeal of the tightrope analogy lay in its capacity to point to the limitations of learning as a uniquely Japanese modality of engagement with financial markets and theories and techniques of finance. In order to appreciate the full significance of this analogy (and what came after learning), however, I turn to an examination of the efforts undertaken by Tada and his fellow traders to learn Euro-American financial knowledge and technology, as well as the unintended consequences of those efforts.

Since its inception in 1987 under Aoki, Sekai Securities' proprietary trading team's predominant modality of engagement with Euro-American investment banks was learning. But there was also a nationalistic undertone to this modality. Sekai traders compared Aoki to the legendary Salomon Brothers head trader Shigeru Myojin, who famously earned $31.45 million dollars in 1996.[5] Aoki's traders proudly told me that, unlike Myojin, Aoki had rejected lucrative offers from several U.S. investment banks. They reasoned that, as a former anti–Vietnam War student activist, Aoki did not want to work for an American firm. Aoki's ambition, rather, was to create a Japanese version of U.S. investment banks' proprietary trading. This meant introducing Wall Street–style proprietary trading *without* a Wall Street–style incentive structure. In setting this goal for himself, Aoki was following postwar Japan's dominant mode of "catching up with and overtaking" (*oitsuke oikose*) Europe and the United States.

At the time of the Sekai proprietary trading team's establishment, the Japanese economy as a whole seemed poised, in the popular imagination, to take a leadership role in the global economy, given the strength of the Japanese manufacturing sector. Nevertheless, those within the securities industry saw themselves as lagging far behind their Euro-American counterparts. Aoki's initiative was animated by an appreciation of the time lag between Japanese and Euro-American financial markets in terms of the availability of financial instruments and technologies, and a knowledge lag between Japanese and Euro-American firms concerning expertise about these instruments and technologies. In other words, Aoki's trading team was framed conceptually by the temporal orientation of modern Japan as *in step with and yet behind* Europe and the United States. As in the manufacturing sector, this temporal orientation was experienced in the modalities of learning by copying, adapting, and refining Euro-American knowledge, technologies, and skills. There was a doubleness, then, to this time lag: just as Sekai and other Japanese securities firms were behind Euro-American investment banks and modeled themselves after those firms, they also perceived themselves to be behind and making a model of the Japanese manufacturing firms whose successes had led to the glories of the bubble years.

As I mentioned in chapter 1, Aoki had spent four years in Sekai's New York branch before establishing his team, acquiring skills and experiences to bring back to Tokyo. In New York, Aoki learned that it was impossible to trade futures and options without a knowledge of advanced mathematics, and without computer programs and a large financial database. Aoki therefore recruited a team of young engineers, mathematicians, and computer scientists from manufacturing firms and graduate programs, and he encouraged them to learn all they could from what they saw as superior Euro-American knowledge of financial economics and financial engineering. Under Aoki's leadership, these young mathematicians and engineers turned traders meticulously studied the basics of financial economics. For example, they read and discussed among themselves John Cox and Mark Rubinstein's *Options Markets* (1985), John Murphy's *Technical Analysis of the Futures Markets* (1986) and other English-language books on trading techniques and philosophies and theories of derivatives valuation. Sekai's research wing, along with Aoki's team once it was formed, translated and published state-of-the-art academic articles by American financial economists in Japanese securities industry journals (see Miyazaki and Riles 2005: 322).

Aoki's initiative was part of Sekai's broader collective effort to acquire "know-how" (*no-hau*) of derivatives trading from its Euro-American counterparts. Since the mid-1980s, Sekai Securities had heavily invested in derivatives research and development. In January 1993, Sekai's research wing, whose main task since its inception in August 1989 had been to develop financial products and trading models for Sekai's institutional clients, also established a liaison center in San Francisco through which it funded the research projects of a number of American financial economists. Some of these collaborative endeavors, such as a project to develop program trading models specifically for Japanese stock markets, helped the firm to expand its business with domestic institutional investors and to justify further investment in similar projects to import, adapt, and refine state-of-the-art technologies and research results from the United States. The research wing also invited U.S.-based financial economists to conduct in-house seminars for Sekai traders and analysts in Tokyo. From the late 1980s until the early 1990s, learning—including observation, experience, translation, adaptation, and refinement—was the mode by which Aoki and his traders experienced the global financial markets.

Learning was so central to the Sekai team's engagement with the market that it served as a site of internal politics. One case in point was the team's 1992 collaboration with a financial economist from the University of California, Berkeley, business school. Sekai sent a junior trader and a researcher to San Francisco to work with the Berkeley professor for approximately five months. The goal was to develop a pricing model and a pricing program for "exotic options." Exotic options are options tailored to a particular investor's needs, and they contain elements—such as a mechanism by which the value of the option contract changes according to changes in the market values of the contract's multiple underlying assets—that make their pricing complicated. In the early 1990s, Euro-American investment banks in Tokyo started introducing exotic options to Japanese institutional investors, and Aoki's team decided to follow by acquiring the pricing techniques required to market these products to its institutional clients. The central problem in pricing exotic options concerned how to solve more complicated differential equations than those contained in standard options pricing formulas. Sekai paid the Berkeley business school professor $3,000 a day for this work.

On the surface, the goal of the collaboration was straightforward and was successfully achieved. The junior trader, Nagai, recalled in April 2000 that, upon his return from San Francisco, the team was able to price exotic options competitively vis-à-vis Euro-American investment banks by using a solution he had developed with the Berkeley economist. However, Hayashi, a senior trader and an applied mathematician trained at the University of Tokyo who had overseen the collaboration, told a different story. He confided to me in April 2000 that, from his point of view, the main purpose of the project had not been to invent new solutions. Instead, he argued, the goal had been to convince Nagai, a recent graduate from a computer engineering program at another university, to accept Hayashi's general solution to the differential equations required for the pricing of these exotic options. The senior trader insisted that he himself had already known the solution because he had solved similar differential equations as a graduate student in applied mathematics. What is interesting is that this personal rivalry between the two traders over a mathematical problem prompted an international collaborative project, which in turn translated into handsome financial support for an American academic while also reconfirming the privileged status of financial economics as knowledge imported from the United States into Japanese markets.

Sekai Securities traders also gradually began to see a contradiction in their efforts to acquire knowledge, technologies, and skills from Euro-American investment bankers and financial economists. They had been asked to learn to trade like traders at Euro-American investment banks without the compensation structures linking their performance to their salary. Many of the traders in the Sekai derivatives team increasingly became dissatisfied and demoralized by this fact.

From 1992 to 1996, Sekai's derivatives team collaborated with a Chicago options trading firm I will call Windy City Options. Aoki arranged a team of Chicago options traders to be stationed in Osaka to engage in arbitrage operations in the Nikkei 225 options markets using Sekai's facilities. Windy City Options initially sent two traders and an assistant. From Sekai's point of view, the goal of the collaboration was to allow what Jean Lave and Etienne Wenger call "legitimate peripheral learning" to occur in an artificially created "community of practice" (Lave and Wenger 1991; see also Bushe and Shani 1991) and acquire options trading techniques through direct observation.[6]

Two young Sekai Securities traders, Takahashi and Yamashita, were assigned to observe the Chicago traders. Takahashi recalled in July 2000 that the Windy City Options traders were rigorously following the rules they set for themselves (see also Miyazaki and Riles 2005: 323). He noted the Chicago traders' "stoic" and "disciplined" engagement with the market. His impression was that the Windy City Options traders repeated the same form of trading over and over again, accumulating small profits one transaction at a time. The Chicago team made a consistent profit of 500 to 700 million yen per year (approximately $4.5 to $6.3 million at the exchange rate of the time). Takahashi observed that they were not interested so much in changing their strategies as the market changed as in changing markets when one market ceased to be profitable. When arbitrage opportunities disappeared in one market, the Chicago traders would move to another market. They were simply repeating what worked until it ceased to work (July 2000).

The most important lesson Takahashi and Yamashita took from their observations was not that the Chicago traders adhered to the principle of discipline, however. The Sekai traders already knew that discipline was a fundamental principle of trading. As Takahashi put it, "there was nothing new" in what he saw the Windy City Options traders do (July 2000). Ironically, the most important lesson the Sekai traders learned was that they would never be able to do what they observed the Chicago traders doing because of the difference in their respective incentive structures. Sekai paid the Windy City Options traders much more than it paid its Japanese traders. Yamashita noted, "We were also traders, but [the Chicago traders] were earning 1 million yen to 1.5 million yen a month." At the time, he earned only 300,000 yen a month after taxes. He continued: "[When I learned of that difference,] I was shocked." Takahashi also found the difference in their incentive structures "stressful" (July 2000). Both Yamashita and Takahashi left their positions shortly after this experience. Yamashita quit the firm in 1996 to go to business school in the United States, and he later started up a trading system development venture. Takahashi entered into a joint venture Sekai set up with a U.S. investment bank in 1998. What impeded Sekai traders' "learning," in the two young traders' perception, was the lack of monetary incentive in their work environment. In their view, in order to pursue arbitrage opportunities in a disciplined manner like the Chicago options traders, they would need to be financially compensated. For them, discipline did not make sense in a situation in which winning or losing did not make much personal difference.

When Sekai's Japanese traders said that they had nothing to learn from American traders, however, they did not necessarily mean that they could do what American traders could do. Rather, they meant that learning was the wrong modality of being in the market and the wrong form of engagement with trading and the skills and technologies it required.

By the time of my fieldwork in 1998, Sekai traders shared a deep sense of Japan's "defeat" (*haisen*) to "foreign capital" (*gaishi*), or Euro-American capital. Sekai's proprietary trading team had stopped training new traders and was even considering terminating trading altogether. Instead, Sekai traders planned to invest in American hedge funds, allowing American hedge fund managers to do the trading for them. This near-complete retreat from trading had been anticipated by Sekai's failed last-minute effort to globalize its derivatives operations in the mid-1990s. Sekai had sent its traders to London and New York in order to start up operations necessary to make its derivatives business more competitive internationally. One trader from Sekai's derivatives team was sent to New York to study stock lending practices in the U.S. markets. Another trader was sent to London to explore new kinds of trading, such as tax arbitrage, a form of arbitrage aiming to exploit differences in capital gains taxes imposed by different countries and jurisdictions. The most important goal of this globalization project, however, was to assemble the best traders from Euro-American investment banks. This meant a radical change from Aoki's original goal of creating a Japanese version of Wall Street–style proprietary trading. Sekai even hired a well-known French derivatives specialist as the head trader of its global operations. But Sekai Securities itself was financially crumbling, and the trend in the financial markets also was shifting from proprietary trading to principal finance, an investment banking activity focusing on investing in or financing a business venture. During my fieldwork in 1998 Sekai Securities initiated a negotiation with a U.S. financial group, and the future of Sekai's proprietary team became uncertain.

Sekai traders' sense of defeat resonated with the general mood resulting from Japan's "big bang," the comprehensive financial reforms and deregulation programs that began to materialize in 1998, as well as the long recession following the collapse of the stock market bubble in the early 1990s. In the late 1990s, the Japanese media debated which Japanese financial institutions would be "winners" (*kachigumi*) and "losers" (*makegumi*) in the deregulated Japanese financial markets. In order to compete in this new environment, in which the presence of Euro-American investment banks was rapidly increasing, some Japanese banks and securities firms began to break away from *keiretsu,* the networks of affiliated trading, manufacturing, and banking corporations that were widely recognized as the backbone of Japan's postwar economic development (see, e.g., Gerlach 1992; see also Johnson 1984; Katz 1998), and reorganize themselves into new alliances. Around this time many Japanese financial institutions also adopted what they perceived to be a more Euro-American system of compensation for their employees. Financial industry insiders seemed to agree that without the assistance of Euro-American capital, and without emulating Euro-American firms' business models, few Japanese financial institutions could survive the current wave of deregulation. Sekai Securities's management was no exception.

Many economic analysts and journalists described the sudden intrusion of foreign capital and some of the institutional features of Euro-American investment banks (especially their compensation structures) into the Japanese financial industry in the late 1990s as a "second occupation" (*daini no senryo*) (see, e.g., Iida and Mizuno 1998; Mizuno 1998; Oshita 1998). As the allusion to the American occupation following World War II suggests, Japanese market professionals expressed considerable ambivalence about the Euro-American expansion into Japan's financial markets and the associated imposition of Euro-American practices and values (see also Miyazaki and Riles 2005: 323). On the one hand, it was a frustrating moment for Japanese financial market insiders, like Aoki, who had believed in their capacity to compete with their Euro-American counterparts without embracing the entire range of Euro-American practices and values. On the other hand, like the American military occupation of Japan, it was an opportunity for change and renewal (see, e.g., Dower 1999).

Many Sekai traders trained under Aoki took up this opportunity to refashion themselves into risk-taking neoliberal subjects. In particular, what concerned them was the question of "incentive" (*insentibu*). Up to this point, traders' salaries at Japanese securities firms had not been enhanced by the kinds of bonuses and other compensation schemes that were common in Euro-American investment banks. In the Japanese system, traders could rely on permanent employment in which their earnings would increase in proportion to their age, and incentives were defined not narrowly in terms of monetary compensation but broadly in terms of age-based promotions and competitions (see Aoki 1988). Many Sekai traders recognized that they had worked on a different form of incentive within a longer-term scheme of compensation, and they were also aware that the new "Euro-American" standards came at social, cultural, and personal costs: under these compensation schemes, workers could be fired once they ceased to be useful. It is also important to note that the Sekai traders believed that the overregulation of the Japanese financial markets had prevented them from acting as rational economic actors. From their point of view, regulation typically created mispricing and anomalies that they could exploit. But what preoccupied Sekai traders in the late 1990s was the apparent lack of incentive inside the Japanese firm. For many Sekai traders, the idea of incentive seemed to constitute a critical component of the condition in which their capacity to become disciplined rational economic actors might be fully realized. An unintended consequence of their various learning projects was their awareness of the limitations of learning as a modality of engagement with the market. This resulted in a renewed appreciation of the power of money through the rhetorical emphasis on incentive. In this shift from learning to incentive, they also began to apprehend "America" as a signifier of a new form of subjectivity, rather than an object of learning and refinement. Whereas learning assumed the ability of Japanese learners to learn Euro-American skills and technologies without being transformed by what they learned, the new engagement with America entailed the transformation of their own modes of being and becoming.[7]

In deploying the tightrope analogy, therefore, Tada sought to suggest that the Sekai derivatives team's approach to trading through learning and education was misdirected. When Tada discussed the limits of learning, he did not simply identify the limits of a particular kind of learning, such as classroom learning or text-based learning. Instead, he pointed to the limits of learning generally, as well as the particular ontological directionality of learning. For Tada, the limits of learning were the limits of Japan, and thus learning emerged as a historically specific mode of engagement with the market that ultimately had to be abandoned. In other words, learning as a modality of engagement had failed.[8] This failure produced a radical shift from learning to incentive, wherein the naked power of money emerged as an attractive option.

THE TEMPORALITIES OF ARBITRAGE

The sense of defeat that Sekai traders shared in the 1990s was not new. Sekai traders had already experienced a sense of defeat by their Euro-American counterparts at the beginning of their careers as derivatives traders. Sekai's arbitrage team launched its index arbitrage operations in the Nikkei 225 futures markets in 1988 and made a handsome profit. By the end of 1991, the size of the team's Nikkei 225 index arbitrage operations had increased to 200 billion yen, in terms of its exposure in the cash market. But it was evident to Sekai arbitrageurs that they were not able to compete with traders at Euro-American investment banks.

There were many reasons for the Sekai arbitrageurs' lack of competitiveness. First, they immediately detected clear disparities in risk taking between themselves and their Euro-American counterparts. As an example, they pointed to the contrasting approaches of traders at Sekai and Euro-American investment banks to mundane technological problems, which prevented the Japanese traders from quickly buying and selling orders for an arbitrage operation. At that time trading at the Tokyo Stock Exchange had not been completely mechanized, and traders and their assistants were forced to fill out individual order forms for the hundreds of stock purchases that each act of index arbitrage required. The forms were then transferred to another section of the firm in the firm's headquarters, whose work consisted of transmitting all orders to the stock exchange through punched paper tape.[9] Each time they did so, however, they found that Euro-American investment banks had beaten them to their goal. In index arbitrage, the time it took to execute orders to buy the basket of individual stocks that corresponded to the index made all the difference. Sekai traders suspected that Euro-American investment banks had beaten them by either transmitting orders more directly or receiving index futures market price information more quickly somehow.[10] As Aoki told me in retrospect, "Foreign capital is go-getting. They look for prey. They have that instinct. The Japanese body doesn't know that instinct. Americans, the animals, have that instinct. They just look at Japan as a place with a lot of prey. Americans will do what would be illegal in the U.S. markets in the Tokyo market, while we Japanese cannot do it. Those Japanese who move to foreign firms do the same. So maybe it's Japanese culture [that holds us back]" (October 1998).

Second, and perhaps more significantly, in many Sekai traders' view, Euro-American investment banks' proprietary trading teams seemed to be able to do whatever it took to construct a large position as soon as they detected an arbitrage opportunity. Unlike Japanese firms, Euro-American investment banks were able to use their global booking centers to quickly mobilize all available resources worldwide in order to capitalize on any profit opportunity anywhere. Aoki observed in May 2011 that, like other major Japanese securities firms, Sekai Securities could not overcome its "regionalist" (*kyotenshugi*) mentality, in which the firm's overseas offices (in New York, London, and Hong Kong) focused on their own regional business, and these regional offices were not integrated into an effective global operation. Within this regionalist framework, Sekai and other firms focused their energies on introducing financial technologies and techniques from Europe and the United States into the Japanese markets and offering new investment opportunities and tools to Japanese institutional investors. The basic orientation of their efforts, then, shared with other projects the modality of catching up with and overtaking their U.S. counterparts.

In particular, Aoki's team was unable to compete with Euro-American investment banks in index arbitrage operations in the early 1990s due to the team's inability to access the offshore stock lending markets for Japanese company shares. At that time, there was no stock lending market in Japan, but there was a vibrant lending market for Japanese company stocks in New York, which, Aoki told me in May 2011, Sekai arbitrageurs became aware of in late 1990. Euro-American investment banks were able to mobilize much larger funds for their arbitrage operations in Japan than Japanese securities firms that were restricted by the firms' capital. This meant that the size of Sekai's arbitrage positions needed to be kept at a certain preset level, and often Sekai arbitrageurs needed to close their trading positions before the prices converged due to an expected market event triggering a margin call in excess of the limits allocated to their arbitrage operations. As one trader, Koyama, recollected, "We were just watching how foreign firms collected money so easily after we closed our positions prematurely. [The traders at foreign firms] were so different. They could take huge risks. We were not like them" (February 2000).

On a more personal level, however, Sekai arbitrageurs experienced their defeat by their Euro-American counterparts in temporal terms. As I have explained, arbitrage entails a distinctive temporal orientation. At least in theory, in seeking to exploit arbitrage opportunities, arbitrageurs make those opportunities disappear and thereby move the market toward a condition of no arbitrage. Arbitrageurs also assume that the market has a general tendency to move toward efficiency that they equate with a condition of no arbitrage, due to the work of arbitrage itself. This prompts arbitrageurs to seek to sharpen their calculations in order to search for less obvious arbitrage opportunities in the same market. Alternatively, arbitrageurs could seek similar opportunities in other markets.

When arbitrage opportunities seemed to have disappeared on the Nikkei 225 Index in the early 1990s, Sekai securities arbitrageurs shifted their attention to another index, the TOPIX Index. The appeal of TOPIX as compared to the Nikkei 225 lay in its complexity. Because it would be impossible to buy all the stocks included in TOPIX, as the traders had done with the 225 stocks that made up the Nikkei 225, arbitrage in TOPIX required a far more complex method of replication:

in order to find arbitrage opportunities, the traders would have to construct a basket of selected stocks that would move in price in the same way as the index as a whole—they would have to replicate the index virtually. This demanded complex computer simulations and statistical modeling. From 1992 until 1995, some of the Sekai traders invested their energy and time in this issue, researching how to refine models for constructing the best basket of stocks for TOPIX arbitrage trading.

There was a certain correspondence between Sekai derivatives traders' institutional commitment to learning and their professional commitment to arbitrage, and their respective temporal orientations. As described earlier, unlike their Euro-American counterparts, who habitually received a share of the profits they earned, Sekai traders received no financial incentives. Their wages were calculated according to seniority, and their jobs were secure. Their intense motivation to succeed, therefore, stemmed from their longer-term commitment to learning and refinement and their sense of competition (cf. Cole 1979; Nonaka and Takeuchi 1995; Vogel 1979; see also Aoki 1988).

And it is here that the complexity of arbitrage trading had its appeal. In 1991, for example, Koyama developed a computer model for forecasting the movements of the Nikkei 225 Index futures market. The program proved very successful, and the firm's management, delighted with the results, asked Koyama to develop further programs of the same kind for other indexes. Koyama refused. As he recalled, "Rules for futures trading are too easy. . . . It is all about how to handle past market data. As a game, it was not so interesting" (February 2000). For Koyama, speculation, and technical analysis for speculative trading, was simple, and once his trading strategy was shared with the rest of the team, he himself would be replaceable.

Instead, Koyama turned to options trading and arbitrage using options. The appeal of options trading to Koyama lay in its complexity and the temporal orientation of arbitrage (February 2000). Whereas speculation required predicting future market movements, arbitrage was agnostic about where the market would go but entailed a faith that whatever its future position was, it would be a position of equilibrium and efficiency. One could say that arbitrage represented an anticipation of *retrospection*—a moment at which the endpoint would be given. For believers in the efficient-market hypothesis, anomalies—that is, arbitrage opportunities—are moments predestined to reach closure. In Koyama's opinion, finding such anomalies was a more complex intellectual process than engineering rules for predicting the future, and therein lay the appeal.

As I have described, therefore, arbitrage is oriented both toward self-closure and toward complexity, which in turn has a specific relationship to the temporality of learning—that is, the temporality of being behind. In other words, the refinement of modeling required by this turn to complexity was an extension of the strategy of learning and copying that had always followed from being behind. This strategy is predicated on a linear, cumulative form of knowledge formation. In the common understanding of Sekai traders, it was precisely this strategy of refinement that had been the secret of Japan's economic success in the postwar era (see Rohlen 1992).

Indeed, Ibuka, one of the traders in charge of Sekai's TOPIX arbitrage operation in the early 1990s, was proud of his refinement of the model for replicating the movements of TOPIX. Originally trained in mechanical engineering, Ibuka joined Aoki's team in 1988, teaming up with Sasaki in index arbitrage operations. For Ibuka, the craftsman-like dimension of this work had a great deal of appeal. He repeatedly told me that he and his team had been able to construct the world's most accurate model for replication of TOPIX (April 2000).

In retrospect, however, to some Sekai traders, the fit between the propensity for refinement in the temporal orientation of being behind and the propensity for complexity in arbitrage foiled their successes. Tanaka rediscovered the simplicity of arbitrage when he moved to a European securities firm in 1998. He teamed up with another trader in the new firm and engaged in trading convertible bonds. Tanaka's team made large profits in 1999. In 2000, he told me that all he had needed to do to become a successful trader was to repeat what worked until it ceased to work in a particular market, and then to repeat that again in another market. In his view, the Sekai team's commitment to refinement of replication was completely misguided. To his surprise, Tanaka discovered that traders at foreign firms were not particularly interested in constructing complex models:

> Japanese traders tend to examine their trading model very carefully, like people at manufacturing companies used to do when they developed vacuum cleaners. Japanese are really good at it and are content to say that they are simply trying hard, whether they make or lose money. To tell you the truth, that kind of attitude does not take you too far in the world of derivatives. In fact, foreign firms have knowledge of all the fancy theories about trading but we traders [at foreign firms] do not pay attention to half of what we

> are told about those theories. We just keep repeating whatever method has been effective. . . . [When I was at Sekai,] a senior trader lost a million dollars in a single day, and our boss was summoned by the firm's executives. Our boss came back and told the trader to present a paper listing points for improvement in his trading method. Here [in a foreign firm] one just loses one's job if one loses money. . . . Sekai traders have placed too much emphasis on theories. There is no point in studying theories. Theories exist for the purpose of making money. There is no point in refining one's trading model just for the sake of its refinement. (May 2000)

In contrast, trading at a foreign firm was like jazz improvisation, Tanaka said. When something ceased to work, or when arbitrage opportunities were foreclosed, foreign traders just tried something else. I want to emphasize here that the contrast Tanaka drew between refinement and improvisation, as modalities of trading, was a contrast between temporal orientations. Japanese traders' attraction to complex models was an effort to extend the temporal orientation of being behind that had worked so well for Japan's manufacturing sector, which was predicated on a correlation between time spent in learning from past mistakes and future successes and achievements. In contrast, Tanaka's allusion to jazz improvisation reflected his acute sense of the irrelevance of such cumulative time to the financial market and "the purpose of making money." If the strategy of refinement had an academic orientation, Tanaka's rendering of trading as improvisation emphasized an artistic quality, in which every moment was unique and succeeded or failed for itself.

Tanaka's awareness of the incongruity between the temporal orientation of the Japanese workplace and the financial market reflected a broader sense shared by other members of the team that collective experience and extensive time spent trading did not necessarily lead to success in the market. Moreover, the experience of arbitrage's self-closing and self-canceling orientation intensified Sekai traders' awareness of the distinctively short time horizon of the trading profession. They shared a belief that they would not be able to remain active in the profession for a long time and that the end of their trading careers was fast approaching (see H. Miyazaki 2010b). For Sekai arbitrageurs, the inevitability of an endpoint of arbitrage amplified on a daily basis their sense of the fast-approaching endpoint of their own trading careers.

In fact, by 1998, some of the members of Aoki's derivatives team had stopped trading altogether. Sudo, a trader who worked under Tada in the mid-1990s, left the firm in early 1998 for a foreign consulting firm, where he provided advice to securities firms on reorganization, employment, and other aspects of their business unrelated to trading. He recalled:

> In 1997, the market was [so volatile] that I realized that the outcome of one's trading depended on one's sheer luck or innate talent. Sometimes I would go to the toilet and come back to my desk to find that my gains had tripled or quadrupled or that I had made huge losses. When I thought that I had devoted my life to this kind of profession, I felt empty. . . . In this profession, the length of one's experience does not contribute to one's value. I thought that it might be better to move to a profession where one's skills correlate to the time and effort one has spent. (February 2000)

Nonaka, another member of Tada's team during the mid-1990s, remained at Sekai after the team was disbanded but was transferred to a newly established section devoted to investing in start-up companies. Nonaka had been a particularly successful trader skilled in a trading strategy commonly known as the long-short strategy, which entails identifying correlations between certain undervalued and overvalued stocks and simultaneously buying low and selling high. However, he told me that he had lost interest in trading because he had found the market limiting:

> There is something deeper in the world of stocks than trading, and that is growth. This is a much deeper world than the world of winning and losing. . . . Trading is always about yourself. . . . The time span of trading is two to three weeks at the longest. The market moves every day. There is no time for self-reflection. Investing in business enterprises is different. The real question is whether these business enterprises will grow. . . . Trading is fun because every day you get results [from your actions]. Even if you don't think or don't act, you can make yourself believe that you are working because the market moves [and generates results]. . . . In this world of investment, unless you move, nothing happens. (May 2000)

In different ways, both Sudo and Nonaka discussed a particular effect of securities trading on their sense of time. What generated this sense for them was neither the pace of the market nor its level of abstraction, but the incongruity between the temporal orientation of work in the Japanese context and the continually self-closing character of trading. Sudo and Nonaka sought to ground their work in another kind of temporal orientation, that of personal and corporate growth.

I have examined a variety of techniques by which Sekai derivatives traders sought to reorient themselves in response to temporal incongruities of many kinds.[11] My attention to this temporal nexus of entities of different domains derives from efforts in science and technology studies to examine the process by which different properties and possibilities of machines, concepts, theories, and other artifacts, temporal and otherwise, converge and diverge, or are foregrounded and backgrounded over time (see, in particular, Latour and Woolgar [1979] 1986; Pickering 1995: 113–156). In particular, my approach resonates with Sharon Traweek's study of Japanese physicists' experience of incongruity between "the negotiable and cumulative 'beamtime'—pulses of the accelerator beam—and the intractable and limited lifetimes of their careers, their detectors, and their ideas" (Traweek [1988] 1992: xi).

Temporal incongruity has long been an anthropological concern. For example, in his study of Algerian peasants' perception of time, Pierre Bourdieu discusses the incongruities of "traditionalist" and modernist conceptions of the future (Bourdieu 1963). More recent examples include Theodore Bestor's study of the Tsukiji seafood market and Karin Knorr-Cetina and Urs Bruegger's study of currency traders in Zurich. Both of these studies focus on the problem of "coordination" with regard to intersecting temporalities, or what Bestor terms "timescapes," in the global flow of capital and commodities (Bestor 2001: 92; Knorr-Cetina and Bruegger 2000: 162–163). My concern with temporal incongruity also centers on the intersecting temporal properties and possibilities contained in economic concepts and practices, but my focus is on a situation in which different temporal properties of economic knowledge and action become visible to individual actors themselves (see also H. Miyazaki 2004b). What is at stake, in other words, is the question of when and how temporal incongruity becomes evident from the viewpoint of market participants, and what uses they make of that incongruity.

I have suggested that these temporal incongruities derived from the intersecting temporalities of financial instruments, market strategies, organizational practices, and personal life choices. Certain temporal features of arbitrage resonated strongly with certain temporal features of work inside the Japanese firm, but that resonance itself generated a sense of incongruity for some. Yet, from a broader perspective, it can also be said that temporal incongruity was already inherent in the Japanese institutional self-location of being behind. A popular understanding of the growth of the postwar Japanese economy points to a pervasive strategy of copying and exceeding American technology and knowledge. At the very moment at which the collective determination of Japanese manufacturing firms to catch up with their American counterparts had produced such spectacular economic growth that it threatened to foreclose the very gap that had sustained this coordinated goal, finance replaced manufacturing and thereby re-created a temporal gap between reality and the ideal, between Japan and its model, "America," and once again situated Japan as "being behind." The temporal gap that had served as Japanese manufacturing firms' ontological foundation had been created anew.

The example of Sekai's proprietary trading team showcases the encounter between the wider temporal gap that defined the Japanese condition in the late 1980s and the particular temporal orientations of arbitrage and securities trading as a profession. What compelled Sekai Securities traders to make these diverse life choices was not the increased speed of economic transactions nor the associated heightened degree of abstraction and alienation of labor from production process prompted by what James Carrier and Daniel Miller have termed "virtualism" (Carrier and Miller 1998a). Rather, it was the temporal incongruity deriving from the intersecting temporalities of Japan's location vis-à-vis the United States, of the Japanese workplace, and of trading strategies themselves. For different members of the team, however, the articulation of these temporal orientations resulted in the emergence of a variety of possibilities, such as refinement, improvisation, and personal and economic growth. But there was another kind of ending that awaited Sekai traders.

CHAPTER 4

Economy of Dreams

During the 1999 New Year's holidays, Tada was busy comparing his options for his future. Disillusioned by Sekai Securities' abandonment of derivatives trading, Tada decided to leave the firm. He had two options: he could move to another Japanese securities firm, or he could leave the world of large Japanese corporations altogether.

As he considered his options, Tada turned to his spreadsheet program. The Excel spreadsheet had long been an essential tool for traders like Tada, but this time, Tada ran the program for a new purpose—to determine his own worth. Using the program, Tada calculated the total amount of his future income and pension, as well as his expenses, under three different scenarios: In the first scenario (Case 1), in which he continued to work for a Japanese firm, he would receive an annual average salary of 8 million yen (approximately $71,400 at the exchange rate of the time). In the second scenario (Case 2), in which he would barely earn what he needed to cover his annual expenses, his annual income would be reduced to 5 million yen (approximately $44,600), the amount that he assumed, for the sake of simplification, to be his average annual expenditure.[1] In the third scenario (Case 3), he would stop working altogether and live on his savings.[2]

Tada was surprised to find that he simply was not worth very much. He calculated that he would need at least 210 million yen (approximately $1.875 million) to stop working at age fifty-five. This goal would be unattainable at the average annual income of a so-called

現在高	10000							
年齢	46							
	使用額	年金1	年金2	*手取*	*金利*	65才必要金額	60才必要金額	55才必要金額
CASE1	500	120	180	800	0.02	16000	18500	21000
CASE2	500	120	180	500	0.02	16000	18500	21000
CASE3	500	60	150	0	0.02	17500	20000	22500
打止								

	年齢	西暦	CASE1				CASE2				CASE3			
			手取	手取累積	変化	残高累積	手取	手取累積	変化	残高累積	手取	手取累積	変化	残高累積
1	46	1999	800	800	500	10500	500	500	200	10200	0	0	−300	9700
2	*47*	2000	800	*1600*	510	11010	500	1000	204	10404	0	0	−306	9394
3	*48*	2001	800	*2400*	520	11530.2	500	1500	208.1	10612.1	0	0	−312	9081.88
4	*49*	2002	800	*3200*	531	12060.8	500	2000	212.2	10824.3	0	0	−318	8763.52
5	*50*	2003	800	*4000*	541	12602	500	2500	216.5	11040.8	0	0	−325	8438.79
6	*51*	2004	800	*4800*	552	13154.1	500	3000	220.8	11261.6	0	0	−331	8107.56
7	*52*	2005	800	*5600*	563	13717.1	500	3500	225.2	11486.9	0	0	−338	7769.71
8	*53*	2006	800	*6400*	574	14291.5	500	4000	229.7	11716.6	0	0	−345	7425.11
9	*54*	2007	800	*7200*	586	14877.3	500	4500	234.3	11950.9	0	0	−351	7073.61
10	*55*	2008	800	*8000*	598	15474.9	500	5000	239	12189.9	0	0	−359	6715.08
11	*56*	2009	800	*8800*	609	16084.4	500	5500	243.8	12433.7	0	0	−366	6349.39
12	*57*	2010	800	*9600*	622	16706	500	6000	248.7	12682.4	0	0	−373	5976.37
13	*58*	2011	800	*10400*	634	17340.2	500	6500	253.6	12936.1	0	0	−380	5595.9
14	*59*	2012	800	*11200*	647	17987	500	7000	258.7	13194.8	0	0	−388	5207.82
15	*60*	2013	120	*11320*	−20	17966.7	120	7120	−116	13078.7	60	60	−336	4871.97
16	*61*	2014	120	*11440*	−21	17946	120	7240	−118	12960.3	60	120	−343	4529.41
17	*62*	2015	120	*11560*	−21	17925	120	7360	−121	12839.5	60	180	−349	4180
18	*63*	2016	120	*11680*	−22	17903.5	120	7480	−123	12716.3	60	240	−356	3823.6
19	*64*	2017	120	*11800*	−22	17881.5	120	7600	−126	12590.6	60	300	−364	3460.07
20	*65*	2018	180	*11980*	37.6	17919.2	180	7780	−68.2	12522.4	150	450	−281	3179.28
21	*66*	2019	180	*12160*	38.4	17957.5	180	7960	−69.6	12452.8	150	600	−286	2892.86
22	*67*	2020	180	*12340*	39.2	17996.7	180	8140	−70.9	12381.9	150	750	−292	2600.72
23	*68*	2021	180	*12520*	39.9	18036.6	180	8320	−72.4	12309.5	150	900	−298	2302.73
24	*69*	2022	180	*12700*	40.7	18077.4	180	8500	−73.8	12235.7	150	1050	−304	1998.79
25	*70*	2023	180	*12880*	41.5	18118.9	180	8680	−75.3	12160.4	150	1200	−310	1688.76

26	*71*	2024	180	*13060*	42.4	18161.3	180	8860	−76.8	12083.6	150	1350	−316	1372.54
27	*72*	2025	180	*13240*	43.2	18204.5	180	9040	−78.3	12005.3	150	1500	−323	1049.99
28	*73*	2026	180	*13420*	44.1	18248.6	180	9220	−79.9	11925.4	150	1650	−329	720.99
29	*74*	2027	180	*13600*	45	18293.6	180	9400	−81.5	11843.9	150	1800	−336	385.41
30	*75*	2028	180	*13780*	45.9	18339.4	180	9580	−83.1	11760.8	150	1950	−342	43.1177
31	*76*	2029	180	*13960*	46.8	18386.2	180	9760	−84.8	11676	150	2100	−349	−306.02
32	*77*	2030	180	*14140*	47.7	18434	180	9940	−86.5	11589.5	150	2250	−356	−662.14
33	*78*	2031	180	*14320*	48.7	18482.6	180	10120	−88.2	11501.3	150	2400	−363	−1025.4
34	*79*	2032	180	*14500*	49.7	18532.3	180	10300	−90	11411.4	150	2550	−371	−1395.9
35	*80*	2033	180	*14680*	50.6	18582.9	180	10480	−91.8	11319.6	150	2700	−378	−1773.8
36	*81*	2034	180	*14860*	51.7	18634.6	180	10660	−93.6	11226	150	2850	−385	−2159.3
37	*82*	2035	180	*15040*	52.7	18687.3	180	10840	−95.5	11130.5	150	3000	−393	−2552.5
38	*83*	2036	180	*15220*	53.7	18741	180	11020	−97.4	11033.1	150	3150	−401	−2953.5
39	*84*	2037	180	*15400*	54.8	18795.9	180	11200	−99.3	10933.8	150	3300	−409	−3362.6
40	*85*	2038	180	*15580*	55.9	18851.8	180	11380	−101	10832.5	150	3450	−417	−3779.8
41	*86*	2039	180	*15760*	57	18908.8	180	11560	−103	10729.1	150	3600	−426	−4205.4
42	*87*	2040	180	*15940*	58.2	18967	180	11740	−105	10623.7	150	3750	−434	−4639.5
43	*88*	2041	180	*16120*	59.3	19026.3	180	11920	−108	10516.2	150	3900	−443	−5082.3
44	*89*	2042	180	*16300*	60.5	19086.9	180	12100	−110	10406.5	150	4050	−452	−5534
45	*90*	2043	180	*16480*	61.7	19148.6	180	12280	−112	10294.6	150	4200	−461	−5994.7
46	*91*	2044	180	*16660*	63	19211.6	180	12460	−114	10180.5	150	4350	−470	−6464.6
47	*92*	2045	180	*16840*	64.2	19275.8	180	12640	−116	10064.1	150	4500	−479	−6943.8
48	*93*	2046	180	*17020*	65.5	19341.3	180	12820	−119	9945.39	150	4650	−489	−7432.7
49	*94*	2047	180	*17200*	66.8	19408.1	180	13000	−121	9824.3	150	4800	−499	−7931.4
50	*95*	2048	180	*17380*	68.2	19476.3	180	13180	−124	9700.79	150	4950	−509	−8440
51	*96*	2049	180	*17560*	69.5	19545.8	180	13360	−126	9574.8	150	5100	−519	−8958.8
52	*97*	2050	180	*17740*	70.9	19616.7	180	13540	−129	9446.3	150	5250	−529	−9488
53	*98*	2051	180	*17920*	72.3	19689.1	180	13720	−131	9315.22	150	5400	−540	−10028
54	*99*	2052	180	*18100*	73.8	19762.9	180	13900	−134	9181.53	150	5550	−551	−10578
55	*100*	2053	180	*18280*	75.3	19838.1	180	14080	−136	9045.16	150	5700	−562	−11140

FIGURE 2. Image of the spreadsheet Tada used to calculate his future retirement probability, comparing three different cases of income, pension, and expenses.

salaryman such as himself. Even if he continued to work until he turned sixty, he discovered, he would not be able to earn enough money for his retirement.

What prompted Tada to make these calculations? Tada's calculations took cues from a brand of neoliberalism as it was widely received in Japan in the late 1990s. Japan's neoliberal economic reform began in the 1980s under the leadership of Prime Minister Yasuhiro Nakasone with a set of privatization and deregulation programs, including the privatization of the country's railway and telecommunication systems. Japan's "big bang" financial reforms, initiated in 1996, entailed a radical reconception of Japanese subjectivity and ultimately of Japanese society. Reformers championed the "strong individual" (*tsuyoi kojin*) willing to take risks (*risuku*) and responsibility (*sekinin*) as the antidote to the "company man" (*kaisha ningen*) devoted to the promotion of the collective interest of his company (see, e.g., Dore 1997; cf. Ito 1996; Koike [1991] 1996).[3]

In the late 1990s, the move to calculate one's own worth (*jibun no nedan*) emerged as one of the characteristic activities of the strong individual that the Japanese government vigorously promoted as part of its neoliberal reform programs. It is important to note that the gender of the strong individual was male in the popular imagination.[4] The strong individual represented the future as against the company man of the past. The strong individual would be always conscious of his own present market value in contrast to the lifetime employee, who viewed his contribution from a "long-term" perspective. The strong individual would grab opportunities as they presented themselves instead of waiting for the Japanese economy to recover, as he might have done during the "lost decade" (*ushinawareta junen*) of Japan's economic recession of the 1990s. In conjunction with this emphasis on risk and individual responsibility, a series of concepts such as "logic" (*ronri*), "rationality" (*gorisei*), "risk" (*risuku*), and "trust" (*shinrai*) served for Japan's winner-hopefuls as an impetus for searching for a new modality of engagement with their employers, markets, and society (see, e.g., Nihon Keizai Shinbunsha 1999; Yamagishi 1998).

The transformations in conceptions of subjectivity associated with these reforms were defined in temporal terms. As Japan's leading financial newspaper, *Nihon Keizai Shinbun,* proclaimed in 1999, in a series of feature articles entitled "New Capitalism Has Arrived," risk and so-called self-responsibility (*jiko sekinin*) were to be the new norms of the market (Nihon Keizai Shinbunsha 1999). The kind of subjectivity expected to emerge in this new form of capitalism, according to the newspaper, was "a strong individual who can withstand the burden of freedom" (Nihon Keizai Shinbunsha 1999: 2), that is, an actor who acts on the basis of short-term and long-term rational calculation aimed at the maximization of profit, rather than on the basis of social obligations.

Business magazines and newspapers ran numerous articles urging Japanese businessmen to calculate their worth (see, e.g., Fujiwara 1998; Noguchi 1998; Okamoto, et al. 1998). This calculation was evidence, in the popular imagination, of the strong individual's rationality, risk taking, and self-responsibility. The act of calculating one's worth was imagined as a social and personal component of wider neoliberal economic reforms. This trend reflected broader changes in Japanese employment practices as company layoffs began to replace the permanent employment system.

Indeed, in the debate throughout the 1990s surrounding Japan's plan for financial reforms and questions of how to transform the "Japanese system" into a more globally competitive one, the notion of risk emerged as a key concept for understanding a new form of capitalism. Many Japanese economists and commentators attributed Japanese market participants' failure in the global financial market to their inability to handle risks properly (e.g., Nihon Keizai Shinbunsha 1999; see also Yamagishi 1998; Yamagishi, Cook, and Watabe 1998).

On the surface, Tada's calculation could be understood as a simple act of rational retirement planning, a standard Euro-American practice newly introduced to Japan as a consequence of changed economic conditions and through the influx of U.S. capitalist values associated with neoliberal economic reform. In Tada's understanding, however, the spreadsheet represented something subtly different: the culmination of his own wider pursuit of objectivity (*kyakkansei*) and logicality (*ronrisei*). A full appreciation of the significance of Tada's calculation demands an examination of the character of his evolving personal dreams and his associated sensibility about ends of all kinds, reminiscent of arbitrage's orientation toward its own end.

AN AUTOMATIC TRADING MACHINE

In 1988, at age thirty-five, Tada came to Sekai's derivatives trading team from a major steel company where he had worked as a plant engineer. An electronic engineer and a graduate of one of Japan's most prestigious private universities, Tada was one of many mathematicians and engineers who left manufacturing for the financial sector during the last phase of Japan's "bubble" economy. Tada quickly rose to become one of the principal figures in Sekai's proprietary trading team and in the Japanese derivatives markets as a whole.

What had attracted Tada to finance was not the promise of a higher salary. At that time, Japanese securities firms, such as Sekai Securities, paid only slightly more than manufacturing companies, and, as I discussed earlier, one's salary as a trader was not pegged to one's performance. Rather, Tada left the steel company, he told me, because he "was not sure how [his] labor as a plant engineer contributed to [the growth of] the company." In contrast, he said, in the world of financial trading, "the distance between mathematics and money [was] very close" (November 1998). In other words, it was the direct effect of the intellectual work of the trader on the firm's earnings that attracted him. Money served for Tada as an important index of the value of his intellectual labor.

Tada was soon placed in charge of managing the trading strategies of the other mathematicians and engineers who had joined the derivatives team. As a manager, Tada demanded that the traders demonstrate a complete commitment to a particular model of "logicality" (*ronrisei*). Tada instructed his traders to logically interrogate their trading strategies by performing extensive computer simulations to test their trading models against "all other possible scenarios" (*subete no shinario*). He debated the results of these tests with them every week and turned down proposals that, in his opinion, lacked logical justification.

From Tada's point of view, the power of logic inhered in its use as a constraint on intuitive impulses. Tada demanded that traders do exactly what their models were telling them to do, even if this contradicted their intuition. Sometimes this negation of one's larger sense of good judgment worked and sometimes it did not, but to Tada this was of lesser consequence. What was important to him was that the strategies were logically conceived and logically followed. Only then could failures become the source of further learning, as traders returned to their simulations to investigate what they had failed to take into account in constructing their models. Like the idea of discipline discussed in chapter 3, therefore, for Tada, logicality demanded a conscious negation of one's own future agency, binding one's future self to predetermined trading strategies or rules.

For some traders, this emphasis on logicality became so all-encompassing that they began to apply it to their thinking about themselves and their futures. Yamashita, a trader mentioned in chapter 3, told me in March 2000 that while working under Tada, he began to try to think logically about every facet of his life. Applying this method of decision making perfected by the trading team, he set out rules to govern his future actions and committed himself to sticking to those rules even when his common sense or pressure from colleagues or friends suggested a different course of action. He felt "superior" to others when he was able to follow these rules and act "logically." He boasted to me that he applied the same principle to even the largest decisions of his career. For example, by 1993, he had set a date on which, if the Nikkei 225 index had fallen below a certain level, he would quit Sekai Securities. As I discussed in chapter 1, by 1993 Sekai's index arbitrage operations had become less profitable. In Yamashita's view, the securities industry's profitability correlated with long-term market trends. Whereas ordinary people intuitively wanted to believe that the market condition would improve when they saw stock prices go up a little, Yamashita had decided to approach the markets and his own career on a longer temporal horizon and more objectively: "By that time, I had learned to see everything logically. I learned from books and conversations with other people that only losers [*makegumi no hito*] make decisions on the basis of their intuition" (March 2000). The logicality of his decision partially derives from his calculation of the level of the Nikkei 225 index that should prompt him to quit trading as his profession, but it largely inheres in his determination not to change his prior commitment arbitrarily. The decision in turn led him to begin to prepare himself for further education and training. Yamashita was admitted to an American business school in the spring of 1996 and quit Sekai that May.

However, Tada's "cult of logical reasoning" met some resistance within the team. Disagreement with his approach focused on his emphasis on logicality as the paradigm of rational reasoning. Young traders tended to favor a more pragmatic notion of efficiency (*koritsusei*). The weekly ritual of producing endless simulations and justifications for one's trading strategies placed far too much emphasis on logic (*ronri*) at any cost, they said, and it lacked efficiency, particularly in terms of the allocation of their time.

The effect of this conflict between logicality and efficiency was that Tada's actions often appeared to his younger traders as irrational. For example, they were dissatisfied with his occasional reliance on what they saw as conventional Japanese solutions to organizational problems. Tada's decision to appoint Hayashi, a University of Tokyo–educated mathematician mentioned in chapter 3, as chief trader was a case in point. To Tada, Hayashi's mathematical skills epitomized a commitment to the pure and academic kind of logicality that he sought to imbue in his traders. But although the other traders agreed that Hayashi had a superior knowledge of mathematics, they pointed out that he was not the most profitable trader. They therefore saw his appointment as a reversion to "Japanese" practices of handing out promotions on the basis of seniority and academic background rather than on the basis of demonstrated results.

Likewise, Tada's emphasis on logicality invoked a familiar debate about the merits of individualism versus collectivism. Who should be the proper agent of mathematical calculation and logical reasoning—the individual or the team? Younger traders objected to Tada's requirement that they disclose their trading strategies to him. To them, a rational team is one in which individual effort meets individual reward, and hence members of the team should be engaged in competition with one another to achieve the best results. Tada insisted, instead, that the traders feel no personal stake in their secrets; on the contrary, to Tada, a rational trading team is one in which all team members emulate the team's most successful members.

Younger traders saw in Tada's demands a manifestation of the stereotypical collective decision-making process based on group-oriented values. Such consensus-based practices were being blamed at that time for the inefficiencies of the Japanese corporation specifically and the decline of the Japanese economy more generally. This critique took its cue from a popular debate about temporality. On the one hand, it had become commonplace to assert that the relative merits of individually oriented or collectively oriented organizations depended on whether one took a short- or long-term view of the market. For example, if one favored long-term economic growth, it might make sense to make short-term economic sacrifices for the sake of building social relations with colleagues or clients (see, e.g., Dore 1983). On the other hand, it had become equally commonplace to assert that the speed of the global financial markets now demanded that profits be calculated on a shorter-term basis. If gains and losses were now being assessed based on individual transactions, then individual initiative should be rewarded over relational stability (see, e.g., Omae 1995). This in turn implied a second-order temporal contrast in which collective agency was associated with the past and individual agency was associated with the present and future.

Tada saw this question differently, however. The difference was inherent in his personal dream. Tada's ultimate goal, he confided, was to invent what he termed "an automatic trading machine." As he repeatedly explained with excitement, the full complexity of market movements could be reduced to one or two hundred variables or factors. Although tracking this many variables would be beyond human capacities to process, a computer should be able to do so. Once invented, he surmised, the machine would outperform the entire team. Tada's demand that traders share their trading strategies with him, therefore, was not an end in itself but rather a means of collecting data for the purposes of building this machine. For Tada, the ultimate goal was neither individualism nor collectivism, but rather to do away with traders and managerial relations altogether. Ironically, what looked to younger traders like a preference for collective agency over individual agency was actually Tada's dream of a moment at which human agency altogether would be rendered superfluous—that is, an end to human agency in financial trading.

What I want to emphasize here is the particular temporal directionality of Tada's dream. If the machine displaced the opposition between individualism and collectivism by replacing both models of agency with the agency of the machine, in Tada's view, it also displaced the contrast between short- and long-term perspectives, and more subtly, between the old and the new. Both short- and long-term perspectives on the market were predicated on a certain continuity between past and present; whatever the time frame, they assumed a link between present actions and future consequences. More important, both were models for action in a present moment in which one imagines a series of decisions or transactions that follow one another in time.

What differentiated the temporality of Tada's dream of building a trading machine from both individual and collective conceptions of agency and their related short- and long-term perspectives on the market, in contrast, was the dream's perspective on its own end. In looking forward to the creation of his automatic trading machine, Tada was imagining a moment at which the machine, finally in operation, would displace these chains of temporally linked strategies altogether. The machine would at that moment become the only agent (there would no longer be a need for traders) and its calculations the only act.

What he was doing was assigning traders the task of creating the very means of replacing themselves, thereby undermining the possibility of a future repetition of present strategies. Tada's dream therefore reimagined the present from the perspective of the end, the moment of the machine.[5]

EARLY RETIREMENT

As it turned out, however, the project came to a different kind of end. Following Sekai's decision to disband its derivatives trading team in December 1998, Tada found himself calculating his own worth on his Excel spreadsheet. On the surface, Tada's calculations seemed to oversimplify his financial future. The calculations in the spreadsheet were set up such that the future moment was a function of the conditions of the present. For example, the income Tada posited for each year until retirement was actually his present income, and he did not take into account possible changes to it. Likewise, his expenditures were assumed to be constant and remain at their present level. It might be said that Tada made these presentist assumptions to simplify his calculations, and this no doubt is true. Yet the consequence of this simplification is that the future becomes a function of the present in a very particular way: the future becomes the simple accumulation of multiple instances of the same present.

However, in light of Tada's perspective from the end—manifested in his dream of a trading machine—we can deduce that his fascination with this act of calculation has a different source. In comparing the three scenarios in the spreadsheet, Tada intended to determine his present course of action by reflecting on it from the point of view of the end—in this case, the moment at which he would cease to work. For Tada, retirement was to be the moment when his own market agency would be terminated. In that sense, it paralleled the moment when the trading machine would replace the agency of his traders. The calculations he performed in the spreadsheet were an extension of the temporal logic that had resulted in the dream of the trading machine. The innovation consisted simply in his application of this perspective from the end to an understanding of himself.

As I mentioned earlier, however, the consequence of this calculation was somewhat surprising to Tada. In fact, as it turned out, there was no such end: even if he continued to work for a Japanese corporation until the mandatory retirement age of sixty, the desired end would be unattainable because he would not have earned enough to cover his retirement expenses. In other words, what the spreadsheet as a whole made visible was the distance between the present moment and the moment of the end of agency (in this case, the moment at which he would be released from his work). It was this finding that prompted Tada to choose to take a risk in his own career, to pursue a path different from any of the three scenarios the spreadsheet compared. The spreadsheet induced Tada to reorient the directionality of his knowledge and to abandon logicality as his method.

In January 1999, at the age of forty-seven, Tada left Sekai Securities and the Japanese corporate world altogether. He entered into a partnership with a younger Japanese trader who had worked for an American investment bank, and together they founded a small investment fund. Given Tada's age and standing in the Japanese financial markets, the partnership itself defied Japanese ideas of seniority, and this defiance was amplified in the informal, ad hoc character of their business. Unlike many members of Sekai's derivatives trading team, Tada was single, and he emphasized that he had no financial obligations or expensive desires: "I could just be farming," he told me repeatedly. Working out of a small office, Tada used his substantial personal contacts to gather information about businesses of all kinds in search of potential investment opportunities.

Tada specialized in developing new investment schemes on behalf of wealthy private investors. Many of these schemes entailed investment in start-up companies. This change exposed him to an entirely new order of risk. Not only did he now make his living in a highly volatile sphere of the market, but he began to invest his own funds in these same schemes. In the trading of derivatives, Tada and his traders had been able to rely on publicly available information for the most part. But the venture capital business forced Tada to deal with unknown characters and business ventures for which information was not publicly available. In this context, informally obtained information became crucial to him, and hence so did trust (*shinrai*). As he told me in August 1999:

> In the outside world, you have to think ahead. If you give this person such and such information now, maybe this person will involve you in some good deal in the future. But there are some bad people. Even when you introduce someone to people, you need to think about the risk involved in doing so. People will scream at you, "Why are you mingling with that kind of person?" because large amounts of money are at stake. At a company, the company

> has rules and does all the risk management for you. But in the outside world, anything goes and there are many people who do risky things. . . . Do you know who will tend to do bad things? There aren't too many people who do bad things in order to become rich. But you have to watch those who have debt, who have a woman, or who have been threatened by someone.

This discovery of risk and trust transformed Tada's relations with his former colleagues. Tada frequently phoned former members of his team to ask for information, and in return, he involved some of them in his new schemes. These relationships thus became what he termed "real" relationships: "Japanese always say that they value 'human relationships' [*ningen kankei*]. But the human relationships that they value so much are simply those between friends—[they are] totally different from the relationships between those who are trying to make money together." Trust now replaced logicality as a method and as the means to his end of retirement.

Between 1999 and 2001, Tada often discussed with me his dream of traveling around Asia with a backpack or bicycling around Japan, which he hoped to do once he had accumulated 200 million yen (approximately $1.786 million at the exchange rate of the time). In Tada's understanding, an early retirement of this sort would afford the possibility of "self-realization" (*jiko-jitsugen*), which was the ideal goal of many of his Euro-American counterparts whom he wished to emulate. However, a similarity exists between Tada's dream of an automatic trading machine and his dream of an early retirement. In both dreams, Tada imagined an exit from work, and the possibility of imagining such an exit was predicated on the possibility of seeing an end to his work.

ARBITRAGING JAPAN

"The Japanese social system as a whole was arbitraged," Tada noted in June 2000. As I discussed in chapter 3, for Tada, his team's collective effort to learn the theories and techniques of finance in the context of a Japanese securities firm exposed the limits of the Japanese commitment to learning. The limits consisted in the lack of monetary incentive in the Japanese firm. In discussing the limits of learning in terms of arbitrage, Tada pointed out that Sekai and other Japanese securities firms were too inefficient to compete with their Euro-American counterparts in the global financial markets. The Sekai team's effort to learn theories and techniques of arbitrage, in other words, revealed its own limitations intrinsic to the way it had operated. The difference Aoki sought to create—that is, the difference embodied in Aoki's idea of a Wall Street–style proprietary trading team without a Wall Street–style compensation scheme—became a difference that Euro-American investment banks exploited. Sekai's arbitrageurs were arbitraged, and many of them, like Tada, decided to transform themselves into strong individuals and pursue risk and reward more aggressively in the present. In his own terms, Tada reoriented himself from being a target of arbitrage ("being arbitraged") to being an arbitrageur once again.

Tada told me that his new business enterprise was "just like arbitrage" (June 2000) and that his approach to investment was an extension of his acutely developed arbitrage sensibility. He enthusiastically explained how he could turn a variety of mispriced investments into targets of arbitrage. In his view, the Japanese markets were full of inefficient customary practices and mispriced investments. For example, Tada explained, memberships in golf clubs in Japan are extremely expensive (and hence mispriced) and predicated on norms of exclusivity, prestige, and hierarchy—which, he asserted, have no intrinsic economic value. And yet, he added, many golf clubs are in poor financial condition due to mismanagement. Why not buy and securitize golf courses, manage them efficiently, and sell memberships to the public at large, thereby turning a profit and dealing a blow to the irrational Japanese inclination to overvalue status?

Around 2000, many of Tada's business deals involved securitization. Securitization schemes aim at assembling assets such as bad loans and future cash flows, which are otherwise not easily transferable, into securities that may be divided, consolidated, and traded. In Tada's view, securitization makes previously untradeable assets, cash flows, and associated risks arbitrageable. For example, Tada's fund securitized a small manufacturer's accounts receivable (*urikake saiken*). In a securitization scheme for accounts receivable, typically, a company that wishes to create a cash flow before the payment date of accounts receivable (Company A, hereafter) sells a bundle of accounts receivable at a discount price to a special purpose company set up for the scheme. This special purpose company is usually registered in the Cayman Islands or another tax haven and issues securities to individual investors. The reason for setting up a special purpose company is to avoid the default risk of Company A as well as that of its trading counterparts. Even if Company A or its trading counterparts go bankrupt, investors in this scheme will be protected from creditors.

Tada's motivation for extending arbitrage to various assets, and even to society at large, lay in his faith in the idea of arbitrage—that by making things efficient he was doing good. One late night in March 2000 after many drinks, over which I had described to him my earlier work on the character of faith among indigenous Fijian Christians (H. Miyazaki 2000, 2004b), Tada suddenly became excited. He told me that his ultimate dream was "to help people," and that he believed that this could be done by providing people with a true religion—one that, unlike all the other religions that existed in Japan, did not overcharge its followers. In Japan, he explained, it is difficult to obtain tax-exempt status for a new religion, but he had learned that if one were to buy an existing religious organization, one would also acquire its tax-exempt status. He had already identified several mismanaged religions now in financial trouble. Why not buy one of these together, he proposed to me, and found a religion on the Internet, based upon an anthropological theory of religious faith, that would provide a religious product at an efficient price, and hence fulfill his dream of helping people while also turning a profit?

Recall that Tada understood the Sekai derivatives team's failure as a symptom of Euro-American investment banks' success in arbitraging the entire Japanese financial industry and markets. Tada's renewed faith in the logic of arbitrage was based on his redefinition of his own agency as an arbitrageur of his own society. As Tada's image of arbitrage as a way of life and a blueprint for a better society suggests, arbitrage contains within itself a particular utopian vision—a vision of efficient markets in the form of correct prices (see Polanyi [1944] 1957: 3).

As I have explained, the calculations inherent in arbitrage are predicated on an assumption—a faith—that efficient markets will develop, and hence that equilibrium will be reached at a future point. There is a recursive dimension to this faith because in acting upon this assumption, through his actions in the market, the arbitrageur helps the market to realize its inherent orientation toward efficiency. What is at stake is a particular self-image, in other words, of the arbitrageur as both swept up in the "invisible hand" and *part of* its agency. In this view, the existence of the arbitrageur as rational actor is the condition of possibility for the efficient market that, in turn, makes the arbitrageur disappear.

Tada's dream of creating an automatic trading machine and his later dream of arbitraging Japan's inefficient markets both echo the distinctive temporality of arbitrage oriented toward a condition of no arbitrage. Recall that in theory, arbitrageurs eliminate arbitrage opportunities by exploiting those opportunities. In other words, arbitrageurs work toward a condition of no arbitrage, a hypothetical condition that enables arbitrage in the first place. The circular logic of arbitrage entails a distinctive temporality of a perspective from the end of arbitrage (no arbitrage) and a movement toward that end. As Tada told me, "My dream is to cast a net over the whole world, and to catch it all, in one fell swoop [*ichimodajin*]" (June 2000). What is critical for present purposes is Tada's heroic conception of his mission to drive the market to a condition of no arbitrage in which arbitrageurs like himself might not exist.

A MANUAL FOR TRUST ASSESSMENT

In the summer of 2001, I returned to Japan to discover that Tada was in deep trouble. Although I cannot elaborate on the nature of this trouble, some of the schemes he had devised had gone terribly wrong. Among other things, he had lost a large amount of his personal savings. Tada himself did not tell me about his problems at the time, but he reflected that he had trusted the wrong people. He blamed himself for not being logical enough in the course of entering this new domain of trust and risk. However, his failures also had an intriguing result: he had a new dream. He explained to me excitedly that he was now contemplating the possibility of devising a method to apply logical thinking to calculate other people's trustworthiness:

> I made a mistake. I lacked the capacity to assess the quality of the management and of people. [In the venture capital business] one's ability to manage risk depends on one's ability to evaluate people.... When dealing with investments traded in the market, I always knew where the risks were. But I went into the venture capital business without understanding where the risks were.... You need to do thorough research on what the person [in whose company you consider investing] has done. You interview everyone with whom that person has had a relationship.... My mistake was that I did not do that.... In trading, I had done thorough research. You have to do the same with the quality of the manager of a company. (August 2001)

Logicality was once again emerging as a method for Tada, and trust was emerging as a potential object of calculation and scientific reasoning. Tada's ultimate goal now was to create a manual for venture capital businesses. He believed that he would be able to evaluate quantitatively all elements of a business venture, from the quality of the manager to the business plan.

In the course of our conversation, I asked Tada about the spreadsheet and about the progress he was making toward his retirement goal. "I had the wrong idea," he immediately responded. "Things don't work that way." Tada told me that earning 200 million yen and retiring was no longer his object. He now felt that he wanted to play a bigger game, and to do that, he would need more money. He also said that he wished to recover the losses he had sustained in the previous year. His dream had moved elsewhere, to the idea of developing a model of trust, and his previous dreams had faded into the background.

It is easy to see in this turn the typical pattern of an undisciplined gambler incapable of cutting his losses. However, I prefer to understand this redeployment of logicality as Tada's renewed effort to define a no-arbitrage situation for the situation in which he found himself. His new dream posited the same ultimate displacement of his agency as did his dreams of the trading machine and of early retirement. Once again, his own agency (in the calculation of others' trustworthiness) was to be displaced by a mathematical model. Tada imagined a formal and quantitative method for calculating human trustworthiness independent of his own subjective and intuitive judgment of other people. However, his latest dream also possessed an important difference from his previous dreams. If the movement from the dream of an automatic trading machine to the dream of an early retirement represented a reorientation of his logical method from the market to himself, this latter displacement of his own logical agency (as a judge of character) represented another kind of reorientation: the conversion of his own newly discovered subjective and intuitive method (trust) into the object of logical reasoning.

In the same conversation we had in August 2001, Tada noted that logicality had always been his method. Early in his career at the steel company, he had created a number of manuals rationalizing various procedures in the plant design process. Tada told me, "Many people do not like the idea of creating a manual [because they feel threatened by the idea of disclosing what they know to other people]. But from my point of view, if I make a manual [and write down what I know in it, it is because] I have other higher things to do." In Tada's mind, manuals were just like the automatic trading machine. The purpose of creating manuals was to free himself from one kind of work for other, more interesting kinds of work. The manual for trust assessment in the venture capital business was another manifestation of Tada's vision of an endpoint to his labor. This sense of closure came with an anticipation of other, arguably more interesting and creative, kinds of labor. In this sense, it was merely a means to a higher end. But there is also a clear sense of putting an end to the problem of trust once and for all. This is similar to the simultaneous sense of the end of arbitrage and the infinite extensibility of arbitrage discussed in the previous three chapters.

All of Tada's dreams posited both a strong commitment to work and an equally powerful imagination of an exit from work. Tada's dream of an automatic trading machine pointed to the machine as a replacement for the traders. His spreadsheet calculation and his ensuing foray into the modality of trust and risk taking placed his own favorite method, logicality, in abeyance while pointing to the end of his professional career. Tada's renewed commitment to logicality once again posited what he saw as an objective procedure for calculating trustworthiness as a replacement of his own agency.

Tada's commitment to these dreams was strong enough to define his entire trading team's objectives in the early 1990s, to facilitate his decision to leave Sekai Securities in 1999, and to sustain his energy in the midst of Japan's venture capitalist boom and bust. But it is also important to note that none of his dreams came true. To the extent that all of his dreams can be seen as extensions of his arbitrage sensibility—that is, his commitment to see an end of arbitrage—however, these dreams served as parameters of the extensibility of arbitrage.

In July 2003, Tada was still in trouble, and he even told me that he had lost confidence in logicality as a method:

> Pursuing rationality, that is, having faith in what is right, has been the basis of my confidence. . . . Now my confidence is being shaken. . . . Sometimes I think that my approach to things may be wrong. When things are not going well, I wonder if [my approach to things] is okay. I think that things I have dealt with have been rather simple. I am now facing something complex. Mentally, I am undecided. I cannot see what is absolutely right. I don't know if this [condition] resulted from an internal or external factor but things just don't go as well as I expect.

By the summer of 2005, however, Tada seemed to have rebounded from his loss. His business focus had shifted from venture capitalism and securitization to mergers and acquisitions. A deal he had arranged between a firm manufacturing auto parts and a liquor store chain was exceptionally successful, and he had formally joined the auto parts manufacturer as a financial strategist. Tada seemed to have found a point of equivalence between trust and logicality. He told me:

> Compared to derivatives, [mergers and acquisitions] are not that difficult. They do not require high intelligence. They are more like human sciences. They do not depend on high technology. So many people think that they can do it and go into them. I did everything in that deal with the liquor store. I drafted all the contracts. . . . It all depends on whether you can generate a sense of trust. The difficulty lies there. You have to manage [the relationship between the parties concerned] so that a sense of distrust may not develop. (June 2005)

Tada continued to extend his arbitrage sensibility to new areas of business. In various mergers and acquisitions deals, Tada saw new arbitrage opportunities. For example, when his company bought a school for problem children, he contemplated expanding the business nationwide: "Just like arbitrage, we could swoop up all the problem children in the country" (February 2006). Other targets of "arbitrage" included hospitals and Japanese spirits (*shochu*) distillers. But, as Tada noted, "everyone is computing the value of a company without firm evidence" (February 2006). He also had begun to collaborate with Nagai, the junior trader mentioned in chapter 3. Nagai had left Sekai in 1997 for a reinsurance company, where he worked as an options trader. He later joined the trading software design firm Yamashita had created but had become independent by 2005. Tada and Nagai were contemplating a business venture specializing in applying options pricing models to the valuation of corporations. Here Tada saw a bigger arbitrage opportunity in the midst of Japan's mergers and acquisitions boom (see, e.g., Iwai and Sato 2008; see also Maekawa 2008; RECOF Corporation 2010).

Tada's renewed commitment to arbitrage, and to finance more generally, was partially inspired by the rise and fall during the height of Japan's mergers and acquisitions boom of two prominent figures who advocated the naked power of money: Takafumi Horie, CEO of Livedoor, an Internet-related service provider, and Yoshiaki Murakami, a former Ministry for International Trade and Industry official turned fierce advocate of the shareholder value and CEO of an investment company, M&A Consulting, commonly known as the "Murakami Fund." Both Horie, fondly called "Horiemon" (loosely referring to the beloved Japanese anime character Doraemon), and Murakami, frequently called *mono iu kabunushi* (a shareholder who speaks up), were outspoken about the power of money and ownership. At the height of his fame, Horie appeared on television daily and published numerous books and interviews in which he publicly stated that money could buy anything: "It is money that motivates human beings" (T. Horie [2004] 2005: 71). After Horie and Murakami made a coordinated bid to control Nippon Hoso, a radio station within the Fuji-Sankei Group, a large media conglomerate, the two were arrested in 2006 for multiple counts of violation of the Securities Trading Act and insider trading.[6]

In a conversation we had in February 2006, Tada differentiated himself from Horie. When Tada's company had contemplated buying a large *shochu* producer in November 2005, he heard about Livedoor's interest in the same producer. Tada was surprised to find out the high price Livedoor was offering, and he was skeptical of the way Livedoor was operating. Tada was also shocked to learn about the accounting manipulation Livedoor had been engaged in: "Even if what you have done sounds illegal, it needs to be legal at a closer examination. That is the relationship between legal risk and business. All you need to do is to *arbitrage* between them. If you exceed that, [your business] simply does not make sense" (February 2006).

In Tada's opinion, Horie was right to believe that there was nothing money could not buy. Indeed, money is a leveraging tool and can be used for any purpose, Tada commented. But in his view, it is also important to remember that money is so transparent that it reflects its user's character. Criticizing Horie's public comment about the power of money, Tada remarked, "That is something one should not say even if one believes in it. An adult usually does not say that. So many people destroyed themselves as soon as they said that." Generally speaking, Tada continued, one should not reveal what is going well: "Someone who is making money should not go public. . . . The same is true for arbitrage. As soon as one discloses one's strategy for arbitrage, one ends up being arbitraged by the same method." In Tada's view, "Horie was preoccupied with how to rule the world. He had an illusion that the world belonged to him" (February 2006).

That evening, Tada and I talked for hours at his favorite bar, a place we had visited a couple of times before. The owner and chef of the place, a woman in her fifties, had known Tada for a long time. Our conversations there tended to be personal.[7] We had talked about his closest friend's death, his love affairs, and other private matters. That evening, Tada was cheerful and talkative. He seemed to have just come out of a slump. Tada discussed many other possible interindustry mergers and acquisitions deals. As our conversation continued into the small hours of the night, he began to discuss one of his favorite topics, a possible exit from capitalism: "There is something wrong with today's economy. The basis [of an economy] should be barter. Capitalism is a fraud. It depends upon people's greed. . . . People have begun to sense the limits of this system, but once you are in it, you can't exit from it too easily. . . . But greed destroys civilization. It has already created all kinds of challenges. We are facing important choices. For example, there are environmental problems. Should we make the earth unlivable?" (February 2006).

Tada went on to elaborate his passionate interest in farming, religious healing, and UFOs, which I will turn to in the next chapter. For present purposes, what interests me is how Tada's preoccupation with ends of all kinds, from the end of arbitrage to the end of Japan's inefficient markets, seemed to culminate in his vision of an end of capitalism. His career-long pursuit of an endpoint to his work is related to this vision. Here the tension between the endlessness of arbitrage and its self-closing character manifests itself as the tension between the endlessness and the end of capitalism widely debated in social theory.

Tada's story demonstrates how the act of arbitrage, and its orientation toward a condition of no arbitrage, enhances a sense of an endpoint. Arbitrage's alleged propensity to reach its own endpoint drives arbitrageurs to always be on the lookout for new arbitrage opportunities elsewhere. For arbitrageurs like Tada, arbitrage was infinitely extensible. In (their) theory, arbitrage opportunities could be found everywhere. To the extent that arbitrage is enabled by a hypothetical condition of no arbitrage, however, all extensions of arbitrage entailed the same anticipation of an endpoint. In this sense, arbitrage is based on a simultaneous viewing of arbitrage's endlessness and endpoint.

Sekai arbitrageurs sought to sustain this double vision. Their vision of an exit from arbitrage, work, and capitalism was always predicated on seeing an endpoint to their career but not on actually exiting the market. This is yet another manifestation of arbitrageurs' embrace of ambiguity. Sasaki's dream discussed in chapter 1 is a case in point. Recall that Sasaki's handout and his dream of publishing an academic article on arbitrage were part of his effort to train young arbitrageurs in the sensibility and technique of arbitrage. What is interesting about Sasaki's dream is its anchoring in both arbitrage as a method of trading and arbitrage as a subject of contemplation. That is, his vision of an exit from trading to academic writing took the form of his continued training of new cadres of arbitrageurs.

The options trader Koyama extended the idea of arbitrage to explain all this. In July 2003, at an Italian restaurant in Ginza, Tokyo, he reiterated his trading philosophy, which he had shared with me several times before: "Human thought tends to be linear [*junbari*]. . . . Mine is different. My position focuses on 'spread' [arbitrageable price difference]. It is the position of an arbitrageur. . . . So I do not act emotionally. I just do what I know from my experience works and do it diligently. [What is needed is] discipline to do it through." On that day, however, Koyama had failed to stick to his own rule, and he reflected on what had happened:

> Today began with the worst scenario I had expected, and my nominal losses increased. . . . In retrospect I wish I could have acted differently. I wish I could have executed what I had believed in. I was beaten by the market today, although it was within the range of what I had expected. . . . When I looked at dominant positions in the market this morning, I observed that no one seemed to believe that the Nikkei 225 would go up beyond 9,500 yen. Many people were selling call options on the Nikkei 225 with a strike price of 9,500. [In a call option, if the value of the Nikkei 225 remains below the strike price, the seller of the call option keeps the premium, that is, the price paid for the option. If the value of the Nikkei 225 exceeds the combination of the strike price and the premium, however, the difference becomes the call option buyer's profit. In a call option, therefore, the buyer's losses are limited to the premium paid, while the seller's losses are potentially unlimited.] I did not expect the Nikkei 225 to move too much today but if it moved, I thought, it would go up. . . . If that happened, I reasoned that the sellers of call options with a strike price of 9,500 yen would panic and start buying them back. . . . So I was selling call options with a strike price of 9,500 yen. . . . What happened was that people started buying back the options frantically at the beginning, so the price of this call option started deviating from its theoretical price [and hence the increase in the price of the call option Koyama was selling resulted in unrealized latent losses in his trading position]. . . . My position was hedged [with index futures] . . . but I decided to take more risk [by selling more]. That was a bad trade. I thought that if the market got back to normal, my losses would be reduced. You can see people's weakness in their inability to cut their losses [*songiri*]. [Saddam] Hussein was also like that. He should have withdrawn [from Kuwait] but he was not able to do a loss-cut. . . . This [story] is in *New Market Wizards*. [Schwager says that] it was "a bad trade" [Schwager (1992) 2005: 11–13].

Koyama's reflection on his trade that day was accompanied by complaints about the lack of incentive in his workplace. Koyama's firm had shifted to the merit system two years before, but Koyama's base salary had gone down 30 to 40 percent compared to several years before. Koyama confided to me that he no longer had an incentive to maintain discipline and that he had lost interest in his work:

> I used to have dreams, and I still have dreams, but I feel that I have seen the limits of my capacity. I think that every human is born with a certain capacity, and a truly successful person has a larger capacity. . . . I used to have a will to search for the truth [about the market] but my memory is getting worse, and I have worries at home. Everyone wants to search for a reason that he or she cannot do one thing or another. . . . In order to survive in the market, you have to have a will to search for the truth [*tankyushin*]. You have to face the market seriously [*shinshi ni*] and try to figure out where the opportunities are. I used to be very serious about that sort of thing but I am no longer so. In order to justify that, I say that I am busy with things at home, that my salary does not go up, and so forth.

He went on to say, "If you are given a clear vision for a brighter future, you would work hard now. But without it, why bother? You are arbitraging in your own mind." For Koyama, his only hope was to see his son grow up. Koyama's invocation of arbitrage here is significant. In trying to sustain his commitment to arbitrage, Koyama internalized the idea of arbitrage as a force in his own mind. He used arbitrage sensibility as a modality of engagement with his professional work as an arbitrageur.

Arbitrage is founded on repeated efforts on the part of arbitrageurs to see its endlessness and endpoint. It is predicated on seeing both an endpoint of arbitrage (a condition of no arbitrage) and its infinite extensibility. I argue that arbitrageurs' work focuses on how to keep these opposing perspectives in view. This work sustains arbitrage as arbitrage and arbitrageurs as arbitrageurs. This resonates with the associational logic underlying arbitrage in which profit is made only when two opposing trading positions converge.

The ambiguity inherent in this associational logic in turn enables arbitrageurs to replicate the logic elsewhere. To put it another way, arbitrage can be sustained only through this repeated effort to find arbitrage opportunities outside of finance. But this extensibility of arbitrage is replicated in relation to itself, as in the case of Koyama, when it meets its own limit.

The career trajectories of Tada and other Sekai arbitrageurs showcase efforts on the part of arbitrageurs to see how their professional and personal endpoints could be made to converge. I have repeatedly sought to recapture the arbitrageurs' double vision of ends and endlessness, and my repetition itself replicates the arbitrageurs' repeated efforts to sustain this double vision, gesturing toward a convergence of a sort between my analysis and its object (see also H. Miyazaki 2004b). But, as I have discussed through the case of Tada, the extensions of arbitrage and its sensibilities have not always resulted in convergence. Like Tada's truncated dreams, the extensions of arbitrage often generate a sense of doubt about arbitrage itself. It is now time to see how arbitrage and its double vision may evaporate both for the arbitrageurs themselves and for myself.

CHAPTER 5

The Last Dream

In 2001, Aoki drafted a "business plan" for a hypnotherapy clinic. Entitled "A Holistic Psychotherapy Clinic," Aoki's business plan proposed a clinic that would incorporate Karma treatment, or past-life regression therapy, into the psychiatric treatment of the so-called borderline personality disorder that was widely reported among Japanese youth. Borderline personality disorder usually manifests itself as impulsive behavior out of fear of rejection (see, e.g., Skodol et al. 2002: 936), and it has been widely identified as a cause of suicidal behavior among Japanese youth.[1] The clinic Aoki proposed would be established next to a preexisting hypnotherapy clinic that had been run by a hypnotherapy specialist, Sasajima, since the late 1980s. Aoki's business plan discussed the social significance of the proposed new clinic and outlined problems with preexisting psychotherapeutic practices aimed at tackling borderline personality disorder that were available in Japan. Aoki claimed in the business plan that none of the preexisting methods were capable of dealing satisfactorily with this form of mental disorder. In his view, borderline disorder demanded collaboration between psychiatrists and psychotherapists. The business plan introduced Sasajima's practice and gave a detailed description of his successful treatment of a fifteen-year-old girl. The patient had suffered from borderline personality disorder, which had manifested itself in her repeated attempts to cut her wrists. The business plan also included a financial prospectus for the clinic, a list of services to be provided by the clinic, an organizational chart of the clinic along with a floor plan for the building that would house it, and brief biographical sketches of the psychiatrists and psychotherapists involved in the project, many of whom held or had held appointments with prestigious university hospitals.

Aoki drafted the document in the midst of Japan's "venture capitalist bubble," in which the business plan had emerged as a highly significant genre of writing. Written on a PowerPoint template, Aoki's business plan conformed to a style of presentation increasingly perceived as effective in securing start-up funds in the Japanese business world.[2] Aoki's objective in preparing the business plan was to attract financial investment in the proposed clinic. The initial stated goal was to raise 200 million yen (approximately $1.6 million at the exchange rate of the time), with which the clinic would generate an annual profit of approximately 40 to 50 million yen (approximately $320,000 to $400,000) after the second year of its operation.

Like many of the other business documents I have examined in this book, Aoki's business plan sought to translate his own personal dream into the language of finance. Aoki harbored a long-standing interest in Buddhism and mental health, and he had met Sasajima in the mid-1990s in the context of his more general quest for spirituality. Aoki told me that when he turned forty, in the late 1980s, he felt that he could no longer work as hard as he had up to then. Aoki reflected in February 2000, "When I was young, I did not think too deeply about anything. I was just driven by the sheer power of dashing about [*ikioi*]. But I realized that my body did not move anymore. Something was wrong. I would not be able to work like I had for the previous ten years." Aoki turned at that point to religion. He studied various schools of religious thought, from Buddhism to Hinduism to Christianity. He concluded that all religious movements started as collective hypnosis. That realization led him to explore hypnosis and hypnotherapy, and during that exploration he encountered Sasajima, a well-established hypnotherapy specialist whose practice was often reported on in weekly magazines and daytime television shows.

Aoki's spiritual pursuit was not entirely personal. Since establishing his proprietary trading team inside Sekai Securities in 1987, Aoki had sought to create a workplace where monetary and spiritual goals would be pursued simultaneously. For Aoki, the introduction of Wall Street–style proprietary trading into the Japanese securities firm without explicit financial incentives required the cultivation of what he termed a "diversity of motivations" (*tayo na mochibeshon*). In particular, Aoki encouraged his traders to pursue their interests in "something a little more 'spiritual' [*seishinteki*]" alongside their interests in money and finance:

> When I joined the management [of Sekai in 1992], I thought that [my task] in the context of financial revolution was to transform a conventional securities firm—that is, an old-fashioned firm [based on obsolete principles]—into a firm capable of surviving financial deregulation. I thought that I would need to train necessary staff [for that task]. [In order to achieve that,] I felt that I would need to maintain high motivation among my staff. I did not expect us to be able to do it in the same way as Wall Street [firms] operated. Money would be simply a reward for one's contribution [to the firm's transformation]. I thought that I would need those interested in making money as well as those interested in something a little more spiritual and philosophical. I believed that such diversity of motivations would generate creativity. (August 2001)

It was in this spirit that Aoki introduced his team to a wide range of books, from the economist Katsuhito Iwai's book on Shakespeare's *The Merchant of Venice,* discussed in chapter 1, to the journalist Takashi Tachibana's *Rinshi taiken* (Near death experience), a book about dying patients' experience of the threshold between life and death (Tachibana 1994). At Aoki's encouragement, many of his traders pursued intellectual interests in philosophical, spiritual, and even extraterrestrial matters.

Sekai's management adopted a completely different course of action in 1998, however, entering into a partnership with a U.S. financial group and embracing a performance-based compensation scheme. For Aoki, this move reflected the management's "maniac fascination with foreigners" (*gaijin kabure*) and went against his own deeply held conviction that Japanese had their own way of doing business and would be able to refine those Euro-American methods and ultimately improve and expand upon them. In 1999, Aoki stepped down as an executive officer of the firm in protest.

Aoki's and his traders' interests in spiritual and extraterrestrial matters conforms to a widely accepted observation about the affinity between neoliberalism and New Age spirituality. Religious studies scholars Jeremy Carrette and Richard King draw attention to what they call "a silent takeover of 'the religious' by contemporary capitalist ideologies by means of the increasingly popular discourse of 'spirituality'" (Carrette and King 2005: 2). In their view, this "capitalist spirituality" is not an infusion of religious ethics into business practices, as some business leaders have claimed, but rather an appropriation of "spirituality" as an instrument to support corporate and neoliberal ideologies (p. 129; see also Lau 2000). The penetration of New Age spirituality into mainstream Japanese corporate life likewise is well documented. Noted examples range from the active advocacy of spirituality as a core principle of management by business leaders including Kazuo Inamori, the founder of Kyocera, to Sony's long-standing interest in extrasensory perception. In *Karuto shihonshugi* (Cult capitalism), Takao Saito, a journalist who has written extensively on Japan's economic problems, offers a line of critique similar to Carrette and King's. Saito points to the "curious affinity between our country's [Japan's] corporate world and occultism" (Saito [1997] 2000: 292). In his view, however, these appeals to spirituality are nothing but attempts to use spirituality as a tool of "mind control" and perpetuate a group-oriented work ethic. Saito's point is that what he calls "occult capitalism" is yet another form of postwar Japanese capitalism based on the pursuit of high productivity at the expense of the pursuit of individual and personal happiness (pp. 440–442). Moreover, Saito sharply criticizes corporate spiritualism for its implicitly "authoritarian," elitist, "nationalistic," and latently "eugenic" content (pp. 433–434).

Aoki's insistence on finding an alternative mode of investment banking may point to a more sympathetic view, in which such corporate spirituality could exceed the parameters of efficient management (see, e.g., Nakamaki 2006; Shimazono 2007). In his survey of "company religions" (*kaishakyo*), the anthropologist Hirochika Nakamaki has examined a wide range of forms of religiosity embedded in Japanese corporate culture, from company-sponsored funerals (*shaso*) to business leaders actively advocating religiosity and spirituality as a core principle of management. For example, Konosuke Matsushita, the founder of the Panasonic Corporation (formerly known as Matsushita Electric Devices Manufacturing Company), created a priestly position within the company structure and founded a shrine known as Kongensha celebrating the animistic concept of life force. Likewise, Yukio Funai, a charismatic management consultant for small and medium-sized enterprises, published a book titled *Ego kara Eva e* (From Ego to Eva), which presented an apocalyptic view of capitalism predicting the arrival in the near future of an era in which virtue (*toku*) will replace greed (*yoku*) as the principle of life (Funai 1995; see also Funai 2002). Ultimately, Nakamaki points to the way in which the "religious" components of Japanese corporations have served, and will potentially continue to serve, as a source of resistance to various forms of economic fundamentalism, including the idea of shareholders as owners of companies. In Nakamaki's view, this aspect of Japanese corporations may effectively become a foundation for a Japanese version of corporate social responsibility (Nakamaki 2006: 198–208).

The religious studies scholar Susumu Shimazono also sees a potential for such broad interest in spirituality to generate a critical perspective on capitalism (see, e.g., Shimazono 2000, 2007). Unlike Nakamaki, however, Shimazono does not see this interest as a distinctively Japanese phenomenon. In his view, it is part of a global phenomenon he terms "new spirituality culture" (*shin reisei bunka*), in which individual and personal transformation and healing (*iyashi*) are sought through an interest in spirituality (Shimazono 2007: 48–50, 63). Shimazono's approach to new spirituality culture departs from other, more dominant approaches to New Age spirituality and occultism in a significant way. In Shimazono's view, the "rise of new spirituality culture" stems from the simultaneous "individualization of society" (*shakai no kojinka*) and "increasingly religious quality of individuals" (*kojin no shukyoka*) (pp. 301–306). In particular, Shimazono situates new spirituality culture in the broader context of Japanese intellectual history. He draws attention to the existence of a number of public intellectuals influenced by and actively advocating new spirituality culture by seeking to give intellectual justifications for this global phenomenon.[3] According to Shimazono, these "spirituality intellectuals" (*reisei chishikijin*), in their publications for a broad general audience, have succeeded in replacing progressive intellectuals in post–Cold War Japan by offering Japanese and other non-Western religious and spiritual traditions as new sources of transformative critique (Shimazono 1996: 248; cf. Ivy 1995; Koschmann 1993). Shimazono observes that the success these intellectuals have enjoyed as writers of popular books is an indication of the deep penetration of new spirituality culture into Japanese culture (Shimazono 1996: 267). Although he does not specify clearly what critical perspective these intellectuals have offered, Shimazono implies that new spirituality culture potentially serves as an alternative mode of life to capitalism.[4]

The example of Aoki's derivatives team seems to validate both arguments. On the one hand, Aoki's original goal was to create a distinctively Japanese form of investment banking based not solely on the pursuit of material gain but also on a philosophical and spiritual quest.

Aoki's endeavor entailed a certain culturalist expectation founded on a belief in the moral superiority of Japanese traders relative to their Euro-American counterparts. On the other hand, Aoki's ambition was partially inspired by a broader public interest in spirituality, and Aoki himself admitted that even Wall Street investment bankers were not blindly driven by greed.[5] Indeed, New Age spirituality is closely tied to business elsewhere, not only in the sense of New Age business (see, e.g., Lau 2000) but also in terms of the way ideas such as complexity are anchored simultaneously in business management theories, New Age practices, and scientific theories (see Thrift 2005: 63–67).

From a different point of view, Mary Poovey, Marc Shell, and other humanities scholars have demonstrated that, both historically and philosophically, there are no easy boundaries to draw between the economic, on the one hand, and the social, the cultural, and the theological, on the other hand (see, e.g., Poovey 1998; Shell [1982] 1993a; see also Appadurai 2011; Comaroff and Comaroff 2000; Hirschman [1977] 1997; Maurer 2002b, 2005c, 2006b). My project may be seen as an effort to reach a similar conclusion via another route. However, my focus is not on uncovering hidden linkages between the economic and the noneconomic.

The goal of this chapter is neither to paint an exotic picture of the Japanese business world as intertwined with mystical quasi-religious and spiritual imagination nor to allude, as Shimazono does, to the diffused global convergence of spirituality and business. Instead, I am interested in examining to what extent economic ideas and beliefs and religious ideas and beliefs may be juxtaposed within the framework of arbitrage. My guiding question is this: to what extent can the interests of Aoki and other Sekai traders in spiritual and extraterrestrial matters be explained in terms of their professional commitment to arbitrage and the sensibilities associated with its extension? This is an experiment of a sort in holding two opposing views in anticipation of their convergence, as in arbitrage itself.

In order to explore this question with ethnographic specificity and depth, I examine Aoki's and Tada's interests in spiritual and extraterrestrial matters in terms of their commitment to see an endpoint (to inefficient markets, life, and capitalism) and the ambiguity surrounding such commitment that is brought into focus by both trading and spiritual explorations. The experiment in this chapter is not dissimilar to the long chain of anthropological experiments using cosmology as a heuristic, by scholars including Gregory Bateson ([1936] 1958), Susan

Harding (2000), Edmund Leach ([1954] 1970), Michael Taussig (1997), and Eduardo Viveiros de Castro (1992). Its goal is to see *to what extent* the sensibility Aoki and Tada have cultivated in arbitrage, and in finance more generally, explains or converges with the way they have pursued their personal dreams and intellectual interests in spiritual and extraterrestrial matters. In other words, my goal is to explore the possibility of arbitraging arbitrage.

The diffuse sense of convergence I suggest here gestures toward the so-called affective turn in the humanities inspired by the philosophical work of Gilles Deleuze and Felix Guattari, Brian Massumi, and others (see, e.g., Deleuze and Guattari [1980] 1987; Massumi 2002). In particular, what I have in mind is the political theorist William Connolly's recent analysis of Christian and economic forms of fundamentalism in the United States, in which he attempts to articulate the need for what he calls "emergent causality" (Connolly 2005, 2008): "In politics diverse elements *infiltrate* into the others, metabolizing into a moving complex—Causation as resonance between elements that become fused together to a considerable degree. Here causality, as relations of dependence between separate factors, morphs into energized complexities of mutual imbrication and interinvolvement, in which heretofore unconnected or loosely associated elements *fold*, *bend*, *blend*, *emulsify*, *and dissolve into each other*, forging a qualitative assemblage resistant to classical models of explanation" (Connolly 2005: 870; original emphases).

Connolly's formulation invokes the problematic of causality that Max Weber famously explored in his work. In *The Protestant Ethic and the Spirit of Capitalism,* Weber juxtaposes Protestantism with modern capitalism. To be sure, Weber did not directly posit that the Protestant ethic was a cause of modern capitalism. At most Weber suggested that the religious idea of "calling" somehow gave rise to the secular idea of vocation and work ethic (see Swedberg 2005: 293).[6] The precise content of Weber's argument has been a subject of intense debate, but underlying Weber's methodological concern was his complex understanding of causality sometimes expressed in terms of "elective affinities."[7]

My ethnographic attention focuses on the ambiguous connections and relationality that such elusive causality seeks to capture and the paradoxical way that ambiguity makes explanation powerful. My claim is that ambiguity demands a certain commitment and generates a kind of hope for human relationality (see also Battaglia 2006). The account that follows may give the reader the impression that I use the categories of "economic" and "noneconomic" as if they were distinctive realms to be linked through causality of one kind or another. I do not intend them as such. The categorical contrast of the economic or financial and the religious or spiritual is meant to echo the form of the juxtaposition between two potentially economically linked assets or flows of cash in an arbitrage operation, not to presume the distinctiveness of the two categories. In other words, these categorical constructs serve as a reminder of my commitment to use arbitrage sensibility as my own analytical framework and my present effort to see how far that commitment is sustainable and how it may evaporate.

NO EXIT

In drafting his business plan, Aoki sought the advice of his successor, Tada. As I discussed in chapter 4, Tada left Sekai in 1999 for a small investment fund pooling investors' money and investing in start-up companies. By 2001, Tada had become an experienced evaluator of business plans. Tada immediately dismissed Aoki's plan as unappealing to potential investors. "There is no exit strategy," Tada noted. In other words, the plan did not offer any concrete plans for an initial public offering (IPO). To Tada, Aoki's plan was too vague, and therefore too risky, as an investment proposal.

In response to Tada's criticism, Aoki laughed: "[For Tada,] the only thing that matters is the question of whether a business would lead to an IPO. . . . What concerns him about this business is the fact that a medical entity would not be able to become a publicly traded company and would not be able to distribute profit to investors. . . . This project does not interest him because there is no exit policy" (August 2001).

For Aoki, the proposed project meant something else: it was his "last dream" (*saigo no yume*). He simply found this project immensely fulfilling: "It feels like I am only alive because of this project" (August 2001). Aoki had had a challenging time since he resigned from Sekai Securities in 1999. He served briefly as a figurehead executive of Sekai's subsidiary company specializing in the trust business, but he subsequently quit to join a newly established Internet-based securities trading firm. One of his reasons for joining this firm was his long-term interest in rationalizing trading practices in the Japanese securities markets. There was no public exchange for certain classes of securities, such as local government bonds, which were traded privately between securities firms and institutional investors. Aoki's firm sought to establish an anonymous online environment in which these securities might be traded in public. However, Aoki's renewed effort to rationalize Japan's financial markets was truncated when other major securities firms and market players refused to participate in the online market the firm had created.

This setback was so professionally damaging to Aoki that he gradually lost interest in finance. In the spring of 2001, he became the chief executive officer of an asset management firm that had incurred losses over the last three years, and he was entrusted to rebuild the firm. When we met in August 2001, Aoki began our conversation as he usually did, with a short lecture on the current state of the area of finance on which his new work focused. Our two previous conversations had begun with lectures on the state of the trust business in Japan and the state of Japan's municipal bond markets, respectively. This time, Aoki's opening lecture was on the asset management business. He concluded by saying, "What is sad about this country is that it did not create an environment in which talented people went into the asset management business" (August 2001).

Aoki quickly added, however, that he did not have much passion about this new work. This was when he confided to me, "My last dream [*saigo no yume*] lies elsewhere." He continued, "The market is infinitely interesting but maybe what I want to do at the end of my [professional] life is different." Aoki's "last dream" was to establish the abovementioned clinic incorporating both psychiatry and hypnotherapy. "No matter what, I would like to accomplish this as my last work," Aoki added. He said, "I will try my best to restructure [this asset management firm]. But I have a feeling that I am moving away from finance. I do not see anything in finance that I want to make my last work [*saigo no shigoto*]" (August 2001).

What had prompted Aoki to initiate the hypnotherapy clinic venture was his observations about Japan's economic development since the 1970s and its social consequences. Reflecting on his days of student activism in the 1960s, Aoki told me, "[What was at stake in that movement] was a choice between pursuits of quantity [*ryo*] [in the sense of economic prosperity] and quality [*shitsu*] [of life], and we ended up with that absurd illusion of becoming an economic giant. But at that time there was a chance to pursue quality" (August 2001).

Aoki admitted to me that by the end of the struggle, he had become disillusioned by the ideologically driven nature of the movement and had wanted to experience the real world (*shakai*). But he insisted that because of Japan's choice of quantity in the early 1970s, the country now faced serious social problems, such as the *hikikomori* syndrome, in which teenagers become reluctant to socialize with other people and lock themselves alone in their rooms. Aoki noted, "[These are] problems we cannot easily solve in the way we have dealt with other problems. Now is the time we work together and change [society]" (August 2001). Aoki believed that one thing Japan desperately needed was a new kind of psychotherapy. His "last dream," in other words, was an effort to resurrect his own youthful passion for an alternative to capitalism that would correct the choices he himself had made in the early 1970s. For him, the clinic would serve as an effective solution to one of Japan's most pressing social problems, the problem of youth (see, e.g., Brinton 2011; Genda [2001] 2005; Genda and Maganuma 2004; Yamada 2004).

From Tada's point of view, however, Aoki's perspective was that of someone who had already exited the market. Aoki's lack of interest in economic gains in his hypnotherapy clinic project seemed to prove this view. Tada's insistence on the importance of exit was an articulation of the very concept of arbitrage. In Tada's view, just like ostensibly "risk-free" arbitrage, a business plan needed to make investment in the proposed business sound like *atodashi no janken* ("a delayed play at rock-paper-scissors"), that is, a sure bet. Only through the possibility of exiting (unwinding arbitraging positions) would it be possible for arbitrageurs to sustain their arbitraging positions. Using this reasoning, Aoki's perspective seemed radically different, in that it was based not on a perspective from an end, or future point of convergence, but on an end that had already been achieved.

For Aoki, Tada's concern with having an exit, and his personal preoccupation with the idea of "self-realization" (*jiko jitsugen*), discussed in chapter 4, were nothing but a manifestation of his obsession with Euro-American investment banking culture:

> What does self-realization mean? I don't understand. How could one realize oneself in this world? I just can't get it. People study Buddhism and seek enlightenment. But [they soon realize that] no such thing is possible. There is something common here. There is no such possibility as self-realization. The world is not a place like that. There is no such possibility. What [Tada] means by self-realization is simply making money fast. Make money and retire early. That is the U.S.-style "happy retirement." He calls that

> self-realization, and he can only see things that way. That is not self-realization. (August 2001)

Underlying Aoki's criticism of Tada was Aoki's deep concern with the nature of belief. Aoki went on to criticize Tada's general faith in theories and techniques of finance. As an example of Tada's tendency to believe too much, Aoki discussed the efficient-market hypothesis, a cornerstone of arbitrage operations in which Aoki and his traders specialized. If speculators bet on their own view of the future direction of the market, arbitrageurs are indifferent to what the future may bring. Embracing arbitrage sensibility, in other words, means embracing a different kind of faith than that entailed in an act of wagering. Aoki noted that the efficient-market hypothesis only looked plausible as long as traders had faith in it: "As long as you stick with it, it would be upheld" (August 2001). As I have discussed, arbitrage opportunities are defined in relation to a hypothetical condition of no arbitrage—a condition in which there are no price discrepancies—and arbitrageurs are supposed to drive the market to a condition of no arbitrage by exploring those arbitrage opportunities. Underlying this circular logic is a faith of a subjunctive kind—that is, acting "as if" one believes in arbitrage, or more precisely in the idea of no arbitrage.

Reflecting on the trajectory of the derivatives team he had founded at Sekai, Aoki recalled his encounter with the idea of "relative value trading" in New York during the 1980s, which I discussed in chapter 1. When he heard John Meriwether discuss relative value trading, Aoki felt that "the time will come when relative value trading becomes essential in Japan" (August 2001) because stock prices in the Japanese markets would no longer continue to increase as they had before. Underlying this observation was Aoki's awareness of the limits of believing in and betting on something like the general tendency for the economy to keep growing.

Aoki thought that Tada went too far—he *actually* believed in the logic of arbitrage and of finance. The team committed itself to program trading based on the quantitative method and the efficient-market hypothesis, but in Aoki's view, eventually confronted the limitations of both. Aoki insisted to me that, at the outset, he had stressed to Tada and other junior traders the unknowability of the market. He said, "I told them that what they should learn is how to engage with [*tsukiau*] the market. But things seem to have changed after I left the team [in the early 1990s]" (August 2001). With this comment, Aoki suggests that under Tada's leadership, more emphasis was placed on the ultimate knowability of the market through rigorous scientific reasoning.

In more general terms, Aoki's point was that one should not have faith in any single method: "There is nothing in the world that is worth believing in." Aoki noted:

> People tend to have faith in something. You should not have faith in anything. You should not believe in anything. That applies to the world of psychology. People tend to believe in the Morita method. The Morita method works for some but not for others. [Its effectiveness] changes over time for some [for whom it used to work]. . . . The reason that I have come to think this way is that I made a mistake myself. I mean that I once believed in something. It worked for me for some time and then I got into trouble. There is nothing in the world that is worth believing in. I reached the conclusion that one needs to keep some distance from everything. (August 2001)

Aoki was alluding here to his bitter experience of losing money when he traded derivatives in New York.

When I visited Aoki in February 2000 at Sekai's subsidiary firm, where he then served as CEO, he drew my attention to a picture of Sai Baba, a South India–based holy man and religious leader with numerous followers worldwide, that was prominently displayed in his office. He quickly noted that he had simply received the picture from someone who had met Sai Baba, telling me apologetically, "I am not a follower of Sai Baba. I simply think that there may be such a point of view."[8] Aoki then alluded to the commentary of Genpo Yamamoto (1866–1961), a prominent Japanese Zen Buddhist monk, on *Mumonkan,* a collection of forty-eight Zen koans by Wumen Huikai (Mumon Ekai) (Yamamoto 1960; see also Aitken 1990). Yamamoto maintains that in Zen Buddhism, one does not adhere to any one school of thought, pointing to the following passage at the beginning of *Mumonkan*: "The Buddha mind and words point the way; the Gateless Barrier is the Dharma entry. There is no gate from the beginning, so how do you pass through it? Haven't you heard that things which come through the gate are not the family treasure? Things gained from causal circumstances have a beginning and an end—formation and destruction" (Aitken 1990: 3).

Commenting on this passage, Genpo Yamamoto states:

> "There is no gate in Zen Buddhism." Consider any other teachings of Buddhism. The Lotus sect is founded on the Lotus Sutra and utters "Glory to the Sutra of the Lotus of the Supreme Law!" [*Namumyohorengekyo*] as their

> prayer [*daimoku*]. The Shinshu sect is founded on the three sutras. The Kegon sect is based on the Four Dharma Realms. But there is no foundation in Zen Buddhism. Its foundation is one's disposition [*shonettama*]. . . . The foundation is one's innate capacity and instinct, and so polish the mirror that is inevitably fogging up. (Yamamoto 1960: 2–3)

Aoki's point was that as in Zen Buddhism, in approaching the market, one needed to avoid being captured by any single perspective.

From Tada's perspective, however, it was Aoki who believed too much, and he insisted that faith or belief was not his modality of engagement with the world. Tada himself had a long-standing interest in spiritual and other supernatural matters. He had learned to practice Reiki, healing through power ostensibly transmitted through the palms of one's hands, and had studied numerous other forms of healing and relaxation. In particular, Tada had read widely about remote viewing, ufology (the study of UFOs), and various other techniques for transcending time and space.[9] He had bought a CD from the Monroe Institute, an organization that provides techniques for a process of controlling human consciousness known as Hemi-Sync. The CD supposedly allows its listeners to achieve a condition in which they are asleep while their mind stays awake, arguably the same state that Tibetan Buddhist monks spend years of practice striving to achieve. This state ostensibly enables one to see one's past and communicate with the dead (www.monroeinstitute.org/).

However, Tada claimed that his interest in afterlife and ufology was purely scientific, rather than religious, and was part of his more general "pursuit of truth" (*shinri no tankyu*) (June 2007). Tada's interest in UFOs and other phenomena in which time and space are transcended had much to do with what he perceived as another kind of an end—the end of capitalism. In his view, once the mechanism by which UFOs fly has been figured out, the entire system of capitalism will fall apart, because capitalism revolves around the scarcity of resources, particularly energy resources. Tada noted that, in fact, such techniques for remote viewing had been researched thoroughly by the U.S. military and the CIA, and training manuals had been disclosed. Tada claimed that the United States had acquired technologies from extraterrestrial aliens—the same technologies that kept UFOs flying—that would allow it to do without oil. (February 2006).[10]

Both Aoki and Tada, then, sustained a certain sense of ambiguity about spiritual and extraterrestrial matters. Aoki was explicit about his rejection of any faith-like commitments, but he also saw a certain epistemological parallel between the financial and spiritual worlds. Tada also rejected faith as a modality of engagement with these matters, and he too was immersed in a search for points of convergence among financial, spiritual, and extraterrestrial explorations.

Aoki's and Tada's ambiguous approach to spiritual and extraterrestrial matters resonates with the kind of ambiguity that they had cultivated and sought to sustain in arbitrage. As I discussed in chapter 2, for my arbitrageur-interlocutors, arbitrage was based on a subjunctive, or "as if," faith that allowed them to see simultaneously arbitrage opportunities in the present and a condition of no arbitrage—the end of arbitrage—in the future they themselves would help to realize. A similar kind of ambiguous faith seems to have generated these various visions of an end of life and of capitalism side-by-side with the traders' commitment to theories and techniques of finance.

The relationship between Aoki's and Tada's financial and spiritual quests was itself also ambiguous. When we spoke in 2000, Aoki admitted that he was not entirely clear how his interest in Buddhism, hypnosis, and other religious and spiritual phenomena was related to his professional work: "When I go home, I absolve myself in that world but I do not know how it is connected to the world of business" (February 2000). This explains why he saw his "last dream" and his work as parallel worlds rather than worlds that would ultimately collapse into each other. For Tada, his interest in arbitrage, like his interest in spirituality and extraterrestrial matters, was a pursuit of a kind of truth, in that it depended on an understanding of the mechanism of the markets. At the same time, Tada sometimes expressed his desire to turn spiritual quests into profit-generating work.

In this sense, the debate between Aoki and Tada can be interpreted as yet another manifestation of the double vision entailed in arbitrage. The two traders' critiques of capitalism based on their mutual interest in spirituality points to a radically different meeting of the economic and the spiritual in the midst of global capitalism. Both Aoki's and Tada's critiques of global capitalism point to their shared sense of ambiguity about the possibility of exiting capitalism. From my perspective, what united them was their sustained commitment to ambiguity and associated view of two opposing paths and their future convergence.

The material I have presented in this chapter fits well with Shimazono's observations, mentioned earlier, in that it points to both the potential and limitations of spiritualism as a source of critical imagination. Aoki's psychotherapy project enhances his long-standing personal critique of capitalism while it stops short of breaking away from the world of finance. Likewise, Tada's interest in the extraterrestrial points to the existence of parallel worlds that allowed him to imagine what lies beyond capitalism and life, even as it led him to participate in nothing more than a conspiracy theory. As a result, however, these cases illuminate a specific manifestation of so-called New Age spirituality or new spirituality culture that does not deploy spirituality for either "mind control" or a critique of capitalism.

But the contrasting cases of Aoki and Tada and their interests in spirituality are significant only in relation to the material presented in the previous four chapters concerning the history of the team they led. In this sense, Aoki's and Tada's cases point to the possibility of extending arbitrage and its commitment to embrace ambiguity as a framework for understanding their spiritual and extraterrestrial interests. The debate between Aoki and Tada is a reminder that there is nothing stable about arbitrage and perhaps other theories and techniques of finance. What exists is a continual debate among arbitrageurs about what makes arbitrage arbitrage.[11]

In this chapter, I have discussed Aoki's dismissal of Tada's "faith" in logical reasoning and arbitrage. Aoki's point was that in order to be a good trader, one should not believe in anything. But, paradoxically, he also noted that arbitrage worked as long as one believed in it. In response, Tada rightly pointed out that Aoki's criticism of Tada's faith in logical reasoning and arbitrage was a view from someone who had already exited the market. Tada viewed his own faith in logical reasoning and arbitrage as different from the speculator's leap of faith. Given the market's unknowability, logical reasoning and arbitrage were the only sure things to him. In other words, Tada's faith was the kind of faith entailed in the traders' insistence that their trading was arbitrage, and not speculation, while knowing full well that it could be regarded as speculation.

The tension between Aoki's and Tada's positions points to yet another kind of double vision entailed in arbitrageurs' engagement with the world. For them, arbitrage was predicated on the coexistence of faith and skepticism. Any move toward one side or the other, such as what Aoki detected in Tada's emphasis on logical reasoning, therefore provoked criticism. Tada's countercriticism followed the same logic. We can see here that arbitrage is a modality of engagement that sits on both a qualified faith in itself and a deep skepticism about itself. Arbitrageurs saw such ambiguity as a condition of the possibility of arbitrage. This debate was only sustained by their shared subjunctive faith in arbitrage, however. When that faith fades away, the debate also fades away.

THE END OF ARBITRAGE?

Both Aoki and Tada struggled with Japan's rapidly changing financial landscape. Aoki experienced one setback after another, whereas Tada was deep in highly controversial investment practices, such as *daisansha wariate* ("allocation of newly issued stocks to a third party") involving a financially struggling company. Both Aoki and Tada were preoccupied with immediate personal crises, and arbitrage and other theories and techniques of finance were rapidly receding to the background. The financial crisis of 2007 to 2008 intensified their sense of the irrelevance of the kind of financial knowledge they had sought to master.

By 2005, Aoki's "last dream" itself had confronted a serious obstacle: Sasajima, the hypnotherapy treatment specialist with whom Aoki had collaborated, had had a stroke. Aoki had quit the asset management firm in December 2003 and had moved to a small securities firm specializing in structured finance. Aoki's new work concerned investment schemes involving the trading of real estate. By February 2005, however, Aoki told me, he had decided to quit finance altogether. He thought he had entered what Buddhists would call *rinjuki* (*vânaprasthya*), the phase of retreating into a forest. Along with his career in finance he intended to abandon his last dream. "No one would trust a person without a job," Aoki noted. "I just decided to give up on everything." In the end, however, he decided to stay in finance. In the spring of 2005, he joined a midsize securities firm's principal investment division, which was run by someone he had known for a long time. As he put it, "This time I was able to hold on to a will to contribute to society through my work. If I had really quit [in February], that will probably would have evaporated also" (June 2005). For Aoki, actually ending his career in finance meant an end of his personal dream. The arbitrage-like commitment to two opposing perspectives seemed to have been sustained.

In a long conversation over lunch in June 2007, however, Aoki confided to me that, over the last few years, he had sought the help of a female psychic medium known for her remote viewing power. Aoki had met the medium through Sasajima in the mid-1990s. When the Internet trading firm ran into trouble in 2001, Aoki thought of this psychic medium and phoned her. Even before Aoki explained the situation to her, the medium told Aoki that she would seek her god's advice. She told Aoki to give up on the firm that he was heading at the time. Aoki was taken aback because he had been just thinking about closing down the firm. He told me that he did not understand how the medium had been able to foresee the trouble he had confronted professionally. This experience convinced him to seek her advice more regularly in the future.

When Aoki was recruited to the asset management firm, he called up the medium again. She told Aoki that the opportunity would not yield much, but she advised him to take it up. So he did. Aoki sought her advice again just before he resigned from the asset management firm. The medium immediately figured out that Aoki was in conflict with someone in the company and told him to quit the firm right away and take up the position at the small securities firm. She told him that he would need to keep on going by "linking" (*tsunageru*) one opportunity to another. That advice made him feel better, he said: "otherwise, I would have been shattered to pieces" (June 2007). Every time he was offered a new job, he called up the medium and she told him to accept the offer, while saying that it would not be easy for him. She told him that there would not be anything exciting for a while but that he would not be deprived of an opportunity. Aoki characterized his life as "a life linking one work to another" (*shigoto wo tsunagu jinsei*) (June 2007). This is why Aoki had refused to stop taking up one appointment after another. As it turned out, it was not the sensibility of ambiguity and associated sense of possibility for convergence he cultivated in arbitrage and finance, but his faith in the medium's assuring words, that sustained his will to work and dream this time.

Recall this book's opening episode. In late July 2010, Tada declared that finance was nothing but "fraud" and arbitraging of knowledge—that is, arbitraging those who are not informed of the real consequences of finance. Tada commented on the significance of the global financial crisis originating from the collapse of the U.S. subprime mortgage markets: "[The crisis] revealed a simple fact, that is, that finance is nothing but a fraud." But Tada also framed this fraud in terms of arbitrage: "As it has turned out, finance was the arbitrage of knowledge gaps between those who know [those in the financial industry] and those who don't [the public], not arbitrage between markets, and this fact has been revealed" (July 2009). There was nothing in Tada's words that reflected his past will to "arbitrage" Japan (Japan's inefficient system). The possibility of transforming himself from an object of arbitrage to an active agent of arbitrage had evaporated. For him, finance, in the sense of the arbitrage of knowledge, had ended.

The appreciation of one kind of end echoed that of yet another kind of end. Our conversation took place at our favorite bar in Roppongi. The original owner of the bar had passed away earlier that year. The woman, whom her patrons affectionately called "Mama," was significant in Tada's personal life. He had originally been taken to the bar by a close female friend of his, an investment banker who committed suicide several years later. The new owner, a former frequent customer of the bar, had kept the business going, but as we munched on the food he prepared for us, both Tada and I quietly acknowledged to each other how much we missed Mama's distinctive elegance and hospitality.

The trajectory of the long debate between Aoki and Tada concerning money, life, and death reflects a broader loss of faith—or ambiguous and subjunctive faith, more precisely—in finance. Their once-shared commitment to the sensibilities of arbitrage was fading away. The loss of faith, albeit of a subjunctive kind, in arbitrage seems to have led Aoki and Tada to lose ambiguity in their personal and professional lives. As they faced increasingly difficult market conditions and the effects of the global financial crisis, they have become more deterministic in their assessments of the world surrounding them. If the technique of arbitrage helped them to keep a double vision of both a clear view of the future and its doubtful credibility, the loss of faith in arbitrage seems to have generated a clearer vision of the known and the unknown.

The end of arbitrage, and the end of finance, increasingly became apparent for many other Sekai traders whose professional lives I have examined in this book. For example, in June 2007, Sasaki reflected on his past dreams: "There was a period of time in the past when I worked with a dream. . . . Mr. Tada sought to create an environment in which all kinds of simulations would be possible [so that his team might create a trading machine interactive with the market]. We all worked with the purpose of creating that sort of thing."

As I discussed in chapter 1, Sasaki sought to sustain a dream in his new position in a Japanese megabank by training new cadres of arbitrageurs. But by 2007, Sasaki had abandoned his dream of publishing an article on financial mathematics. In reminding me of the fact that the dream he used to share with Tada and other traders was misguided, Sasaki was alluding to the fact that the kind of convergence of professional and personal intellectual lives Sasaki had sought in his past dreams turned out to be impossible. This was partially due to the change that Sasaki saw in the Japanese workplace. Sasaki noted that Japanese corporations had begun to separate their employees' professional lives from their personal lives:

> [After the bubble economy,] Japanese society changed. We all felt that Japan had been defeated. Japanese companies used to be family-like. The company would intrude into your private life. [But things are not like that anymore.] In the past I would take home boring tasks, but nowadays, if you did that, you would be accused of taking the company's proprietary information out of the company. In the past I used to try to acquire personal addresses of my colleagues including those working in other sections of the company than mine, but nowadays all such information is regarded as private and unavailable. Personally, however, things have become easier as a result of the clear separation of the private world and the workplace. We now know that the world exists as a result of various different coexisting things. What I think about at home is different from what I think about at work. (June 2007)

As a result of this separation, Sasaki had shifted his intellectual energy to his own personal weekend study of mathematics. Sasaki still retained his dream of contributing to society, but his new dream was decoupled from his professional work. His ambition focused on developing a free computer program to assist daily reading and thinking for businesspeople like himself. The resonance between the sensibilities of arbitrage and his past dreams in terms of their shared commitment to see convergence between two comparable movements (prices, cash flows, professional and personal intellectual interests, and so on) seemed to have evaporated.

Tanaka, the convertible bond trader at a European investment bank mentioned in chapters 2 and 3, was asked to leave the bank in 2005. The strategy he once analogized to jazz improvisation had ceased to work in the convertible bonds markets. In retrospect, he told me in March 2010, what he was doing was not arbitrage at all. Rather, in his opinion, the trading of convertible bonds was like the Harlem Globetrotters' performance of passing a ball from one player to the next. The market of convertible bonds issued by Japanese corporations was small; in his estimate, there were only one hundred participants in the market, mostly proprietary traders trading for investment banks and hedge fund managers. In 2005, convertible bonds were irrationally overpriced. Tanaka noted that traders had started passing the same bond around and around while knowing that it was a "bomb," meaning that at some point it could not be sold to anyone. The market suddenly crashed, and Tanaka incurred large losses.

Tanaka was unable to find employment for two years. He was eventually hired by a Japanese securities firm and became deputy director of the firm's equity division. As a result of his experience in the convertible bonds markets, he was disillusioned with the idea of arbitrage. As noted in chapter 2, Tanaka was not entirely sure whether he was engaged in arbitrage or speculation in the convertible bonds markets, but this time his ambiguity disappeared. In his view, arbitrage was nothing but a fiction. Instead, he had started advocating speculation, and as deputy head of the equity division, he had his own proprietary trading account that he used to bet on certain stocks as a speculator. In the summer of 2010, however, the firm suddenly closed Tanaka's account, and his career as a trader ended.

The end of arbitrage was both more abrupt and somewhat more emancipating for others. In March 2010, the options trader Koyama was informed by his firm's management that the fund he had managed would be closed. He was asked whether he wanted to quit the firm or be transferred to another section as an analyst, and he was given two weeks to make up his mind. He discussed his future with his wife. She asked him whether he wanted to continue to work as a trader. He was not sure. One day he happened to receive an email announcement of a workshop featuring options traders from foreign firms. It suddenly dawned on him that these options traders were ten or more years younger than he was and had traded options for over ten years. He had never thought of his age, but he came to the conclusion that he should retire from trading. Koyama confided to me that he had felt "God's hands" (April 2010). His fund's annual return had been 4 or 5 percent and he had been stressed about the low performance of the fund. He wanted to close the fund but would not be able to initiate the process himself. When he was told that his fund would be closed and be refunded to investors, Koyama felt relieved. The arbitrageur of his own mind was not able to make up his mind. He sustained his ambiguous faith through the metaphor of arbitrage itself until his career as an arbitrageur ended rather abruptly.

Perhaps many Sekai arbitrageurs had already anticipated arbitrage's endpoint in their initial encounter with and excitement about the idea of arbitrage. As I have repeatedly pointed out in this book, after all, arbitrageurs had only an "as if" faith in arbitrage. In this sense, the end of arbitrage was inevitable. Moreover, in more general terms, arbitrageurs knew that arbitrage was predicated on the idea of no arbitrage, an endpoint to arbitrage. There was nothing surprising about the situation in which arbitrage was no longer possible, although the situation in which Sekai arbitrageurs found themselves late in the first decade of the twenty-first century was far from a condition of no arbitrage or market efficiency. From one point of view, everything looks like arbitrage. From another point of view, there is no arbitrage. And this viewing of the two opposing positions itself is part of arbitrage. To sustain that view demands a commitment to or faith in the sensibilities of arbitrage. But that possibility is quickly fading, for both my trader-interlocutors and myself.

CHAPTER 6

From Arbitrage to the Gift

In his 2000 book, *Nijuisseiki no shihonshugiron* (A theory of capitalism for the twenty-first century), Katsuhito Iwai, the economist and public intellectual whose analysis of *The Merchant of Venice* served as an important source of inspiration for Sekai Securities arbitrageurs, situated speculation and its destabilizing force at the heart of capitalism. Writing in response to the global financial crises that shook the world in the late 1990s, Iwai first examined consequential shifts in the debate about East Asian capitalism between 1997 and 1998. He argued that the failure of the Long-Term Capital Management hedge fund in September 1998 had changed economists' view on East Asian economies:[1] "[After the collapse of Long-Term Capital Management,] it was increasingly argued that the most significant cause of the financial crisis should be found not in those East Asian countries' domestic factors but in excessively 'speculative activities' of hedge funds and transnational investment banks that move funds from one financial market to the next all over the world in search of short-term gains. . . . Economists were relieved because they were finally able to identify the real 'culprit' that had caused the financial crises. The name of the 'culprit,' of course, was the speculator" (Iwai 2000: 11).

Iwai was being ironic here; in his view, the speculator was nothing but a "scapegoat." Iwai went on to contemplate the nature of speculation. He drew attention to the famous beauty contest analogy that Keynes put forward in *The General Theory of Employment, Interest, and Money.* Like a newspaper beauty contest in which readers aim to choose "the average preferences of the competitions as a whole" (Keynes [1936] 1997: 156), Keynes suggested, speculation is "an infinite chain of expectations" (Iwai 2000: 21). Iwai discussed what he termed the "paradox of rationality," the tendency for "individual pursuits of rationality [to] generate irrationality for society as a whole" (p. 23). According to Iwai, the Asian currency crisis was simply one of many manifestations of this paradox. Since capitalism is predicated on the principle of speculation, Iwai declared that capitalism would continue to cause such crises in the future (p. 33). He claimed that the development of financial derivatives simply increased the scale, scope, and speed of this perpetual process (pp. 25–31).

Iwai quickly reminded the reader, however, that the derivatives traders identified as "culprits" in the aftermath of the financial crises of the late 1990s are not necessarily different from ordinary participants in the market economy. In his view, speculation, that is, "buying low and selling high" (p. 11), is "the most essential activity of the market economy" (p. 13).

Recall that in his interpretation of *The Merchant of Venice,* Iwai identified the exploitation of price difference—that is, "buying low and selling high"—as the foundational principle of capitalism since the time of merchant capitalism. There Iwai attended to the way capital "mediates" (*baikai*) different systems of value in its effort to increase itself (Iwai [1985] 1992). In his 2000 book, Iwai called the same principle *speculation.* In his view, those in the market economy cannot but be speculators: "In the market economy, both the production of commodities and the consumption of commodities by nature entail an element of speculation. . . . Speculators are not different species standing in opposition to consumers and producers. Everyone who produces, exchanges, and consumes in the market economy is a speculator in all aspects of his/her existence. The true 'culprit' is us" (Iwai 2000: 13).

Iwai's theory of capitalism has an ironic twist. In his view, because we are all speculators, we cannot avoid continuing to cause crises. Iwai urged his readers to recognize and embrace this "fate" (p. 69), a reference that recalls his earlier analysis of the long-distance trader Antonio's melancholy as an effect of capitalism's exploitation and elimination of difference.

Speculation continues to serve as a dominant framework for critiquing financial capital (see, e.g., Galbraith [1954] 1997; Harvey 1989, 2000; Henwood [1997] 1998; LiPuma and Lee 2004; Shiller [2000]

2001; Strange 1986). The persistent focus on speculation in the critical study of financial markets implies skepticism about the claim by Sekai traders and other financial market professionals that they are not speculators, but arbitrageurs. In this final chapter, I juxtapose Sekai arbitrageurs' philosophical extensions of arbitrage with social theorists' critical engagements with speculation in order to unpack the broader implications of arbitrageurs' ambiguous faith in arbitrage and the intellectual work entailed in sustaining that faith for the critique of capitalism. I preserve the format of my ethnographic account by staying close to Sekai traders' reading lists. In particular, I return to Katsuhito Iwai's work and introduce his collaborator Kojin Karatani, a literary critic and philosopher whose work has been highly influential among Japanese intellectuals of my generation (see Karatani and Iwai 1990).[2] This is an effort on my part to see where the thinking of Sekai traders converges and diverges with my own. I offer this as an example of the possible collaboration and conversation between financial market experts and humanistic social scientists, like myself. I conclude the book with a reflection on the relationship between finance and anthropology and their respective methods, with a view to arbitraging that relationship using the sensibilities of arbitrage I have sought to represent, recapture, and replicate in these pages.

SALTO MORTALE

In a series of essays originally written in Japanese between 1998 and 2000 and published in 2003 as *Transcritique on Kant and Marx*, Kojin Karatani reconstructs a critique of capitalism. Karatani follows Marx to identify a moment of faith—a *salto mortale,* or "fatal jump"—in the production of surplus value, and in this moment of faith Karatani sees an opportunity to interject a countermovement.

In contrast to Iwai's ironic diagnosis of global capitalism, Karatani takes on the more self-consciously normative task of rereading Kant and Marx in search of a program to reconstruct communism after the collapse of the Soviet Union (see also Shimada, Yamashiro, and Karatani 2000). In *Transcritique,* Karatani dismisses deconstruction and other theoretical devices that he admits he himself had once habitually deployed in his critiques of capitalism. In the preface, Karatani elaborates on this impetus to rethink Marx:

> I, too, was part of this vast tendency—called deconstruction, or the archaeology of knowledge, and so on—which I realized later could have critical

> impact only while Marxism actually ruled the people of many nation-states. In the 1990s, this tendency lost its impact, having become mostly a mere agent of the real deconstructive movement of capitalism. Skeptical relativism, multiple language games (or pubic consensus), aesthetic affirmation of the present, empirical historicism, appreciation of subcultures (or cultural studies), and so forth lost their most subversive potencies and hence became the dominant, ruling thought. Today, these have become official doctrine in the most conservative institutions in economically advanced nation-states. (Karatani 2003: x–xi)[3]

Karatani's move to reconsider his own theoretical orientation did not originate from the more commonly noted loss of faith in alternatives to capitalism (see, most notably, Harvey 2000). Rather, the motivation for Karatani's intellectual reorientation derives from the loss of the critical power of theory due to capitalism's appropriation of the very theoretical devices previously used to produce ironic diagnoses of capitalism.[4] Karatani's endeavor focuses on reconstructing critique as what he terms "transcritique," or critique that is "both transcendental and transversal" (Karatani 2003: 4). Karatani also remarks in the preface to *Transcritique* that, "beginning in the 1990s, my stance, if not my thinking itself, changed fundamentally. I came to believe that theory should not remain in the critical scrutiny of the status quo but should propose something positive to change the reality" (p. xii). My aim is not to evaluate Karatani's project and others that recognized the limitations of irony, however. Rather, my purpose is to present an example of the particular kind of utopian vision that is based on such a faith in the possibility of critique.

Central to Karatani's transcritique is Marx's theory of value form. Karatani writes: "The asymmetrical relationship inherent in the value form (between commodity and money) produces capital, and it is also here where the transpositional moments that terminate capital can be grasped. And it is the task of transcriticism to make full use of these moments" (p. 25). Karatani draws particular attention to the following sentence from *Capital* concerning the role of faith in the production of value: "C-M. *First metamorphosis of the commodity, or sale.* The leap taken by value from the body of the commodity into the body of the gold is the commodity's *salto mortale,* as I have called it elsewhere. If the leap falls short, it is not the commodity which is defrauded but rather its owner" (Marx [1867] 1990: 200–201; original emphases). Karatani explains, "Whether or not the commodity is valuable is determined only after the *salto mortale* of the exchange" (Karatani 2003: 190).

In Karatani's view, this moment of *salto mortale* presents an opportunity for a countermovement to intervene. In particular, he argues, "Surplus value that sustains industrial capital can exist, in principle, only thanks to this mechanism that workers *in totality* buy back what they produce. Surplus value is finally realized on the consumption point, the place where capital is confronted by alterity and compelled into a *salto mortale* as a seller of commodities" (p. 289). In other words, "[Capital] has to, at least once, stand in the selling position due to its self-reproductive nature" (p. 207).

From this standpoint, Karatani argues for a movement of consumers and workers "posited in the context of the theory of value form and seen as a transposition from relative value form to equivalent value form (from seller of labor-power commodity to buyer of commodities); and further in the context of the capital's metamorphosis: M-C-M′" (p. 296). Karatani continues:

> The self-reproductive movement of capital will never end by itself; it will continue, no matter what kind of crises it entails. Then, in what way can one stop it? I would propose an idea of combining two endeavors. The first one is to create a form of production and consumption that exists outside the circuit of M-C-M′—the consumers'/producers' cooperative. In this "association of free and equal producers," there is no wage labor (labor-power commodity). In order to make this entity grow and expand, one ought to establish a financial system (or a system of payment/settlement) based on a currency that does not turn to capital, namely that does not involve interest. (p. 297)

Ultimately, Karatani took his own leap of faith to launch what he termed an "associationist movement" to end capitalism, turning to Local Exchange Trading Systems (LETS) as the basis of this movement (pp. 298–300; see also Karatani 2000a). Karatani sees "a ray of hope" (Karatani 2003: xii; see also Karatani 2000b) in this concept. Along with the renowned poststructuralist philosopher Akira Asada and other thinkers, Karatani established the New Associationist Movement (NAM) in 2000 (Karatani 2000b). *Transcritique* was originally his effort to give this movement philosophical underpinnings. NAM was subsequently disbanded a few years later.

What interests me is Karatani's attention to the role of a leap of faith in Marx's theory of value form. According to Karatani, what differentiates Marx from classical economists is Marx's understanding of commodity as a "synthesis": "Like classical economists, Marx, too, claimed that commodity was use-value and [exchange-] value at the same time;

the difference was that he grasped it as a synthesis that might happen in the future. He saw it ex ante facto. Seen in this way, there is no guarantee as to whether the synthesis is realized" (Karatani 2003: 187). And, Karatani adds, "the synthesis is not possible if not for a leap" (p. 189). Here Karatani juxtaposes the leap Marx saw in commodity exchange with the leap Søren Kierkegaard saw in Christian faith (p. 189).[5]

In Karatani's terms, the speculative moment of capital demands yet another kind of speculation. Marx discovered commodity's leap of faith through an analogous leap of faith required to grasp that synthesis. Likewise, Karatani views the task of ending capitalism as demanding a similar speculative leap. This in turn invites a different kind of leap of faith and speculation on his own part, that is, his move to bet on the "principle of the NAM" (see Karatani 2000b).

Iwai and Karatani's positions were simultaneously unique and not so unique. They returned to critiques of classical economics—John Maynard Keynes's *The General Theory of Employment, Interest and Money* ([1936] 1997) and Karl Marx's *Capital* ([1867] 1990), respectively. And they both took on speculation as a target of their critique as well as a modality of critique. In Iwai's view, everyone cannot but be a speculator in capitalism. In Karatani's view, the speculative leap of faith is as essential to critique as it is to the reproduction of capital. The view they hold in common—that capitalism is an endless or perpetual movement—is widely shared among social theorists (see, e.g., Wallerstein 1991).[6] Iwai's ironic stance has been a pervasive position in critiques of capitalism since the 1980s, whereas Karatani's heroic activism has been an increasingly popular mode of argument on the left (see, e.g., Graeber 2011).

In response to the global financial crisis of 2007 to 2008, Iwai and Karatani have recast their respective critiques of capitalism. In a series of essays, Iwai once again points to the relevance of Keynes's beauty contest analogy and describes the current crisis as a demonstration of the inherent instability of capitalism. Iwai also notes that the current crisis has gone more deeply than the crises of 1997 to 1998 in that it has shaken people's belief in money itself. In his opinion, this has manifested itself in the weakening of the U.S. dollar (Iwai 2008). Ultimately, however, Iwai suggests that the crisis only marked the "second end" (Iwai 2011: 261), after the depression of 1929, not the "true end" (p. 262), of laissez-faire capitalism:

> Can this second end really be the true end of laissez-faire? The answer is perhaps "no." People's memories are short, especially on economic matters.

> When all the dust raised by the current global economic crisis has settled down and, with the help of discretionary fiscal and monetary policies as well as stricter rules of financial regulations, global capitalism has regained a certain degree of stability, the advocates of the laissez-faire doctrine are bound to come back and start to rain praise upon the virtue of the "invisible hand." History may then repeat itself, the first time as tragedy, and the second time probably as tragedy too. (p. 261)

Likewise, Karatani emphasizes the "repetitive structure" (*hanpukuteki kozo*) of capital (and the nation-state) and the endlessness of capitalism, which occasionally culminates in a catastrophic crisis, and he once again gestures toward a movement to counter that structure (Karatani 2009). In these writings, both Iwai and Karatani stress the endless quality of capitalism.

I have repeatedly noted arbitrageurs' anticipatory gesture toward both arbitrage's endlessness and the end of arbitrage and explored the implications of that gesture. The self-canceling feature of arbitrage intensifies arbitrageurs' appreciation of this movement toward an end. For Iwai, Karatani, and other critics, capitalism is a form of perpetual movement and the critique of capitalism is an equally infinitely renewable endeavor. By contrast, the Sekai Securities arbitrageurs I have examined in this book have always been conscious of a quickly approaching endpoint to their professional work. While Karatani's project is to perpetuate the possibility of critique, and thus of his own profession, Sekai arbitrageurs were quite willing to imagine an end to theirs. This is where arbitrageurs' ambiguous faith critically differs from Karatani's leap of faith. Arbitrageurs are one step removed from arbitrage itself.

Recall Sasaki's reading of Iwai's interpretation of *The Merchant of Venice* as a theory of arbitrage in contrast to Iwai's later elaboration of a theory of speculation. The question that animates my ethnographic inquiry is: what difference does it make if one calls the principle of capitalism speculation or arbitrage? Moreover, what difference does it make if one defines oneself as a speculator or an arbitrageur? And, ultimately, what does a critique of capitalism look like if it is based on arbitrage rather than speculation? If speculation points to the perpetual motion of capital in the abstract, arbitrage points simultaneously to its own perpetually repeatable possibility as an example of capital's movement and to its own endpoint as an example of the personal and social cost of that movement. Arbitrage's potential as an alternative to speculation as a model for critique lies in this inherent paradox. Its self-canceling tendency perhaps offers a refreshing alternative to speculation as a mode of engagement with capitalism.

In light of my ethnographic observations of Japanese arbitrageurs' conception of arbitrage, however, it is unnecessary to make such a clear-cut distinction between speculation and arbitrage. Embracing arbitrage as a modality of critique means embracing its ambiguous faith, which in turn signals arbitrage's fundamental conceptual instability, and even its own denial, without sacrificing its practical utility. As I have shown, for many Sekai arbitrageurs, the arbitrage sensibility depended on sustaining a double vision of the infinite extensibility of arbitrage (arbitrage opportunities elsewhere) and an endpoint of arbitrage (a condition of no arbitrage as the beginning and endpoint of each arbitrage operation). These two perspectives on arbitrage coexist and support each other. Arbitrage is not possible without an effort to maintain this double vision. This is the *work* that arbitrageurs' ambiguous faith demands. The ambiguity of arbitrage's endpoint allows arbitrageurs to imagine other ends and endpoints, including the ends and endpoints of their own personal life goals, dreams, and fantasies. These ends and endpoints in turn sustain their commitment to arbitrage, albeit in an ambiguous fashion.

Likewise, Sekai arbitrageurs have been aware of the possibility that their arbitrage operations are not arbitrage at all but simply speculation. In chapter 2, I examined their complex views of the relationship between arbitrage and speculation. Even at the height of these traders' stock index arbitrage operations in the late 1980s and the early 1990s, they agreed that differentiating between arbitrage and speculation was difficult. They understood very well the fine line between the two, although they nevertheless insisted that their trading was arbitrage, not speculation.

In other words, arbitrageurs saw both arbitrage and speculation in their "arbitrage operations," whereas critics of capitalism could see only speculation in them. I have argued that this double vision and its possible convergence is what makes arbitrage arbitrage, and not simply speculation. In other words, arbitrage is possible only when it is open to the possibility of its denial or evaporation. In this sense, the difficulty Sekai arbitrageurs began to face in sustaining their ambiguous faith in arbitrage, for a variety of reasons, and their eventual abandonment of arbitrage, had always been anticipated in the fact of their ambiguous faith itself.

This book has been an effort to trace the possibility of arbitrageurs' ambiguous faith in arbitrage to its evaporation (not simply in the hypothetical condition of no arbitrage required for each arbitrage operation but in the intensification of arbitrageurs' self-doubt following the global financial crisis of 2007 to 2008 or other more personal crises). My aim has been to create an ethnographic account that mirrors arbitrageurs' own anticipation of and reflection on the trajectory of their commitment to arbitrage.

The widely shared sense of an end of an era among Sekai arbitrageurs and financial market professionals globally may be one point in the larger incessantly creative and destructive movement of capital. It may simply mean that new generations of financial market professionals need to dream up new utopian dreams and imaginaries. But perhaps it indeed signals an end of something. This may be an occasion for critics of capitalism to stop and withhold their impulse to see history repeating itself. It all depends on whether one sees speculation or arbitrage in the world. And one sees both if one embraces arbitrage's ambiguity.

In this book, I have offered an ethnographic analysis of arbitrage—a core idea, theoretical construct, and strategy in finance—and its particular effects on the Japanese financial markets and certain Japanese financial market professionals. What complicates my account is my deployment of arbitrage as a method of my own inquiry into arbitrage and associated phenomena. As I observe the way Japanese arbitrageurs extend various components of arbitrage to different markets, different spheres of life, and different temporal moments, I also have sought to extend arbitrage (and its extensibility) to my own ethnographic account. I conclude with a reflection on extensibility as an anthropological problem.

ARBITRAGING ANTHROPOLOGY AND FINANCE

In her 2009 bestseller, *Fool's Gold: How the Bold Dream of a Small Tribe at J. P. Morgan Was Corrupted by Wall Street Greed and Unleashed a Catastrophe,* Gillian Tett, a *Financial Times* journalist originally trained in social anthropology, captures the intellectual excitement generated by the development of a new class of derivative products known as credit derivatives. Financial instruments for repackaging default risk into tradable securities, credit derivatives subsequently contributed to the global financial crisis of 2007 to 2008. Tett begins her book with an account of Peter Hancock, the "intellectual godfather" (Tett 2009a: 5) of J.P. Morgan's derivatives team, one of the first groups of investment bankers to launch credit derivatives: "[Hancock] was exceedingly cerebral, intensely devoted to the theory and practice of finance in all its forms. He viewed almost every aspect of the world around him as a complex intellectual puzzle to be solved, and he especially loved developing elaborate theories about how to push money around the world in a more efficient manner. When it came to his staff, he obsessively ruminated on how to build the team for optimal performance. Most of all, though, he loved brainstorming ideas" (p. 6).

Hancock sought to foster an experimental spirit and "teamwork ethos" by "encourag[ing] collaboration and long-term thinking, rather than self-interested pursuit of short-term gains" (p. 7). What drove Hancock and his team instead was a dream of changing the way the economy works through credit derivatives: "Credit derivatives would allow J.P. Morgan—and in due course all other banks, too—to exquisitely fine-tune risk burdens, releasing banks from age-old constraints and freeing up vast amounts of capital, turbo-charging not only banking but the economy as a whole" (p. 48).

Tett's ultimate focus, however, is on the way this dream eventually led to the global financial crisis: "As with all derivatives, these tools were to offer a way of *controlling* risk but they could also *amplify* it. It all depended on how they were used. The first of these results was what attracted Hancock and his team to the pursuit. It would be the second feature that would come to dominate the business a decade later, eventually leading to a worldwide financial catastrophe" (p. 22; original emphases).

In Tett's view, what facilitated the latter course of events was what she terms the "'silo' mentality" (p. 252) of financial market professionals and regulators. In an essay she contributed to the American Anthropological Association's newsletter, *Anthropology News,* Tett analogizes bankers' silo mentality to that of the Tajik villagers she studied as a social anthropology doctoral student: "Bankers (like Tajik villagers) operate as a tightly defined group, with specific cultural patterns and a quasi language (or jargon) of their own. Also like Tajik villagers, bankers are generally trained to think in rigid 'silos' and, as a result, find it hard to see how their overall system operates, or to see the contradictions in their own rhetoric and internal organizations" (Tett 2009b: 6).

Tett asserts the relevance of anthropology not simply in these analytical terms but also in more practical terms. In her view, anthropology, as an endeavor to link "different parts of a social structure" (Tett 2009a: 252), has a distinctive contribution to make to the current debate about financial markets and their regulation—that is, the task of overcoming market participants' silo mentality. Tett suggests at the end of *Fool's Gold* that the lack of a "holistic" perspective on the part of financial market professionals and their observers (economists, regulators, and others) was a cause of the present crisis: "The finance world's lack of interest in wider social matters cuts to the very heart of what has gone wrong. What social anthropology teaches its adherents is that nothing in society ever exists in a vacuum or in isolation. Holistic analysis that tries to link different parts of a social structure is crucial, be that in respect to wedding rituals or trading floors. . . . In recent years, regulators, bankers, politicians, investors, and journalists have all failed to employ truly holistic thought—to our collective cost" (p. 252). By implication, she suggests that financial market professionals break away from their silo mentality by embracing a more anthropological and more holistic perspective.

My present endeavor echoes Tett's explicit and influential call for an anthropological, and holistic, perspective in the ongoing debate about the future of finance and financial markets. In my view, however, what a holistic perspective entails is not a straightforward matter. Anthropological holism has heterogeneous origins and has been a subject of intense debate since the 1920s (see, e.g., Bateson [1936] 1958; Benedict 1934), well before the celebration of partiality in more recent anthropological projects (see, e.g., Marcus 1998; M. Strathern 1992).

My project draws on a paradoxically more ambiguous vision of anthropological holism and in turns offers a more modest, yet more realistic, goal for both financial market professionals and their observers and critics. This vision of holism stems from the anthropology of the gift, one of the most theoretically vibrant and longest-standing anthropological topics. The ultimate goal of my endeavor is to examine the parallel and significantly different ways models of arbitrage and of the gift, and dreams of financial market professionals and of anthropologists, work. Here, extensibility emerges as a critical point of convergence between anthropology and finance. What is at stake is not merely a technical issue within the discipline of anthropology; it is related, rather, to the locus of human hope in the unknown and the unknowable (see H. Miyazaki 2004b, 2010b).

The kind of anthropological holism I seek to invoke in this book is inspired by the brands of holism proposed by two founding figures of anthropology, Bronislaw Malinowski and Marcel Mauss. Although both Malinowski and Mauss articulated their respective brands of holism in their efforts to critique economics, the two foundational texts of economic anthropology they wrote, Malinowski's *Argonauts of the Western Pacific* and Mauss's *The Gift,* advanced radically different intellectual agendas and subscribed to different versions of holism. Yet in my view, both texts posit profound ambiguity as a method for invoking a holistic approach (see also Osteen 2002).

The subject of the gift may sound remote from financial markets, but those who reflect on the gift immediately realize how tricky an act of giving can be. In its anthropological conception, the gift does not represent a small segment of the human economy. Rather, it stands for a distinctive perspective on the entire human economy.

One of the original insights of the anthropology of the gift, which goes back to Malinowski and Mauss, is that gifts and commodities, and giving and barter, cannot be easily demarcated from each other. In treating the *kula* exchange—a circulation of ceremonial objects such as shell necklaces and armbands among islands off the coast of Papua New Guinea—as "a novel type of ethnological fact" (Malinowski [1922] 1984: 510), Malinowski sought to demonstrate the significance of a holistic approach that sees the mundane and the magical on a single analytical plane. In particular, Malinowski drew attention to the coexistence of the *kula* exchange supported by myths and magic and a wide range of other, more mundane forms of exchange. Moreover, in his "complete survey of all forms of payment or present" (p. 176), Malinowski noted, "There are so many transitions and gradations between [barter] and simple gift, that it is impossible to draw any fixed line between trade on the one hand, and exchange of gifts on the other" (p. 176). The primary effect of Malinowski's ethnographic analysis is a blurred boundary between giving and bartering, and between mundane and magical forms of exchange.[7]

In fact, the chief anthropological insight about the gift is not so much the specificity of gifts vis-à-vis commodities as the impossibility of defining the contours of the gift. This impossibility has typically been addressed through the problem of whether a pure gift is possible. To the extent that a gift generates debt and calls for a reciprocal act, a pure gift is not possible (see, e.g., Laidlaw 2000; Parry 1986). As Chris Gregory and others have long argued, the gift cannot be comprehended from a perspective predicated on the idea of a pure gift or on a clear distinction between gifts and commodities (see, e.g., Appadurai 1986b; Gregory 1982; Parry 1986; Thomas 1991). The boundaries between gifts and commodities quickly crumble. A long chain of studies has focused on the work invested by actors in the demarcation of the gift from market and other transactions (see, e.g., Keane 2001; see also Graeber 2001; Munn 1986).

In Marcel Mauss's *The Gift*, arguably the most influential anthropological text ever written, the category of the gift itself is posited as impossible from the outset (Derrida 1992). Mauss set out to solve the problem of why a gift needs to be reciprocated. Mauss argued that a gift carries with it a part of the giver, which in turn demands that it be returned to the giver. More significantly, Mauss posits the gift as a total social fact in which "all kinds of institutions are given expression at one and the same time—religious, juridical, and moral, which relate to both politics and the family; likewise economic ones, which suppose special forms of production and consumption, or rather, of performing total services and of distribution. This is not to take into account the aesthetic phenomena to which these facts lead, and the contours of the phenomena that these institutions manifest" (Mauss [1950] 1990: 3). Not unlike Malinowski's emphasis on "transitions and gradations" between bartering and gift giving, Mauss pays particular attention to the "hybrid" quality of the gift—as an object that contains within itself part of a person, as an act that is simultaneously interested and disinterested, and so forth. Here Mauss emphasizes the ambiguity of the category of the gift itself.

Malinowski's and Mauss's brands of holism have been criticized for their respective incompleteness.[8] But what unites Malinowski's project with Mauss's is the distinctive fuzziness their respective versions of holism create, and this is precisely where Malinowski and Mauss inadvertently shared a method for offering a holistic vision of humanity.[9] It is important to note that this fuzziness results from their shared analytical commitment to the category of the gift. Only through this limited vision were they able to see its expansiveness and extensibility (see H. Miyazaki 2006a; 2010a). In other words, they sought to offer a glimpse of an expanded vision of humanity through an only slightly stretched perspective in which a series of stark analytical contrasts, such as giving and bartering, gifts and commodities, and the gift and the contract are intentionally confounded. It can be said that a strategy of destabilization (rather than a strategy of stabilization) is at work at the heart of these founding figures' projects. Ironically, a holistic vision needs to be expressed through a limited vision (the gift) and a demonstration of how it is not sustainable. In other words, I suggest, the anthropology of the gift is an exercise in making the gift appear in the course of its evaporation.

Anthropological insights about the gift, such as Malinowski's discussion of *kula* exchange and Mauss's insight about the relationship between persons and things in the gift, have been extended to a broad range of contemporary forms of giving, such as donations of blood, human organs, and body parts, and to other forms of exchange, such as financial transactions. For example, in his introduction to the renowned volume *The Social Life of Things,* Arjun Appadurai compares Chicago's commodity futures trading to the *kula* exchange Malinowski studied. In Appadurai's view, there are several areas of commonality between the two forms of "tournament," including their shared "agonistic, romantic, individualistic, and gamelike ethos that stands in contrast to the ethos of everyday economic behavior" (Appadurai 1986a: 50). Likewise, one may be tempted to extend anthropological theories of debt to an analysis of collateralized debt obligations and other recent technical financial instruments for turning debt into tradable entities (cf. Graeber 2011). Yet I suggest that the anthropological impulse to extend the gift to a broader range of phenomena itself finds an analogue in the logics of finance.

My anthropological engagement with finance, therefore, focuses not on the specific point of continuity or disjuncture between market and nonmarket exchange, but rather on the very urge to *extend* the insights of the gift to financial markets. Elsewhere I have argued that this urge is a replication of the ethnographic observation, common since the work of Malinowski and Mauss, that gift giving itself operates on a principle of extension. Ethnographic examples of this range from Malinowski's own observations about the system of the interisland exchange of *kula,* to Mauss's well-known discussion of *hau*—the "spirit of the gift" that moves with the gift and then returns to the giver (Mauss 1990)—to Nancy Munn's discussion of *kula* exchange partners' "spatiotemporal" experience, to the analysis by Andrew Strathern, Marilyn Strathern, and others of interlinked events of exchange (see Merlan and Rumsey 1991; H. Miyazaki 2005a, 2006a, 2010a; Munn 1986, 1990; A. Strathern 1979; M. Strathern 1988). I argue that it is precisely in such extensibility that anthropologists have found a glimpse of a holistic vision of humanity in the gift.

In this book, I have sought to demonstrate the distinctive kind of extensibility that arbitrage affords. The extensibility of arbitrage is translated into the extensibility of the category at another level of analysis, just like the extensibility of the gift is regularly translated into the idea of an analysis, theory, or idea as a gift. The extensibility found in both cases is extensible itself, as the gift has been extended to the history of the idea of contract (Mauss [1950] 1990) or intellectual exchange (Sahlins 1972).

In retrospect, this book is an effort to restage Marcel Mauss's work on the gift on the plane of finance. I have done so not by extending Mauss's insights about the gift or capitalism into an analysis of finance, but by juxtaposing the logic of extension and the sense of extensibility found both implicitly and explicitly in Mauss's discussion of the gift—as well as in the way Mauss's work has been debated in anthropology, philosophy, and other disciplines—with the logic of extension in arbitrage. I have done so only implicitly in the text to avoid replicating the extensible tendency of the gift literature.

This is admittedly a rather "abstract" endeavor. I refer to extensibility at several different levels of analysis in the anthropology of the gift as well as in the sensibilities of arbitrage. This attention to the device or technique underlying the anthropology of the gift owes its inspiration to Marilyn Strathern's long-standing effort to critique Mauss and take the gift to the task of producing different kinds of analytical effect. As *The Gender of the Gift* powerfully demonstrates, Strathern redeploys anthropological tools ("conventions" or "aesthetic constraints"), including the gift-commodity dichotomy, to the project of demonstrating "how an anthropological analysis could flow radically differently within its own aesthetic constraints" (H. Miyazaki 2009: 195). Annelise Riles, a student of Strathern's, has extended this analytical sensibility to other kinds of tools, such as legal techniques and theories (Riles 2010, 2011). In *Arbitraging Japan,* I have sought to offer a glimpse of the power of such attention with regard to certain tools and techniques of finance. My focus is on the relationship between arbitrage and the gift and the kinds of extensibility that distinguish the two.

This understanding of the gift and of arbitrage points to a different anthropological engagement with what Tett has called "silo mentality." Instead of seeking to offer a holistic perspective on financial markets by linking traders to regulators and finance to other facets of economic and social life, I propose to pay attention to what happens in the vicinity of "silo" thinking. The dream shared by Peter Hancock and his colleagues in Tett's account is a case in point. Their dream exceeded the kind of short-term reasoning often attributed to Wall Street investment banking (see, e.g., Ho 2009). In more practical terms, according to Tett herself, Hancock's team also sought to think "laterally" across different organizational sections of their bank. Silo mentality expanded where intellectual excitement was sparked, a sense of loyalty to the team was harnessed, and a dream was shared. All of these slightly expansive and extensible effects within silo thinking drove the team's innovation forward.

The goal of my present exercise then is to find evidence of the way such silo mentality could serve as a source of expansive and extensible thought and imagination, in much the same way as the focus on the gift has inspired expansive anthropological thought and imagination. My project does not claim to present a totalistic or holistic view of financial markets in the sense in which Tett uses the term. Instead, it seeks to follow a sort of silo thinking at work in the vicinity of trading, and the inherent ambiguity that enables and is enhanced by its extensions. In this sense, this project offers an only slightly broadened scope of inquiry enabled by careful attention to ambiguity and associated expansive and extensible thought that lies at the heart of the practice of trading and investment. The book is intended to serve as an ethnographic reminder of such ambiguity and extensibility. I argue that such ambiguity is precisely the locus of expansive thinking and imagination (cf. Law 2004).[10] I have sought to draw ethnographic attention to concrete instances in which financial market professionals' silo thinking generates expansive thought and imagination even beyond finance and the market narrowly defined. My argument is that these instances may not serve as openings for radical subversion, but that they are potential openings for wider conversation, dialogue, and even collaboration. In this book, I have examined a specific kind of silo thinking at work in financial markets—that is, arbitrage, a cornerstone of theories and techniques of finance.

In a series of experimental essays based on Douglas Holmes's ethnographic research inside central banks, Holmes and George Marcus have proposed the category of the "para-ethnographic" as "a means to enter fields of expertise" (Holmes and Marcus 2005: 241). The para-ethnographic is "a kind of illicit, marginal social thought—in genres such as 'the anecdotal,' 'hype,' and 'intuition'—within practices dominated by the technocratic ethos" (p. 237). My ethnographic inquiry has followed Holmes and Marcus's lead to seek a similar point of entry into the world of finance. My entry point is not the para-ethnographic per se, but a particular kind of conceptual extensibility and expansiveness internal to theories and techniques of finance such as arbitrage that, I contend, is analogous to the extensibility and expansiveness long assigned to certain key anthropological concepts, such as the gift. The parallel between the extensibility of arbitrage and the extensibility of the gift may appear to some as a potential target of another arbitrage.

In this book, I have offered a series of comparable perspectives: arbitrage and speculation, universalistic logics (money, finance, and rationality) and particularizing logics (learning and other cultural logics of Japanese organizational knowledge), and arbitrage and the gift. Whether one sees in them an arbitrage opportunity depends on whether one believes in arbitrage, or more precisely, in its ambiguity and associated extensibility.

Here I am juxtaposing the extensibility of the gift with the extensibility of arbitrage with a view to collapsing them into each other (or arbitraging them, if you like). If Malinowski's and Mauss's extensions of the gift category—from pure gifts to barter, and from the gift to the idea of contract, respectively—were exercises in dissolving the distinction between gifts and commodities within the very framework of that distinction, my ethnographic project also seems to have generated an effect of dissolving arbitrage in my own account of Sekai traders' various extensions of the arbitrage category.

There is a fundamental difference in these forms of extension, however. To the extent that the extensibility of the gift leaves the gift as an almost eternal point of return and an inexhaustible source of theoretical inspiration and associated humanism, the extensibility of arbitrage lets arbitrage evaporate along with the kind of faith required to recognize its possibility. Arbitrage is meant to do so in its determination to eliminate arbitrage opportunities, but from another point of view, arbitrage and arbitrage opportunities do not exist in the first place.

Between the substantiveness of human economy that the extensibility of the gift category seems to guarantee for anthropology (Polanyi [1944] 1957, 1957; see also Dalton 1961; Gudeman 2001) and the virtuality of financial markets that the extensibility of the arbitrage category seems to confirm (see Carrier and Miller 1998b), however, something at once self-evident, naïve, and audacious may be lurking. Perhaps that is the excitement and dream without which any of these extensions, my own included, are inconceivable to begin with. This is why there is a sense of possibility in reappreciating the kind of excitement entailed in the logics of finance and their extensibility as a locus of slight expansion of thinking, imagination, and humanity despite all the nightmares such excitement often ends up producing.

This broadened view of finance opens up a space for detecting a kind of affinity that is neither internal nor external to finance in traders' professional and personal intellectual trajectories. It is certainly important to understand the often devastatingly broad and uneven impact that the utopian dreams of financial market professionals have had in the world. But I argue that this space can also enable dialogue between traders and regulators, between financial market professionals and their academic observers and critics (such as economists and anthropologists), and among all of us as thinking subjects whose lives have been affected profoundly by the current financial crisis. In this sense, my account is not so much a story of a dream turning into a nightmare, as a story of a dream potentially inspiring other dreams (see also H. Miyazaki 2004b).

The trajectories of Sekai derivatives traders' extensions of arbitrage and arbitrage sensibility showcase the expansiveness and diversity of thinking in the vicinity of financial transactions. The recognition of such thinking in turn demands a different framework of conversation about the future of finance and financial markets. My references to George Soros in the introduction and J.P. Morgan derivatives specialists in Gillian Tett's account in this chapter are meant to demonstrate how such reflexivity is the norm in the world of finance. In my own reading of Kojin Karatani's critique of capitalism in this chapter, I have sought to engage in a reading and reflexive practice parallel to my interlocutors' in a field slightly closer to my own profession.

In July 2010, Aoki attended a lecture on the anthropology of arbitrage that I delivered in Tokyo. Aoki had dinner with Sasaki a few days after the lecture and the two discussed my analysis of arbitrage and arbitrage sensibility. They pondered why arbitrage would interest an anthropologist. Aoki and Sasaki began to discuss some philosophical implications of arbitrage. In Aoki's view, arbitrage offers a "general theory" of difference and its elimination between value systems. Like arbitrage, different cultural and religious values could be mediated so that people from different values systems could understand each other. Sasaki slightly disagreed, arguing instead that arbitrage offers a method for appreciating difference as such. In his opinion, to the extent that arbitrageurs continually search for new kinds of difference, they assume that arbitrageable difference should exist somewhere. Arbitrage thus contains within itself both a propensity to eliminate already-known differences and a propensity to search for not-yet-known differences. Underlying arbitrage, from Sasaki's perspective, is a potential for cultivating an awareness that the existence of difference is a "natural" (*shizen*) state and is a "source of human vitality" (*jinrui no katsuryoku no gensen*) (August 2011).

The debate between Aoki and Sasaki effectively resurrected the double vision intrinsic to arbitrage—that is, the vision of the endlessness and of the endpoint of arbitrage that they had worked to sustain in their past arbitrage operations. But what is more significant for present purposes is the way Aoki and Sasaki sought to relate the idea of arbitrage to what they thought to be an anthropological question, the question of what to do with cultural and religious difference. This is perhaps a simple reminder that a commitment to theories and techniques of finance, such as arbitrage, can serve as a source of inspiration for thought and imagination beyond finance and the market narrowly defined. Indeed, such seemingly undisciplined expansiveness and extensibility in thought and imagination internal to the logics of finance is a necessary foundation for the reintegration of theories and techniques of finance into our collective futures.

.Yet what was more important for me personally was Aoki and Sasaki's friendly effort to understand my interest in them. In their conversation, they effectively arbitraged finance and anthropology, but they did it in a way that made our long-standing friendship appear. This was a warm and reassuring reminder that it was, after all, their commitment to personal relationships that sustained their commitment to the techniques and logics of finance.

Notes

INTRODUCTION

1. Such ethnographic attention to competing temporal forms is common in anthropology (see Gell 1992; Greenhouse 1996; Guyer 2007; H. Miyazaki 2004b, 2006a; Munn 1990, 1992; Robbins 2001). A typical focus of analysis is the tension between these intersecting temporalities and the creative efforts of specific actors to reconcile them (see, e.g., Bestor 2001; Kelly 1986; H. Miyazaki 2003; Yoneyama 1999, to name a few from the anthropology of Japan).

2. Here I am lumping together old and relatively new anthropological attempts to recognize the efforts of research subjects to interpret, analyze, model, and theorize the world in which they find themselves. To some extent, anthropologists have always been interested in the form and the content of their research subjects' knowledge, but the efforts I have in mind explicitly address the parallel or affinity between the knowledge practices of anthropologists and those of their interlocutors (see Bateson [1936] 1958; Leach [1954] 1970; M. Strathern 1988). Clifford Geertz's interpretive anthropology makes a latent claim for interpretation as a mode by which we struggle to answer common everyday questions about the world in which we find ourselves (Geertz 1973). George Marcus's programmatic efforts to make anthropological knowledge production more collaborative are also anchored in an assumption that anthropologists and their research subjects share both problems and methods (see, e.g., Marcus 1998, 2007).

3. The Black-Scholes formula is an equation for pricing options over time that is predicated on the assumption that options can be accurately hedged by trading underlying assets (Black and Scholes 1973; see also Bernstein [1992] 1993: 215–223; MacKenzie 2006: 127–138).

4. A contextualized account of finance is intended to challenge the universal and universalizing quality of global ideas and ideologies. For example, Thomas Rohlen's ethnography of a Japanese regional bank is one of the earliest attempts to study a financial institution in relation to cultural values (Rohlen 1973, 1974). Likewise, in her anthropological study of the first few years of the Shanghai stock market, Ellen Hertz offers a dense interpretation of what the "stock fever" (*gupiao re*) meant to people in Shanghai (Hertz 1998: 71). Hertz compares the Shanghai stock fever with speculative bubbles and bursts in U.S. and other markets and proposes that the stock fever in Shanghai be understood in relation to numerous other kinds of *re* (fevers) in urban Chinese life:

> Fevers are moments when a particular conception of the relation between the individual and the group in urban Chinese society is given expression. . . . In their strongest form, they make reference to mythical conceptions of power, both the power to do good, as in the cult of Mao or Guan Yu, and the power to harm, as in the Qing dynasty sorcery scare. . . . With fevers, differences between "commoners" are temporarily muted while the commonalities linking "the People" are ritually enacted. *Re* act out the binary class division between "the People" and "the State" which characterizes the tributary mode of production. (p. 81)

Here Hertz powerfully demonstrates the specific symbolic meaning attached to the stock market bubble in Shanghai.

5. This line of thinking is not so remote from the critique of the area-studies framework of Japanese studies that Marilyn Ivy, Victor Koschmann, Naoki Sakai, and others have advanced (see, e.g., Ivy 1995; Koschmann 1996; Sakai 1997). However, my interest is in exploring to what extent seemingly universal logics of finance and seemingly historically specific logics of Japanese culture emerge as alternative explanatory frameworks and are thus analytically arbitrageable (see chapters 5 and 6).

6. Compare this to Immanuel Wallerstein's discussion of the "buddenbrooks phenomenon" (after Thomas Mann's 1901 novel, *Buddenbrooks*), in which "the typical path of transformation in the social patterns of a wealthy family dynasty, from great entrepreneurs to economic consolidator to patron of the arts, and eventually these days to either decadent roué or hedonistic-idealistic dropout" (Wallerstein 1991: 137). I thank Haiyan Lee for drawing my attention to this linkage.

7. My visit to Sekai Securities was arranged by my mother's acquaintance, the father of someone a few years behind me at the high school I graduated from. I was initially introduced to the head of the derivatives product development unit, but that person in turn introduced me to Tada.

8. See Victor Koschmann's discussion of "new academism" during the 1980s (Koschmann 1993).

9. My ethnographic focus on the role of intellectual excitement in the Japanese financial markets resonates with Silvia Yanagisako's ethnographic attention to "sentiments" in Italian family-owned business: "Bourgeois 'economic' actions, like all culturally meaningful actions, are incited, enabled, and constrained by sentiments that are themselves the products of historically contingent cultural processes" (2002: 11).

1. SHAKESPEAREAN ARBITRAGE

1. Throughout the book, unless otherwise noted, all translations from the Japanese are my own.

2. See Mikami and Yotsuzuka (2000) for the two former Salomon Brothers traders' exposition of relative value trading.

3. Katsuhito Iwai received a PhD in economics from the Massachusetts Institute of Technology in 1972 and taught at Yale University before taking up a teaching position at the University of Tokyo's Economics Department in 1981. His books include *Disequilibrium Dynamics: A Theoretical Analysis of Inflation and Unemployment* (1981), *Kaheiron* (A theory of money) (1993), *Nijuisseiki no shihonshugiron* (A theory of capitalism for the twenty-first century) (2000), and *Kaisha wa dare no monoka* (Who owns a company?) (2005). *Venisu no shonin no shihonron* (A theory of capital according to *The Merchant of Venice*) ([1985] 1992) was Iwai's first book for a general audience.

4. Iwai quotes the following two passages from the play:

> In sooth, I know not why I am so sad;
> It wearies me, you say it wearies you;
> But how I caught it, found it, or came by it,
> What stuff 'tis made of, whereof it is born,
> I am to learn;
> And such a want-wit sadness makes of me,
> That I have much ado to know myself. (I, i, 1–7)

And:

> I hold the world but as the world, Graziano—
> A stage where every man must play a part,
> And mine a sad one. (I, i, 77–79)

All quotations from the play are from *The Norton Shakespeare* (Shakespeare 2000).

5. In his book *Shakespeare's Economics,* the economist Henry Farnam notes, "*The Merchant* [*of Venice*] involves more than antagonistic views of usury. It also involves a discussion of the extreme *laissez faire* philosophy of economics. Shylock in a significant sentence says, 'thrift is blessing, if men steal it not' (I, iii, 91 [I, iii, 86 in *The Norton Shakespeare*]). In other words he stands for the night-watchman theory of government. Any piece of clever trickery earns the divine blessing, i.e., is morally right, as long as it does not violate the criminal law" (Farnam 1931: 7).

6. Steven Mentz notes, "One risk of Shell's approach . . . is that it can conflate metaphoric exchange and literal exchange while ignoring the additional meanings that cling to the words used to describe men and money in early modern culture. Early modern explorations of economics usually bear traces of multiple discourses" (Mentz 2003: 179). Mentz's criticism of Shell's work draws on the commentary of the economists Jack Amariglio and David Ruccio on literary critics' use of economic concepts (Amariglio and Ruccio 1999; see also Osteen and Woodmansee 1999: 12).

7. Iwai quotes the following passage: "He hath an argosy bound to Tripolis, another to the Indies; I understand moreover upon the Rialto he hath a third at Mexico, a fourth for England, and other ventures he hath squandered abroad" (I, iii, 15–18).

8. Here Iwai quotes Antonio's response to Shylock, who asks why, when Antonio had previously berated him for being a money-lender, he should lend money to Antonio now:

I am as like to call thee so [dog] again,
To spit on thee again, to spurn thee too.
If thou wilt lend this money, lend it not
As to thy friends; for when did friendship take
A breed for barren metal of his friend?
But lend it rather to thine enemy,
Who if he break, thou mayst with better face
Exact the penalty. (I, iii, 125–132)

9. Iwai quotes Bassanio's own words:

In Belmont is a lady richly left,
And she is fair, and, fairer than that word,
Of wondrous virtues. Sometimes from her eyes
I did receive fair speechless messages.
Her name is Portia
. . . .
For the four winds blow in from every coast
Renowned suitors, and her sunny locks
Hang on her temples like a golden fleece,
Which makes her seat of Belmont Colchis' strand,
And many Jasons come in quest of her.
O my Antonio, had I but the means
To hold a rival place with one of them,
I have a mind presages me such thrift
That I should questionless be fortunate. (I, i, 161–176)

10. "Therefore prepare thee to cut off the flesh./Shed thou no blood, nor cut thou less nor more/But just a pound of flesh. If though tak'st more/Or less than a just a pound . . . Thou diest, and all thy goods are confiscate" (IV, i, 319–327).

11. Iwai juxtaposes this exchange in the trial scene with Jessica's elopement with Lorenzo, where they represent "two variations of alchemic exchange between Jewish and Christian communities" (Iwai [1985] 1992: 42).

12. Iwai points to Portia's remark to Bassanio:

You see me, Lord Bassanio, where I stand,
Such as I am. Though for myself alone
I would not be ambitious in my wish
To wish myself much better, yet for you
I would be trebled twenty times myself,
A thousand times more fair, ten thousand times more rich. (III, ii, 149–154)

Lars Engle notes, "The pattern of credit and debit, payment and profit, is drawn in this play with nearly the precision of an auditor's report, and . . . the character whose actions most shape and exploit this pattern is not Shylock or Antonio but Portia" (Engle 1986: 37).

13. "Profit originates from difference, and profit makes difference disappear. The existence of profit causes long-distance trading to expand and ultimately reduces the difference in prices between regions, the very source of profit in merchant capitalism. [In industrial capitalism,] profit causes industrial capital to accumulate and reduces the difference in value between labor and products of labor. [In post-industrial capitalism,] it prompts imitation of new technology and reduces the difference between present value and future value, the source of profit for an innovative enterprise. To mediate value difference is to eliminate that difference. Capitalism demands that new difference, that is, difference as a new source of profit be searched for all the time. It moves like a perpetual motion. It is a 'dynamic' economic mechanism in its essential sense of the term" (Iwai [1985] 1992: 67–68).

14. Walter Cohen notes that among Shakespeare's plays, *The Merchant of Venice* has generated the greatest diversity of interpretations. Cohen suggests that the play "requires us not so much to interpret as to discover the sources of our difficulty in interpreting, to view the play as a symptom of a problem in the life of late sixteenth-century England" (Cohen 1982: 767). In order to illuminate this problem, Cohen situates the play in both English and Italian contexts. In response to the predominant interpretation of the play in terms of English economic history, in which Antonio and Shylock represent medieval feudalism and capitalism, respectively, Cohen observes that, in light of Venetian history, "the hostility between Antonio, the open-handed Christian merchant, and Shylock, the tight-fisted Jewish usurer, represents not the conflict between declining feudalism and rising capitalism, but its opposite. It may be seen as a special instance of the struggle, widespread in Europe, between Jewish quasi-feudal fiscalism and native bourgeois mercantilism, in which the indigenous forces usually prevailed" (p. 771; cf. Netzloff 2003).

In reversing the dominant economic interpretation of the play, Cohen highlights irreconcilable contradictions intrinsic to it: "In *The Merchant of Venice* English history evokes fears of capitalism, and Italian history allays those fears. One is the problem, the other the solution, the act of incorporation, of transcendence, toward which the play strives" (Cohen 1982: 772). His general point, however, is that "[the play's] formal movement—dialectical transcendence—is not adequate to the social conflict that is its main source of inspiration and one of its principal subjects. Some of the merit of *The Merchant of Venice* ironically lies in the failure of its central design to provide a completely satisfying resolution to the dilemmas raised in the course of the action" (p. 775; cf. Danson 1978).

15. Likewise, in the early twentieth century, some stockbrokers in Tokyo's emergent stock exchange engaged in a similar form of *sayatori* to exploit the difference in the prices of a single security with different delivery dates. (see, e.g., Yamaichi Shoken Kabushikigaisha Shashi Hensan Iinkai 1998: 19–20).

16. Similarly, the economist Mahmoud A. El-Gamal describes the history of Islamic finance as "Shari'a arbitrage" (El-Gamal 2006). El-Gamal associates

arbitrage with attention to "form," or analogical thinking, as contrasted to attention to "substance," or economic reasoning. El-Gamal proposes to recover the latter in Islamic finance (El-Gamal 2006: xii, 20–25; see also Maurer 2006b: 26–27).

Likewise, Phillip Mirowski, a historian of science, identifies arbitrage as a principle for both economic and scientific measurements: "In the marketplace, the prices of most commodities can be stated in terms of prices of other commodities; in physics, most constants can be defined by other constants. The key variable in the market situation is profit; in scientific measurements it is error. In markets, exchange is deemed arbitrage-free when any sequence of trades between commodities, however circuitous, always end up with identical numerical relative prices of the initial and final commodities" (Mirowski 1994: 567).

17. Stephen Gudeman also describes Fredrik Barth's classic paper "Economic Spheres in Darfur" as a study of arbitrage. In that paper, Barth challenges the framework of "spheres of exchange" that Paul Bohannan originally formulated in his analysis of an African economy (Bohannan 1955; see also Guyer 2004). In drawing attention to the increase of entrepreneurial activities seeking to value discrepancies between economic transactions in two different spheres, Barth notes, "entrepreneurs will direct their activity pre-eminently towards those points in an economic system where the discrepancies of evaluation are greatest, and will attempt to construct bridging transactions which can exploit these discrepancies" (Barth [1967] 2000: 158). Gudeman interprets Barth's account as follows: "Local entrepreneurs, interested in securing a money profit, could mobilize costless labor for their projects. They offered (in the traditional fashion) beer, made from the subsistence millet crop, to those who labored in their fields; but the entrepreneurs purchased the inexpensive millet, and they used the low-cost labor to plant their profitable cash crops rather than more millet. One sphere thus grew by debasing the other, and profit was made by strategic exchanges or arbitrage between different economic spheres" (Gudeman 2001: 142n20). Gudeman's discussion of arbitrage is framed in terms of his broader discussion of profit, innovation, and accumulation via Schumpeter's discussion of entrepreneurship. Here Gudeman's premise is that "arbitrageurs are not innovators but calculators of risk and rewards; innovators create value, arbitrageurs use calculations of risk and rewards; innovators create value, arbitrageurs use calculations to gather part of this value" (p. 107).

More recently, Jane Guyer draws attention to the widespread practices of "temporal arbitrage" enabled by technical and legal "formalities," such as payment scheduling, in Nigeria (Guyer 2004: 163–164).

18. Ethnographic attention to a modality is increasingly common. For example, in his study of the Zambian Copperbelt, James Ferguson defines his object of study as "a mode of conceptualizing, narrating, and experiencing socioeconomic change and its encounter with a confounding process of economic decline" (Ferguson 1999: 21).

19. To the extent that my account follows the divergent uses to which the idea of arbitrage is put, the divergent meanings arbitrage acquires in different

contexts, and its consequences for its users' intellectual, professional, and personal trajectories (see H. Miyazaki 2003, 2005b), it may recall the "social life of things" approach developed by Arjun Appadurai and others (see Appadurai 1986b; especially, Kopytoff 1986). But here my intent is to emulate the shape of Sasaki's handout.

2. BETWEEN ARBITRAGE AND SPECULATION

1. This is in accordance with the settlement rules of the Osaka Stock Exchange introduced in March 1989 and implemented after September 1990. See "Special Rules for Business Regulations and Brokerage Agreement Related to Index Futures" (Osaka Stock Exchange), http://www.ose.or.jp/f/general_cms_pages/10669/wysiwyg/ru06.pdf, accessed June 7, 2012. See also Osaka Shoken Torihikijo 2011.

2. See, e.g., "Nibanzoko wo saguru tenkai-ka?" (In search of a second bottom?), *Nihon Keizai Shinbun,* January 13, 1990, 16; "Saiteitorihiki sage hakusha" (Arbitrage has spurred the downfall [of stock prices]), *Nihon Keizai Shinbun,* February 22, 1990, 3; "Puroguramu baibai ga sage kasoku" (Program trading has accelerated the downfall [of stock prices]), *Asahi Shinbun,* February 22, 1990, 9; "Kappatsuka suru saiteitorihiki" (Arbitrage is becoming more frequent), part 1–4, *Nihon Keizai Shinbun,* February 23, 1990, 20; February 24, 1990, 16; February 27, 1990, 20; February 28, 1990, 20; "Kabuka oyure ni toshika azen" (Investors stunned by the stock price fluctuations), *Asahi Shinbun,* February 27, 1990, 3; "Nikkeiheikin, shijo 2-banme no sage: Owarine 28,000 yen ware sunzen" (The Nikkei 225's fall [of April 2nd] was the second biggest in history: [Yesterday's] closing price was almost below 28,000 yen), *Nihon Keizai Shinbun,* April 3, 1990, 1. See also Y. Miyazaki (1992: 200–201, 204–211).

3. Commenting on the debate about index arbitrage in Japan, Merton Miller, a Nobel laureate and an important figure in financial economics, points out that foreign firms were arbitraging Japan's high commissions:

> Brokerage commission on common stocks can be expected to be higher than those on index futures if only because the broker's costs of handling and processing stock orders are greater. But thanks to MOF's [the Japanese Government Ministry of Finance's] brokerage cartel policies of high, fixed retail stock commissions, the cost to the customer for establishing or adjusting diversified portfolios of equities, was not just three or four times higher with stock than with futures, as is the case currently in the United States, but anywhere from thirty to fifty times higher! Higher to *outside* customers, that is. But not, of course, to any foreign arbitrage firms with membership on the Tokyo Stock Exchange. Members could buy stocks directly, without paying commissions, and then hedge by selling futures to ordinary Japanese investors. The futures contracts, though quoted at a substantial premium to theoretical cash value, were still a bargain for *Japanese* investors relative to direct stock purchases at full retail commissions. (M. Miller 1997: 31–32; original emphases)

4. Hull has eliminated the term "riskless" in his definition of arbitrage in a subsequent edition of the textbook, but the overall nuance of the definition

remains the same: "Arbitrage involves locking in a profit by simultaneously entering into transactions in two or more markets" (Hull 2000: 14).

5. Contrasting arbitrage with speculation in terms of their divergent approaches to risk has long been a standard practice in writings about financial markets. For example, in his *Speculation on the Stock and Produce Exchanges of the United States*, Henry Crosby Emery notes, "Arbitrage, at least in the case of securities, is not speculation at all. If both prices are actually known at the same moment, to buy at one price and sell at another is not to take a risk, and so is not speculation. It is trade" (Emery 1896: 138). Likewise, Max Weber characterizes arbitrage as an operation based on precise calculation and therefore a virtually riskless operation: "The 'arbitrageur' seeks a profit in that he simultaneously sells a good at a place where it is, at that moment, able to be sold at a higher price, while he buys it at a place where it is to be had more cheaply. His business is therefore a pure example of calculating the numbers.... When things are correctly calculated, there is no other risk involved, but, when one compares the volume of transactions with the gain that is being sought, there are therefore also relatively modest chances for profit" (Weber [1924] 2000: 344–345). In contrast, speculation "is no example of pure and simple calculation—for, [the speculator's] success is dependent upon the onset of the expected *change* in the general price of the specific good—and the speculator must take into account the circumstances that possibly contribute to that" (Weber [1924] 2000: 345, original emphasis).

6. For example, proponents of organized securities trading sought to distinguish speculation from gambling by arguing that speculation stabilized prices and therefore enabled exchange-based trading to be used by hedgers (see, e.g., Crump 1874; Huebner 1910, 1911). For more comprehensive treatments of the long chains of debates about the distinction between gambling and speculation, see, e.g., Brenner (1990: 90–112), de Goede (2005: 47–85), and Lurie (1979).

7. For nuanced discussions of different versions of defense of LTCM's trading strategy, see de Goede (2005: 135–137) and MacKenzie (2006: 218–242).

8. Here volatility serves as an indicator of the anticipated future price fluctuations of the underlying stock of a convertible bond. The calculation of volatility is one of the most important procedures in convertible bond arbitrage.

9. Leach's work constitutes a critique of the typologizing of social systems characteristic of the structural functionalist school of British social anthropology: "My own view is that equilibrium theory in social anthropology was once justified but that it now needs drastic modification. We can no longer be satisfied with attempting to set up a typology of fixed systems" (Leach [1954] 1970: 284–285). Instead, seeing that "every real society is a process in time" (p. 5), Leach seeks to capture its dynamism: "I hold that it should be possible for anthropologists to develop methods for the analysis of changing social systems which avoid metaphysical generalisations" (p. 285). In order to achieve this goal, Leach follows Hans Vaihinger's work *The Philosophy of "As If"* ([1924] 2000), redeploying the static mode of modeling derived from structural functionalism with a qualification that such models are "as if" models: "Candid recognition that social systems are not necessarily naturally stable need not

compel the structurally minded social anthropologist to abandon all his traditional techniques of analysis, for he will still be justified in continuing his use of scientific fictions" (p. 285). In other words, for Leach, these fictional models constitute merely a means to an end (see Riles 2004a, 2010, 2011), that is, the goal of depicting society as a dynamic process.

10. There is nothing surprising about the delicate relationship of belief to doubt itself. As Tanya Luhmann notes in her ethnography of contemporary witchcraft practices, people believe in magic while knowing that it is inherently irrational to do so (Luhmann 1989). Similarly, arbitrageurs believe in the particular kind of rationality underlying arbitrage while knowing that it is irrational to do so.

11. Here I am particularly inspired by William Kelly's elegant effort to capture the coproduction and copresence of nostalgia and rationalization in rural Japan during the late 1970s and early 1980s (Kelly 1986).

12. Many of the traders inherited Aoki's view of the market, although in Aoki's own view some of his traders had overextended it (see chapter 5).

13. Here I refrain from citing the articles for the sake of protecting the traders' identity.

14. Despite the protestation of Aoki, Sasaki, and other industry insiders, a series of regulatory measures took effect between 1990 and 1992. The margin required for futures trading was increased from 9 percent to 15 percent on August 24, 1990, from 15 percent to 20 percent on January 31, 1991, from 20 percent to 25 percent on June 27, 1991, and finally from 25 percent to 30 percent on December 18, 1991. Ironically, however, this period turned out to be the most speculative trading period for the Nikkei 225 futures market. The trading volume of the Nikkei 225 futures contracts in 1991 was 21.643 million contracts, and the face value of the trading was 536.73 trillion yen. (Here I am relying on various undated documents provided by Osaka Stock Exchange officials in October 1998.) Moreover, the index futures were continually overpriced, and in many traders' view, there were numerous arbitrage opportunities (see also Tokyo Shoken Torihikijo 2002: 665–667).

15. "Shisu no sentaku, shijo ni makaseyo: Royama Shoichi Osakadai kyoju ni kiku" (Let the market choose the best index: An interview with professor Royama Shoichi, Osaka University), *Nihon Keizai Shinbun*, December 23, 1992, 3.

16. Ibid.

17. Stigliz concludes his book *Freefall* with the following remark: "Will we seize [the financial crisis as] the opportunity to restore our sense of balance between the market and the state, between individualism and the community, between man and nature, between means and ends? We now have the opportunity to create . . . a new society in which each individual is able to fulfill his aspirations and live up to his potential, in which we have created citizens who live up to shared ideals and values, in which we have created a community that treats our planet with the respect that in the long run it will surely demand" (Stiglitz 2010: 296–297).

18. For anthropological analyses of the practical uses to which ambiguity and techniques of ambiguation are put in other ethnographic settings, see, e.g.,

Battaglia (1997); Brenneis (1986); Herzfeld (1997); Keane (1997); H. Miyazaki (2004a, 2004b).

3. TRADING ON THE LIMITS OF LEARNING

1. For example, in her ethnographic study of derivatives traders in Chicago, the anthropologist Caitlin Zaloom draws attention to the "quasi-religious" commitment of the traders she studied to the idea of discipline:

> Discipline is an ethical system and profit-making strategy. It is a method both for engaging the market and being accountable to it. Maintaining discipline allows traders to allay the dangers of acting in the market. . . . Humility in relation to the market demands the recognition that success can be perilous. A trader's claim to special knowledge or access to the mysteries of the market invites retribution. There is a fine distinction between maintaining a basic confidence in one's ability to interact with the market and an arrogance that will draw its wrath. A disciplined trader knows that the market takes away the earnings of the arrogant trader: loss is the penalty for the breakdown of discipline. (Zaloom 2006: 139)

2. In the concluding chapter of a sequel to the book, Schwager notes: "There are two basic reasons why discipline is critical. First, it is a prerequisite for maintaining effective risk control. Second, you need discipline to apply your method without second-guessing and choosing which trades to take. I guarantee that you will almost always pick the wrong ones. Why? Because you will tend to pick the comfortable trades. . . . As a final word on this subject, remember that you are never immune to bad trading habits—the best you can do is to keep them latent. As soon as you get lazy or sloppy, they will return" (Schwager [1992] 2005: 466).

3. Behind Sekai Securities' success in establishing itself quickly in the Chicago futures markets was a young and energetic trader, Ishida. Ishida had worked under Aoki in Sekai's New York office from 1983 until 1984 before moving to Chicago, where he played a leading role in Sekai's operations from 1985 until 1990. Ishida told me in September 2001 that he had been able to trade easily in the Chicago Board of Trade pits thanks to his prior experience serving as a floor trader (*badachi*) at the Tokyo Stock Exchange. An informal and friendly person fascinated with American life, Ishida also made friends with a number of local Chicago traders and was able to facilitate Sekai's entry into Chicago's futures markets.

4. In the 1990s, when Japanese corporations served as a new model of management, the focus on learning emerged as the most important location of the Japanese economy's strength. The apparent success of Japanese corporations served as evidence of the need for a shift to knowledge as the focal point of management (see, e.g., Drucker 1971; Nonaka and Takeuchi 1995; see also see Abegglen and Stalk 1985: 119–147). In their influential book *The Knowledge-Creating Company,* Ikujiro Nonaka and Hirotaka Takeuchi theorize the process of knowledge creation in Japanese corporations, developing the notion of a "knowledge-creation spiral" and drawing attention to the way tacit knowledge is translated into explicit knowledge through "externalization" and

"internalization" (Nonaka and Takeuchi 1995; see also Nonaka, Konno, and Toyama 2001: 14).

5. "Salomon Trader Was Paid $31.45 Million," *New York Times*, April 8, 1997, www.nytimes.com/1997/04/08/business/salomon-trader-was-paid-31.45-million.html, accessed January 5, 2011.

6. Lave and Wenger observe that "learners inevitably participate in communities of practitioners and that the mastery of knowledge and skill requires newcomers to move toward full participation in the sociocultural practices of community" (Lave and Wenger 1991: 29). This move to situate learning in what they call a "community of practice" is ultimately predicated on their view that "learning is an integral and inseparable aspect of social practice" (p. 31). As William Hanks points out in his commentary on Lave and Wenger's thesis, therefore, in their view, "learning is a way of being in the social world, not a way of coming to know about it" (Hanks 1991: 24).

7. For an account of diverse responses to and consequences of the general convergence of Japanese and American styles of human resource management during the 1990s, see Jacoby (2005).

8. This is a familiar process of culturally essentialist objectification—that is, the objectification of a certain practice as an emblem of Japanese society to be rejected as obsolete (see, e.g., Thomas 1991). Of course, Japanese corporations' business strategies have been much more complex and diverse (see, in particular, Aoki 1988, 1994). My focus here, however, is on the way the popular conception of the Japanese business strategy of imitating and innovating Euro-American ideas served as a concrete model for action for certain Japanese economic actors.

9. After 1985 stock trading at the Tokyo Stock Exchange was computerized gradually, but it remained only partially mechanized until 1999 (Tokyo Shoken Torihikijo 2002: 609–614, 818–826). For example, until the mid-1990s, traders at securities firms did not have full direct access to the exchange's trading and price information systems (p. 820).

10. I was not able to verify this independently.

11. In her study of the "culture" of Wall Street, Karen Ho also draws attention to the temporal dimensions of work on Wall Street. In particular, Ho examines Wall Street investment bankers' misrecognition of the stability of their employment in terms of the cycles of the markets rather than in terms of downsizing prompted by the promotion of the shareholder value, the very value they were advocating in the market. She is concerned with the way a particular kind of presentism has resulted from Wall Street bankers' cultural emphasis on smartness and high-reward systems and their lack of future orientation (Ho 2009: 250–252).

4. ECONOMY OF DREAMS

1. Tada assumed an interest rate of 2 percent.

2. This was a purely hypothetical scenario for the sake of comparison. Tada did not have anything specific in mind with this scenario.

3. This general trend reached its height in the early 2000s when Prime Minister Junichiro Koizumi, backed by his personal popularity, forcefully

advanced the privatization of the country's postal and postal savings services. During Koizumi's term from 2001 to 2006, neoliberalism was linked explicitly with a particular brand of individualism and an image of Japan's renewal through a collective embrace of "pain" (*itami*) associated with reform (see H. Miyazaki 2002).

4. Karen Kelsky's ethnography of Japanese businesswomen working in Euro-American firms suggests that professional Japanese women, who have always been outside the lifetime employment system, have long defined themselves as embodying the attributes of the strong individual, such as risk taking and self-responsibility (Kelsky 2001).

5. To the extent that machine or algorithmic trading is now widely practiced, Tada's dream has been realized. Sasaki, who in the early 1990s pursued Tada's dream of building a trading machine, was part of his bank's project to make its machine trading system more energy-efficient and eco-friendly in 2010 (August 2010).

6. In February 2005, the Livedoor Group acquired approximately 35 percent of all Nippon Hoso shares and became the largest shareholder of Nippon Hoso (Nikkei Keizai Shinbunsha 2005: 14–18). Lehman Brothers had agreed to provide 80 billion yen (approximately $770 million) in exchange for Livedoor's convertible bonds. Livedoor's ultimate goal was to control Fuji Television Network. Murakami's fund had acquired approximately 16 percent of the Nippon Hoso shares by the fall of 2004 and apparently coordinated with Livedoor in Livedoor's bid to become the majority shareholder of Nippon Hoso (pp. 25–26, 145–149). In response, Nippon Hoso announced that it would issue special new shares (*shinkabu yoyaku ken*) to be owned by the Fuji-Sankei Group (pp. 78–80). Livedoor and Fuji-Sankei eventually reached an agreement to form an alliance (pp. 125–127). Horie allegedly exaggerated Livedoor's profit while selling his own shares in the market. Following the arrest of Horie, Murakami was also arrested for insider trading in June 2006. Murakami's fund, once a major shareholder of Nippon Hoso, was said to have encouraged and subsequently profited from Livedoor's plan to acquire control of the radio station (see, e.g., Oshika [2006] 2008).

7. Tada often told me that our conversations were good opportunities for him to evaluate his own life choices "objectively" (*kyakkanteki ni*). Tada's interest in objectivity resonates with the recurrent emphasis on the importance of logical thinking in his stories. In a somewhat analogous way, the anthropologist Ruth Behar explains that her ethnographic interlocutor, Esperanza, afforded her "a status analogous to the priest as a redemptive listener of her confession" (Behar 1990: 253). Where Behar's interlocutor sought redemption, however, my conversations with Tada offered him opportunities to reassess his past decisions and reorient his knowledge.

5. THE LAST DREAM

1. See, e.g., "Kyokaisei pasonariti shogai: Utsu nado heihatsu, shindan muzukashiku" (Borderline personality disorder: It is often accompanied by

depression and other mental conditions and is difficult to diagnose), *Nihon Keizai Shinbun*, January 14, 2011, evening edition. According to this report, 60 percent of attempted suicides are attributable to borderline personality disorder.

2. David Kirsch, Brent Goldfarb, and Azi Gera dispute the significance of business plans in influencing venture capitalists' funding decisions (Kirsch, Goldfarb, and Gera 2009).

3. In Shimazono's view, these "spirituality intellectuals" include anthropologist Keiji Iwata, philosopher Takeshi Umehara, Jungian psychologist Hayao Kawai, economic anthropologist Shin'ichiro Kurimoto, and religious studies scholar Shin'ichi Nakazawa (Shimazono 1996: 250).

4. Naoki Kashio, an anthropologist of religion and an emerging spirituality intellectual, goes further, suggesting that the personal quest for the expansion of consciousness may serve as a catalyst for radical change in the nature of sociality and society (Kashio 2010a; see also Kashio 2010b; cf. N. Horie 2009).

5. In their study of a large Korean conglomerate, Roger L. Janelli and Dawnhee Yim analyze the relationship between Confucianism and capitalism in South Korea in terms of "a variety of mutually supportive relationships between cultural understandings and the defense or pursuit of material gain" (Janelli and Yim 1997: 123).

6. See also the prominent Japanese economic historian Hisao Otsuka's discussion of Max Weber's *The Protestant Ethic and the Spirit of Capitalism* (Otsuka 1966, 1994).

7. According to Richard Swedberg, "the most common interpretation . . . is that 'elective affinity' is used by Weber to express the fact that two sets of social facts or mentalities are related to each other or gravitate to each other—even though no direct and simple causality between the two can be established" (2005: 83).

8. Direct witnessing of Sai Baba's miraculous power plays a significant role in the development of devotion to the holy man among his followers (see Klass 1991: 121–122, 146–153).

9. Tada had read Joseph McMoneagle's book on remote viewing, *The Ultimate Time Machine: A Remote Viewer's Perception of Time, and Predictions for the New Millennium* (1998), in English several years before, in addition to various other publications on the subject. Tada also recommended to me Jean-Jacques Velasco and Nicolas Montigiani's book (2008) as a reliable source of information about UFOs.

10. See Battaglia (2006) for various examples of apocalyptic and yet optimistic engagements with the extraterrestrial.

11. Bill Maurer notes, "Islamic banking . . . is not simply a collection of diverse and sometimes contradictory efforts to avoid riba, but the debate over riba itself, instantiated not only in discussions and arguments but in contractual forms and transactions" (Maurer 2006b: 101). The specific significance of debate in Islam aside (see, e.g., Fischer and Abedi 1990), Maurer's insight is relevant here.

6. FROM ARBITRAGE TO THE GIFT

1. According to Iwai, the collapse of the Soviet Union in 1991 meant to students of economics that "the world entered the 'age of Adam Smith'" (Iwai 2000: 5). For example, Iwai cites the rhetoric of the 1993 World Bank report on the "East Asian miracle" (World Bank 1993), which argues that the economic success of East Asian countries can be attributed to their "'market-friendly' economic policies" (Iwai 2000: 7; see, e.g., World Bank 1993: 10). He then draws attention to the first shift in this discourse on East Asian economies that occurred in the aftermath of the Asian currency crisis of 1997:

> The sudden financial crisis at the end of the twentieth century surprised and confused people. In particular, those economists who worship Adam Smith as their founding father were deeply surprised and deeply confused. That is because the scope, degree and speed of the crisis were so far removed from Adam Smith's vision of the market economy.
>
> Following the collapse of socialism, the world should belong to Adam Smith. Why on earth doesn't the market's "Invisible Hand" work smoothly?
>
> Immediately following the East Asian currency crisis, many of those economists who had praised East Asia's "market friendly" policies, sought the cause of the crisis in those "anti-market" institutions and policies remaining in East Asian economies. If you follow Adam Smith's teaching, the market does not lead to equilibrium and stability because the market's "invisible hand" . . . is constrained for some reason. The market may be underdeveloped because of irrational customs and institutions. Alternatively, the market may be distorted by arbitrary policy interventions and regulations. (Iwai 2000: 9)

2. Kojin Karatani is a literary critic and philosopher who was born in 1941. His English-language books include *Architecture as Metaphor* (1995), *Origins of Modern Japanese Literature* (1993), and *Transcritique on Kant and Marx* (2003).

3. Reflecting on *Owarinaki sekai* (The world without an end), his 1990 collaboration with Iwai, Karatani remarked in a roundtable discussion recorded in April 1999:

> [The dialogue with Iwai] was held around the time of the collapse of the Soviet Union. At that stage, I believe, I wanted to say that whereas Soviet-style state capitalism had usually been regarded as communism or socialism, communism did not exist there. Rather, I wanted to say, communism would emerge in the process of the advancement of global capitalism. However, after the collapse of the Soviet Union and the Gulf War, such an ironic endorsement of global capitalism has lost its irony. It has become a simple endorsement [of global capitalism]. For example, the critical edge that Derrida and Deleuze had had up to that point was lost. Of course, because Derrida and Deleuze were well aware of this fact, they declared that they were Marxists. . . . The radical meaning that those thoughts had had up to the 1980s was lost after 1990, and I had to rethink Marx at that point. (Shimada, Yamashiro, and Karatani 2000: 53)

4. This is precisely the condition of knowledge in the so-called new economy to which Luc Boltanski and Ève Chiapello, Douglas Holmes and George

Marcus, Nigel Thrift, and others draw attention, albeit in different ways and for different theoretical purposes (see, e.g., Boltanski and Chiapello [1999] 2005; Holmes and Marcus 2005; Thrift 2005).

5. As Matt Tomlinson points out, however, Kierkegaard's conceptualization of "leap" reflects the paradox of Christian faith entailed in the ambiguous tension between human agency and divine agency (Tomlinson 2010: 756n4).

6. In their 1990 book, *Owarinaki sekai* (The world without an end), Karatani and Iwai repeated the point that Iwai had made in his interpretation of *The Merchant of Venice,* that capitalism is a form of "perpetual motion" (*eikyu undo*) that defers its own end by continually searching for and eliminating difference on ever new spatial, conceptual, or temporal horizons (Iwai [1985] 1992: 68). These two well-known Japanese public intellectuals' dialogue on the nature of capitalism took place at a moment in which the collapse of the Soviet Union and the triumph of global capitalism were widely perceived to be imminent. In their dialogue, however, Iwai and Karatani insisted that there was nothing new about these unfolding events. In their view, since the time of merchant capitalism, capitalism has always exploited differences of all kinds and eliminated boundaries of all kinds. Thus, they argued that the collapse of socialist regimes was simply a replication of this recurring pattern in the movement of capital.

7. This view of *Argonauts of the Western Pacific* may contradict the use Arjun Appadurai has made of the foundational text in his pioneering anthropological analysis of the production of value in the derivatives markets, in which he draws attention to several common features of the *kula* exchange and the commodity futures markets. Appadurai focuses on the way both forms of exchange are separated from more mundane forms of exchange: "In both cases, the tournament occurs in a special arena, insulated from practical economic life and subject to special rules. In both cases, what are exchanged are tokens of value that can be transformed into other media only by a complex set of steps and only in unusual circumstances. In both cases, there are specific ways in which the reproduction of the larger economy is articulated with the structure of the tournament economy.... Perhaps most important, in both cases, there is an agonistic, romantic, individualistic, and gamelike ethos that stands in contrast to the ethos of everyday economic behavior" (Appadurai 1986a: 50).

8. See, e,g., Gregory Bateson's *Naven* for the impossibility of putting parts into a whole (Bateson [1936] 1958); the work of Annette Weiner for her critique of Malinowski's work (Weiner 1976); and the works of Jane Fajans, Fred Myers, and Terence Turner for their critique of Maussian total social facts (Fajans 1993; Myers 2001; Turner 1989).

9. In *Argonauts of the Western Pacific,* Malinowski brought economy into view as an important object of ethnographic research under the banner of what he termed "New Humanism" (Malinowski 1922; see also Young 2004: 547). In his 1922 *Economica* article, "Ethnology and the Study of Society," Malinowski argued for "the need of studying all the phases of native life . . . attractive and ugly, sensational and commonplace alike" (Malinowski 1922: 217; emphasis removed). For him, economy was the least sensational and most mundane

dimension of social life, and one that anthropologists had largely ignored up to then (p. 218).

10. This type of insistence on finding unexpected openings within a seemingly closed and overdetermined space has been common in critical theory. For example, many ongoing proposals aim to subvert global capitalism from within by focusing on the openings that capitalism has brought into view. These proposals range from efforts by Fredric Jameson and others to uncover utopian content in the midst of mass culture (see, e.g., Jameson 1991; see also Ivy 1995: 243–247; Robertson 1998; Treat 1996: 284–285 for similar efforts in terms of Japanese mass culture) to the call by Michael Hardt and Antonio Negri and others for attention to the emancipatory potential in the rhetoric of globalization itself (see, e.g., Hardt and Negri 2000; Karatani 2003; see also Coronil 2000; Turner 2002: 76–77). Here ambiguity is regarded as a common marker of such openings.

References

Abegglen, James C., and George Stalk. 1985. *Kaisha, the Japanese Corporation.* New York: Basic Books.

Abolafia, Mitchel Y. 1996. *Making Markets: Opportunism and Restraint on Wall Street.* Cambridge, Mass.: Harvard University Press.

Adachi, Tomohiko, and Motonari Kurasawa. 1993. "Stock Futures and Options Markets in Japan." In *Japanese Capital Markets: New Developments in Regulations and Institutions,* ed. Shinji Takagi, 403–425. Oxford: Blackwell.

Aitken, Robert. 1990. *The Gateless Barrier: The Wu-Men Kuan (Mumonkan).* San Francisco: North Point Press.

Akerlof, George A., and Robert J. Shiller. 2009. *Animal Spirits: How Human Psychology Drives the Economy, and Why It Matters for Global Capitalism.* Princeton, N.J.: Princeton University Press.

Allison, Anne. 1994. *Nightwork: Sexuality, Pleasure, and Corporate Masculinity in a Tokyo Hostess Club.* Chicago, Ill.: University of Chicago Press.

Amariglio, Jack, and David F. Ruccio. 1999. "Literary/Cultural 'Economies,' Economic Discourse, and the Question of Marxism." In *The New Economic Criticism: Studies at the Intersection of Literature and Economics,* ed. Martha Woodmansee and Mark Osteen, 381–400. London: Routledge.

Aoki, Masahiko. 1988. *Information, Incentives, and Bargaining in the Japanese Economy.* Cambridge: Cambridge University Press.

———. 1994. "The Japanese Firm as a System of Attributes: A Survey and Research Agenda." In *The Japanese Firm: The Sources of Competitive Strength,* ed. Masahiko Aoki and Ronald Dore, 11–40. Oxford: Oxford University Press.

———. 2010. *Corporations in Evolving Diversity: Cognition, Governance, and Institutions.* Oxford: Oxford University Press.

Appadurai, Arjun. 1986a. "Introduction: Commodities and the Politics of Value." In *The Social Life of Things: Commodities in Cultural Perspective,* ed. Arjun Appadurai, 3–63. Cambridge: Cambridge University Press.

———, ed. 1986b. *The Social Life of Things: Commodities in Cultural Perspective.* Cambridge: Cambridge University Press.

———. 2011. "The Ghost in the Financial Machine." *Public Culture* 23(3): 517–539.

Auden, W.H. 1991. "Brothers and Others." In *The Merchant of Venice: Critical Essays,* ed. Thomas Wheeler, 59–78. New York: Garland.

Avril, Philippe. 2000. *Nihon no ekuiti deribatibu* [Equity derivatives in Japan]. Tokyo: Sigma Base Capital.

Banta, Martha. 1993. *Taylored Lives: Narrative Productions in the Age of Taylor, Veblen, and Ford.* Chicago, Ill.: University of Chicago Press.

Barth, Fredrik. (1967) 2000. "Economic Spheres in Darfur." In *Entrepreneurship: The Social Science View,* ed. Richard Swedberg, 139–160. Oxford: Oxford University Press.

Bateson, Gregory. (1936) 1958. *Naven: A Survey of the Problems Suggested by a Composite Picture of the Culture of a New Guinea Tribe Drawn from Three Points of View.* 2nd ed. Stanford, Calif.: Stanford University Press.

Battaglia, Debbora. 1997. "Ambiguating Agency: The Case of Malinowski's Ghost." *American Anthropologist* 99(3): 505–510.

———, ed. 2006. *E.T. Culture: Anthropology in Outerspaces.* Durham, N.C.: Duke University Press.

Beck, Ulrich. 1992. *Risk Society: Towards a New Modernity.* London: Sage Publications.

Behar, Ruth. 1990. "Rage and Redemption: Reading the Life Story of a Mexican Marketing Woman." *Feminist Studies* 16(2): 223–258.

Benedict, Ruth. 1934. *Patterns of Culture.* Boston: Houghton Miffin.

Benston, Alice N. 1991. "Portia, the Law, and the Triparitite Structure of *The Merchant of Venice.*" In *The Merchant of Venice: Critical Essays,* ed. Thomas Wheeler, 163–194. New York: Garland.

Bernstein, Peter L. 1992. *Capital Ideas: The Improbable Origins of Modern Wall Street.* New York: Free Press.

Bestor, Theodore. 2001. "Supply-Side Sushi: Commodity, Market, and the Global City." *American Anthropologist* 103(1): 76–95.

Beunza, Daniel, Iain Hardie, and Donald MacKenzie. 2006. "A Price is a Social Thing: Towards a Material Sociology of Arbitrage." *Organization Studies* 27(5): 721–745.

Beunza, Daniel, and David Stark. 2004. "Tools of the Trade: The Socio-Technology of Arbitrage in a Wall Street Trading Room." *Industrial and Corporate Change* 13(2): 369–400.

———. 2005. "How to Recognize Opportunities: Heterarchical Search in a Trading Room." In *The Sociology of Financial Markets,* ed. Karin Knorr-Cetina and Alex Preda, 84–101. Oxford: Oxford University Press.

Black, Fischer S., and Myron Scholes. 1973. "The Pricing of Options and Corporate Liabilities." *Journal of Political Economy* 81(3): 637–654.

Boesky, Ivan F. 1985. *Merger Mania: Arbitrage: Wall Street's Best Kept Money-making Secret.* Ed. Jeffrey Madrick. New York: Holt, Rinehart and Winston.

Bohannan, Paul. 1955. "Some Principles of Exchange and Investment among the Tiv." *American Anthropologist* 57(1): 60–70.

Boltanski, Luc, and Ève Chiapello. (1999) 2005. *The New Spirit of Capitalism.* Trans. Gregory Elliott. London: Verso.

Borovoy, Amy. 2010. "Japan as Mirror: Neoliberalism's Promise and Costs." In *Ethnographies of Neoliberalism,* ed. Carol Greenhouse, 60–74. Philadelphia: University of Pennsylvania Press.

Bourdieu, Pierre. 1963. "The Attitude of the Algerian Peasant toward Time." In *Mediterranean Countrymen: Essays in the Social Anthropology of the Mediterranean,* ed. Julian Pitts-Rivers, 55–72. Paris: Mouton.

Brenneis, Donald. 1986. "Shared Territory: Audience, Indirection and Meaning." *Text* 6: 339–347.

Brenner, Menachem, Marti G. Subrahmanyam, and Jun Uno. 1991a. "Arbitrage Opportunities in the Japanese Stock and Futures Markets." In *Japanese Financial Market Research,* ed. William T. Ziemba, Warren Bailey, and Yasushi Hamao, 439–465. Amsterdam: Elsevier Science.

———. 1991b. "Stock Index Futures Arbitrage in the Japanese Markets." In *Japanese Financial Market Research,* ed. William T. Ziemba, Warren Bailey, and Yasushi Hamao, 411–438. Amsterdam: Elsevier Science.

Brenner, Reuven. 1990. *Gambling and Speculation: A Theory, a History, and a Future of Some Human Decisions.* With Gabrielle A. Brenner. Cambridge: Cambridge University Press.

Brinton, Mary. 2011. *Lost in Transition: Youth, Work, and Instability in Postindustrial Japan.* Cambridge: Cambridge University Press.

Butler, Judith. 2010. "Performative Agency." *Journal of Cultural Economy* 3(2): 147–161.

Bushe, Gervase R., and Abraham B. Shani. 1991. *Parallel Learning Structures: Increasing Innovation in Bureaucracies.* Reading, Mass.: Addison-Wesley.

Callon, Michel. 1998a. "An Essay on Framing and Overflowing: Economic Externalities Revisited by Sociology." In *The Laws of the Markets,* ed. Michel Callon, 244–269. Oxford: Blackwell.

———. 1998b. "Introduction: The Embeddedness of Economic Markets in Economics." In *The Laws of the Markets,* ed. Michel Callon, 1–57. Oxford: Blackwell.

———. 2005. "Why Virtualism Paves the Way to Political Impotence: A Reply to Daniel Miller's Critique of *The Laws of the Markets.*" *Economic Sociology European Electronic Newsletter* 6(2): 3–20.

———. 2010. "Performativity, Misfires and Politics." *Journal of Cultural Economy* 3(2): 163–169.

Callon, Michel, Yuval Millo, and Fabian Muniesa, eds. 2007. *Market Devices.* Malden, Mass.: Blackwell.

Carrette, Jeremy, and Richard King. 2005. *Selling Spirituality: The Silent Takeover of Religion.* London: Routledge.

Carrier, James G., and Daniel Miller. 1998a. "Introduction." In *Virtualism: A New Political Economy,* ed. James G. Carrier and Daniel Miller, 1–24. Oxford: Berg.

———, eds. 1998b. *Virtualism: A New Political Economy.* Oxford: Berg.

Choy, Timothy. 2011. *Ecologies of Comparison: An Ethnography of Endangerment in Hong Kong.* Durham, N.C.: Duke University Press.

Cohen, Walter. 1982. "*The Merchant of Venice* and the Possibilities of Historical Criticism." *ELH* (English Literary History) 49(4): 765–789.

Cole, Robert E. 1979. *Work, Mobility, and Participation: A Comparative Study of American and Japanese Industry.* Berkeley: University of California Press.

Comaroff, Jean, and John L. Comaroff. 2000. "Millennial Capitalism: First Thoughts on a Second Coming." *Public Culture* 12(2): 291–343.

Comaroff, John L., and Jean Comaroff. 1992. *Ethnography and the Historical Imagination.* Boulder, Colo.: Westview.

Connolly, William E. 2005. "The Evangelical-Capitalist Resonance Machine." *Political Theory* 33(6): 869–886.

———. 2008. *Capitalism and Christianity, American Style.* Durham, N.C.: Duke University Press.

Coronil, Fernando. 2000. "Towards a Critique of Globalcentrism: Speculations on Capitalism's Nature." *Public Culture* 12(2): 351–374.

Cox, John, and Mark Rubinstein. 1985. *Options Markets.* Englewood Cliffs, N.J.: Prentice-Hall.

Crump, Arthur. 1874. *The Theory of Stock Exchange Speculation.* 3rd ed. London: Longmans, Green, Reader and Dyer.

Dalton, George. 1961. "Economic Theory and Primitive Society." *American Anthropologist* 63(1): 1–25.

Danson, Lawrence. 1978. *The Harmonies of The Merchant of Venice.* New Haven, Conn.: Yale University Press.

Dattel, Eugene R. 1994. *The Sun That Never Rose: The Inside Story of Japan's Failed Attempt at Global Financial Dominance.* Chicago, Ill.: Probus.

de Goede, Marieke. 2005. *Virtue, Fortune and Faith: A Genealogy of Finance.* Minneapolis: University of Minnesota Press.

Deleuze, Gilles, and Felix Guattari. (1980) 1987. *A Thousand Plateaus: Capitalism and Schizophrenia.* Trans. Brian Massumi. Minneapolis: University of Minnesota Press.

Derrida, Jacques. 1992. *Given Time: I. Counterfeit Money.* Chicago, Ill.: University of Chicago Press.

Dore, Ronald. 1983. "Goodwill and the Spirit of Market Capitalism." *British Journal of Sociology* 34(4): 459–482.

———. 1997. "Japan's Reform Debate: Patriotic Concern or Class Interest? Or Both?" *Journal of Japanese Studies* 25(1): 65–89.

Dower, John W. 1999. *Embracing Defeat: Japan in the Wake of World War II.* New York: W.W. Norton.

Draper, John W. 1935. "Usury in *The Merchant of Venice.*" *Modern Philology* 33(1): 37–47.

Drucker, Peter F. 1971. "What We Can Learn from Japanese Management." *Harvard Business Review,* March–April, 110–122.

Dybvig, Philip H., and Stephen A. Ross. 1987. "Arbitrage." In vol. 1 of *The New Palgrave: A Dictionary of Economics,* ed. John Eatwell, Murray Milgate, and Peter Newman, 100–106. London: Macmillan.

El-Gamal, Mahmoud A. 2006. *Islamic Finance: Law, Economics, and Practice.* Cambridge: Cambridge University Press.

Elster, Jon. 2000. *Ulysses Unbound: Studies in Rationality, Precommitment, and Constraints.* Cambridge: Cambridge University Press.

Elyachar, Julia. 2005. *Markets of Dispossession: NGOs, Economic Development, and the State in Cairo.* Durham, N.C.: Duke University Press.

Emery, Henry Crosby. 1896. *Speculation on the Stock and Produce Exchanges of the United States.* Studies in History, Economics and Public Law, vol. 7, no. 2. New York: Columbia University.

Endlich, Lisa. (1999) 2000. *Goldman Sachs: The Culture of Success.* New York: Touchstone.

Engle, Lars. 1986. "'Thrift Is Blessing': Exchange and Explanation in *The Merchant of Venice.*" *Shakespeare Quarterly* 37(1): 20–37.

Ewald, François. 1991. "Insurance and Risk." In *The Foucault Effect: Studies in Governmentality,* ed. Graham Burchell, Colin Gordon, and Peter Miller, 197–210. Chicago, Ill.: University of Chicago Press.

Fackler, Martin. 2010. "Japan Goes From Dynamic to Disheartened." *New York Times,* October 16. www.nytimes.com/2010/10/17/world/asia/17japan.html, accessed June 6, 2012.

Fajans, Jane. 1993. "Introduction." In *Exchanging Products: Producing Exchange* (Oceania Monographs 43), ed. Jane Fajans, 1–13. Sydney: Sydney University Press.

Fama, Eugene. 1970. "Efficient Capital Markets: A Review of Theory and Empirical Work." *Journal of Finance* 25(2): 383–417.

Farnam, Henry W. 1931. *Shakespeare's Economics.* New Haven, Conn.: Yale University Press.

Ferguson, James. 1999. *Expectations of Modernity: Myths and Meanings of Urban Life on the Zambian Copperbelt.* Chicago, Ill.: University of Chicago Press.

Fischer, Michael M.J., and Mehdi Abedi. 1990. *Debating Muslim: Cultural Dialogues in Postmodernity and Tradition.* Madison, Wis.: University of Wisconsin Press.

Fisher, Melissa S. 2010. "Wall Street Women: Engendering Global Finance in the Manhattan Landscape." *City and Society* 22(2): 262–285.

Fisher, Melissa S., and Greg Downey, eds. 2006. *Frontiers of Capital: Ethnographic Reflections on the New Economy.* Durham, N.C.: Duke University Press.

Fourcade-Gourinchas, Marion, and Sarah L. Babb. 2002. "The Rebirth of the Liberal Creed: Paths to Neoliberalism in Four Countries." *American Journal of Sociology* 108(3): 533–579.

Friedman, Milton. 1953. *Essays in Positive Economics.* Chicago, Ill.: University of Chicago Press.

Frost, Peter J., Larry F. Moore, Meryl Reis Louis, Craig C. Lundberg, and Joanne Martin, eds. 1985. *Organizational Culture.* Beverly Hills, Calif.: Sage.

Frost, Peter J., Walter R. Nord, and Linda A. Krefting, eds. 2004. *Managerial and Organizational Reality: Stories of Life and Work*. Upper Saddle River, N.J.: Pearson Education.

Fujiwara, Yasuko. 1998. "Jibun no nedan" [One's own worth]. *Asahi Shinbun* (Western Japan edition), September 16, 22.

Funai, Yukio. 1995. *Ego kara eva e: Chikyu ga kawaru, jinrui ga kawaru* [From Ego to Eva: The Earth is changing, and humanity is changing]. Tokyo: PHP Kenkyujo.

———. 2002. *Danmatsuma no shihonshugi* [Death throes of capitalism]. Tokyo: Tokuma Shoten.

Galbraith, John Kenneth. (1954) 1997. *The Great Crash 1929*. Boston: Houghton Mifflin.

Geertz, Clifford. 1973. *The Interpretation of Cultures*. New York: Basic Books.

———. 1979. "Suq: The Bazaar Economy in Sefrou." In *Meaning and Order in Moroccan Society: Three Essays in Cultural Analysis,* ed. Clifford Geertz, Hildred Geertz, and Lawrence Rosen, 123–313. Cambridge: Cambridge University Press.

———. 1982. "The Way We Think Now: Toward an Ethnography of Modern Thought." *Bulletin of the American Academy of Arts and Sciences* 35(5): 14–34.

Gell, Alfred. 1992. *The Anthropology of Time: Cultural Constructions of Temporal Maps and Images*. Oxford: Berg.

Genda, Yuji. (2001) 2005. *A Nagging Sense of Job Insecurity: The New Reality Facing Japanese Youth*. Trans. Jean Connell Hoff. Tokyo: International House of Japan.

Genda, Yuji, and Mie Maganuma. 2004. *Nito: Furita demo naku shitsugyosha demo naku* [The NEET (Not in Employment, Education or Training): Neither freeters nor unemployed]. Tokyo: Gentosha.

Gerlach, Michael. 1992. *Alliance Capitalism: The Social Organization of Japanese Business*. Berkeley: University of California Press.

Graeber, David. 2001. *Toward an Anthropological Theory of Value: The False Coin of Our Own Dreams*. New York: Palgrave.

———. 2011. *Debt: The First 5,000 Years*. New York: Melville House.

Greenhouse, Carol. 1996. *A Moment's Notice: Time Politics Across Cultures*. Ithaca, N.Y.: Cornell University Press.

———. 2010. "Introduction." In *Ethnographies of Neoliberalism,* ed. Carol Greenhouse, 1–10. Philadelphia: University of Pennsylvania Press.

Gregory, Chris A. 1982. *Gifts and Commodities*. London: Academic Press.

Gudeman, Stephen. 2001. *The Anthropology of Economy*. Malden, Mass.: Blackwell.

Guyer, Jane. 2004. *Marginal Gains: Monetary transactions in Atlantic Africa*. Chicago, Ill.: University of Chicago Press.

———. 2007. "Prophecy and the Near Future: Thoughts on Macroeconomic, Evangelical and Punctuated Time." *American Ethnologist* 34(3): 409–421.

Hanks, William F. 1991. "Foreword." In *Situated Learning: Legitimate Peripheral Participation*, by Jean Lave and Etienne Wenger, 13–24. Cambridge: Cambridge University Press.

Hardie, Iain. 2004. "The Sociology of Arbitrage: A Comment on MacKenzie." *Economy and Society* 33(2): 239–254.

Harding, Susan F. 2000. *The Book of Jerry Falwell: Fundamentalist Language and Politics*. Princeton, N.J.: Princeton University Press.

Hardt, Michael, and Antonio Negri. 2000. *Empire*. Cambridge, Mass.: Harvard University Press.

Harrison, J. Michael, and David M. Kreps. 1979. "Martingales and Arbitrage in Multiperiod Securities Markets." *Journal of Economic Theory* 20(3): 381–408.

Harrison, J. Michael, and Stanley R. Pliska. 1981. "Martingales and Stochastic Integrals in the Theory of Continuous Trading." *Stochastic Processes and Their Applications* 11(3): 215–260.

Harrison, Paul. 1997. "A History of an Intellectual Arbitrage: The Evolution of Financial Economics." *History of Political Economy* 27 (supplementary issue): 172–187.

Harvey, David. 1989. *The Condition of Postmodernity: An Enquiry into the Origins of Cultural Change*. Oxford: Blackwell.

———. 2000. *Spaces of Hope*. Berkeley: University of California Press.

———. 2005. *A Brief History of Neoliberalism*. Oxford: Oxford University Press.

Hayek, Friedrich A. (1948) 1980. *Individualism and Economic Order*. Chicago, Ill.: University of Chicago Press.

Hein, Laura. 2004. *Reasonable Men, Powerful Words: Political Culture and Expertise in Twentieth-Century Japan*. Washington, D.C.: Woodrow Wilson Center Press.

Henwood, Doug. (1997) 1998. *Wall Street: How It Works and for Whom*. London: Verso.

Hertz, Ellen. 1998. *The Trading Crowd: An Ethnography of the Shanghai Stock Market*. Cambridge: Cambridge University Press.

Herzfeld, Michael. 1997. *Cultural Intimacy: Social Poetics in the Nation-state*. New York: Routledge.

Hirschman, Albert O. (1977) 1997. *The Passions and the Interests: Political Arguments for Capitalism Before Its Triumph*. Princeton, N.J.: Princeton University Press.

Ho, Karen. 2009. *Liquidated: An Ethnography of Wall Street*. Durham, N.C.: Duke University Press.

Holmes, Douglas. 2009. "Economy of Words." *Cultural Anthropology* 24(3): 381–419.

Holmes, Douglas, and George Marcus. 2005. "Cultures of Expertise and the Management of Globalization: Toward the Refunctioning of Ethnography." In *Global Assemblages: Technology, Politics, and Ethics as Anthropological Problems*, ed. Aihwa Ong and Stephen Collier, 235–252. Malden, Mass.: Blackwell.

Horie, Norichika. 2009. *Rekishi no naka no shukyoshinrigaku: Sono shisho keisei to fuchi* [The psychology of religion in history: Its formation and placement]. Tokyo: Iwanomishoten.

Horie, Takafumi. (2004) 2005. *Kasegu ga kachi: Zero kara hyaku oku boku no yarikata* [Those who make money are winners: My method for earning 10 billion yen from nothing]. Tokyo: Kobunsha.

Huebner, S.S. 1910. "Scope and Functions of the Stock Market." *Annals of the American Academy of Political and Social Science* 35(3): 1–23.

———. 1911. "The Functions of Produce Exchanges." *Annals of the American Academy of Political and Social Science* 38(2): 1–35.

Hull, John C. 1997. *Options, Futures, and Other Derivatives.* 3rd ed. Upper Saddle River, N.J.: Prentice Hall.

———. 2000. *Options, Futures, and Other Derivatives.* 4th ed. Upper Saddle River, N.J.: Prentice Hall.

Hull, John C., and Alan White. 2010. "Ratings Arbitrage and Structured Products." Working paper, University of Toronto. www.rotman.utoronto.ca/~hull/DownloadablePublications/RatingsCriteria.pdf. Accessed November 14, 2010.

Iida, Tsuneo, and Takanori Mizuno. 1998. *Kin'yu haisen wo koete* [Overcoming defeat in the financial war]. Tokyo: Toyokeizai.

Ito, Hideshi. 1996. "The Economics of the 'Company Man.'" *Japanese Economics Studies* 24(6): 29–55.

Ivy, Marilyn. 1993. "Formations of Mass Culture." In *Post-war Japan as History,* ed. Andrew Gordon, 239–258. Berkeley: University of California Press.

———. 1995. *Discourses of the Vanishing: Modernity, Phantasm, Japan.* Chicago, Ill.: University of Chicago Press.

Iwai, Katsuhito. 1981. *Disequilibrium Dynamics: A Theoretical Analysis of Inflation and Unemployment.* New Haven, Conn.: Yale University Press.

———. (1985) 1992. *Venisu no shonin no shihonron* [A theory of capital according to *The Merchant of Venice*]. Tokyo: Chikumashobo.

———. 1993. *Kaheiron* [A theory of money]. Tokyo: Chikuma Shobo.

———. 2000. *Nijuisseiki no shihonshugiron* [A theory of capitalism for the twenty-first century]. Tokyo: Chikumashobo.

———. 2005. *Kaisha wa dare no mono ka* [Who owns a company?]. Tokyo: Heibonsha.

———. 2008. "Jiyuhonin wa daini no shuen" [The second end of laissez-faire]. *Nihon Keizai Shinbun,* October 24.

———. 2011. "The Second End of Laissez-Faire: The Bootstrapping Nature of Money and the Inherent Instability of Capitalism." In *New Approaches to Monetary Theory: Interdisciplinary Perspectives,* ed. Heiner Granssmann, 237–266. London: Routledge.

Iwai, Katsuhito, and Takahiro Sato. 2008. *M&A kokufuron: Yoi kaishabaishu to wa do iu koto ka* [M&A for the wealth of the nation: What would a good buyout look like?]. Tokyo: Purejidentosha.

Jacoby, Sanford M. 2005. *The Embedded Corporation: Corporate Governance and Employment Relations in Japan the United States.* Princeton, N.J.: Princeton University Press.

Jameson, Fredric. 1991. *Postmodernism, or, The Cultural Logic of Late Capitalism.* Durham, N.C.: Duke University Press.

Janelli, Roger L., and Dawnhee Yim. 1997. "The Mutual Constitution of Confucianism and Capitalism in South Korea." In *Culture and Economy: The Shaping of Captalism in East Asia,* ed. Timothy Brook and Hy V. Luong, 107–124. Ann Arbor: University of Michigan Press.

Johnson, Chalmers. 1984. *MITI and the Japanese Miracle: The Growth of Industrial Policy, 1925–1975.* Berkeley: University of California Press.

Karatani, Kojin. 1993. *Origins of Modern Japanese Literature.* Trans. Brett de Bary. Durham, N.C.: Duke University Press.

———. 1995. *Architecture as Metaphor: Language, Number, Money.* Trans. Sabu Kohso. Cambridge, Mass.: MIT Press.

———, ed. 2000a. *Kanonaru komyunizumu* [Possible communism]. Tokyo: Ota Shuppan.

———, ed. 2000b. *Genri* [The principle (of the Non-Associationist Movement)]. Tokyo: Ota Shuppan.

———. 2003. *Transcritique on Kant and Marx.* Trans. Sabu Kohso. Cambridge, Mass.: MIT Press.

———. 2009. "Kokka to shihon: Hanpukuteki kozo wa sekaitekina kibo de sonzai suru" [Nation-States and Capital: Their repetitive structure operates on a global scale]. *Shukan Asahi,* April 30 [published as a special issue of *Asahi Journal*], pp. 27–29.

Karatani, Kojin, and Katsuhito Iwai. 1990. *Owarinaki sekai: Kyuju nendai no ronri* [The world without an end: the logic of the 1990s]. Tokyo: Ohtashuppan.

Karatzas, Ioannis, and Steven E. Shreve. 1988. *Brownian Motion and Stochastic Calculus.* New York: Springer-Verlag.

Kashio, Naoki. 2010a. *Supirichuariti kakumei: Gendai reiseibunka to hirakareta shukyo no kanosei* [Spirituality revolution: Contemporary spiritual culture and the possibility of open religiosity]. Tokyo: Shunjusha.

———. 2010b. *Supirichuaru raifu no susume* [A proposal for spiritual life]. Tokyo: Bungeishunju.

Katz, Richard. 1998. *Japan: The System That Soured: The Rise and Fall of the Japanese Economic Miracle.* Armonk, N.Y.: M.E. Sharpe.

Keane, Webb. 1997. *Signs of Recognition: Powers and Hazards of Representation in an Indonesian Society.* Berkeley: University of California Press.

———. 2001. "Money Is No Object: Materiality, Desire, and Modernity in an Indonesian Society." In *The Empire of Things: Regimes of Value and Material Culture,* ed. Fred R. Myers, 65–90. Santa Fe, N.M.: School of American Research.

———. 2010. "Minds, Surfaces, and Reasons in the Anthropology of Ethics." In *Ordinary Ethics: Anthropology, Language, and Action,* ed. Michael Lambek, 64–83. New York: Fordham University Press.

Kelly, William W. 1986. "Rationalization and Nostalgia: Cultural Dynamics of New Middle-class Japan." *American Ethnologist* 13(4): 603–618.

———. 1998. "Learning to Swing: Oh Sadaharu and the Pedagogy and Practice of Japanese Baseball." In *Learning in Likely Places,* ed. John Singleton, 265–285. New York: Cambridge University Press.

Kelsky, Karen. 2001. *Women on the Verge: Japanese Women, Western Dreams.* Durham, N.C.: Duke University Press.

Kestenbaum, David. 1999. "Death by the Numbers." *Science,* n.s., 283 (5406): 1244–1247.

Keynes, John Maynard. (1936) 1997. *The General Theory of Employment, Interest, and Money.* Amherst, N.Y.: Prometheus Books.

Kirsch, David, Brent Goldfarb, and Azi Gera. 2009. "Form or Substance: The Role of Business Plans in Venture Capital Decision Making." *Strategic Management Journal* 30(5): 487–515.

Klass, Morton. 1991. *Singing with Sai Baba: The Politics of Revitalization in Trinidad.* Prospect Heights, Ill.: Waveland.

Knorr-Cetina, Karin. 1981. *The Manufacture of Knowledge: An Essay on the Constructivist and Contextual Nature of Science.* Oxford: Pergamon.

Knorr-Cetina, Karin, and Urs Bruegger. 2000. "The Market as an Object of Attachment: Exploring Postsocial Relations in Financial Markets." *Canadian Journal of Sociology/Cahiers canadiens de sociologie* 25(2): 141–168.

———. 2002. "Global Microstructures: The Virtual Societies of Financial Markets." *American Journal of Sociology* 107(4): 905–930.

Knorr-Cetina, Karin, and Alex Preda, eds. 2005. *The Sociology of Financial Markets.* Oxford: Oxford University Press.

Kobayashi, Kazuko. 1993. *Shoken* [Securities]. Tokyo: Nihon Keizai Hyoronsha.

Koike, Kazuo. (1991) 1996. *The Economics of Work in Japan.* Tokyo: LTCB International Library Foundation.

Kondo, Dorinne K. 1990. *Crafting Selves: Power, Gender, and Discourses of Identity in a Japanese Workplace.* Chicago, Ill.: University of Chicago Press.

Kopytoff, Igor. 1986. "The Cultural Biography of Things: Commoditization as Process." In *The Social Life of Things: Commodities in Cultural Perspective,* ed. Arjun Appadurai, 64–91. Cambridge: Cambridge University Press.

Koschmann, J. Victor. 1993. "Intellectuals and Politics." In *Post-war Japan as History,* ed. Andrew Gordon, 395–423. Berkeley: University of California Press.

———. 1996. *Revolution and Subjectivity in Postwar Japan.* Chicago, Ill.: University of Chicago Press.

Krugman, Paul. 2008. *The Return of Depression Economics and the Crisis of 2008.* London: Penguin.

Kunimura, Michio. 1990. "Saiteitorihiki wa kabukaboraku wo kasoku shinakatta" [Arbitrage did not accelerate the stock·price crash." *Ekonomisuto* [Economist], March 27, 22–25.

Laidlaw, James. 2000. "A Free Gift Makes No Friends." *Journal of the Royal Anthropological Institute,* n.s., 6 (4): 617–634.

Latour, Bruno. 1987. *Science in Action: How to Follow Scientists and Engineers through Society.* Cambridge, Mass.: Harvard University Press.

———. 1993. *We Have Never Been Modern.* Trans. Catherine Porter. Cambridge, Mass.: Harvard University Press.

Latour, Bruno, and Steve Woolgar. (1979) 1986. *Laboratory Life: The Construction of Scientific Facts.* 2nd ed. Princeton, N.J.: Princeton University Press.

Lau, Kimberly J. 2000. *New Age Capitalism: Making Money East of Eden.* Philadelphia: University of Pennsylvania Press.

Lave, Jean, and Etienne Wenger. 1991. *Situated Learning: Legitimate Peripheral Participation.* Cambridge: Cambridge University Press.

Law, John. 2004. *After Method: Mess in Social Science Research.* Oxon, U.K.: Routledge.

Leach, Edmund. (1954) 1970. *Political Systems of Highland Burma: A Study of Kachin Social Structure.* London: Athlone Press.

Lee, Benjamin, and Edward LiPuma. 2002. "Cultures of Circulation: The Imaginations of Modernity." *Public Culture* 14(1): 191–213.

Lépinay, Vincent-Antonin. 2007a. "Decoding Finance: Articulation and Liquidity around a Trading Room." In *Do Economists Make Markets? On the Performativity of Economics,* ed. Donald MacKenzie, Fabian Muniesa, and Lucia Siu, 87–127. Princeton, N.J.: Princeton University Press.

———. 2007b. "Parasitic Formulae: The Case of Capital Guarantee Products." In *Market Devices,* ed. Michel Callon, Yuval Millo, and Fabian Muniesa, 261–283. Malden, Mass.: Blackwell.

———. 2011. *Codes of Finance: Engineering Derivatives in a Global Bank.* Princeton, N.J.: Princeton University Press.

Lewis, Michael. 1989. *Liar's Poke : Rising through the Wreckage on Wall Street.* New York: Norton.

———. 1999. "How the Eggheads Cracked." *New York Times Magazine,* January 24.

LiPuma, Edward, and Benjamin Lee. 2004. *Financial Derivatives and the Globalization of Risk.* Durham, N.C.: Duke University Press.

Lowenstein, Roger. 2000. *When Genius Failed: The Rise and Fall of Long-Term Capital Management.* New York: Random House.

Luhmann, Tanya. 1989. *Persuasions of the Witch's Craft: Ritual Magic in Contemporary England.* Cambridge, Mass.: Harvard University Press.

Lurie, Jonathan. 1979. *The Chicago Board of Trade, 1859–1905: The Dynamics of Self-Regulation.* Urbana: University of Illinois Press.

Lynch, Michael. 1985. *Art and Artifact in Laboratory Science: A Study of Shop Work and Shop Talk in a Research Laboratory.* London: Routledge and Kegan Paul.

MacKenzie, Donald. 2001. "Physics and Finance: S-Terms and Modern Finance as a Topic for Science Studies." *Science, Technology, and Human Values* 26(2): 115–144.

———. 2003a. "An Equation and Its Worlds: Bricolage, Exemplars, Disunity and Performativity in Financial Economics." *Social Studies of Science* 33(6): 831–868.

———. 2003b. "Long-Term Capital Management and the Sociology of Arbitrage." *Economy and Society* 32(3): 349–380.

———. 2006. *An Engine, Not a Camera: How Financial Models Shape Markets.* Cambridge, Mass.: MIT Press.

———. 2009. *Material Markets: How Economic Agents Are Constructed.* Oxford: Oxford University Press.

MacKenzie, Donald, and Yuval Millo. 2003. "Constructing a Market, Performing Theory: The Historical Sociology of a Financial Derivatives Exchange." *American Journal of Sociology* 109(1):107–145.

MacKenzie, Donald, Fabian Muniesa, and Lucia Siu, eds. 2007a. *Do Economists Make Markets? On the Performativity of Economics.* Princeton, N.J.: Princeton University Press.

———. 2007b. "Introduction." In *Do Economists Make Markets? On the Performativity of Economics,* ed. Donald MacKenzie, Fabian Muniesa, and Lucia Siu, 1–19. Princeton, N.J.: Princeton University Press.

Maekawa, Ayumi. 2008. "Nihon kigyo no M&A doko" [Trends in M&A involving Japanese companies]. Mizuho Research, December. www.mizuho-ri.co.jp/research/economics/pdf/research/r081201enterprise.pdf. Accessed November 16, 2010.

Mahathir, Mohamed, and George Soros. 1997. "Mahathir vs. Soros." *Far Eastern Economic Review,* October 2, 32.

Malinowski, Bronislaw. 1922. "Ethnology and the Study of Society." *Economica* 6: 208–219.

———. (1922) 1984. *Argonauts of the Western Pacific: An Account of Native Enterprise and Adventure in the Archipelagoes of Melanesian New Guinea.* Prospect Heights, Ill.: Waveland.

March, James G. 2010. *The Ambiguities of Experience.* Ithaca, N.Y.: Cornell University Press

March, James G., and Johan P. Olsen. 1976. *Ambiguity and Choice in Organizations.* Bergen, Norway: Universitetsforlaget.

Marcus, George E. 1998. *Ethnography through Thick and Thin.* Princeton, N.J.: Princeton University Press.

———. 2007. "Ethnography Two Decades After Writing Culture: From the Experimental to the Baroque." *Anthropological Quarterly* 80(4): 1127–1145.

Markowitz, Harry M. 1999. "The Early History of Portfolio Theory: 1600–1960." *Financial Analysts Journal* 55(4): 5–16.

Marx, Karl. (1867) 1990. *Capital: A Critique of Political Economy.* Vol. 1. Trans. Ben Fowkes. London: Penguin.

Massumi, Brian. 2002. *Parables for the Virtual: Movement, Affect, Sensation.* Durham, N.C.: Duke University Press.

Maurer, Bill. 1995. "Complex Subjects: Offshore Finance, Complexity Theory, and the Dispersion of the Modern." *Socialist Review* 25 (3/4): 113–145.

———. 1999. "Forget Locke? From Proprietor to Risk-bearer in New Logics of Finance." *Public Culture* 11(2): 365–385.

———. 2002a. "Anthropological and Accounting Knowledge in Islamic Banking and Finance: Rethinking Critical Accounts." *Journal of the Royal Anthropological Institute* 8(4): 645–667.

———. 2002b. "Repressed Futures: Financial Derivatives' Theological Unconscious." *Economy and Society* 31(1): 15–36.

———. 2003a. "Please Destabilize Ethnography Now: Against Anthropological Showbiz-as-Usual." *Reviews in Anthropology* 32: 159–169.

———. 2003b. "Uncanny Exchanges: The Possibilities and Failures of 'Making Change' with Alternative Monetary Forms." *Environment and Planning D: Society and Space* 21(3): 317–340.

———. 2005a. "Due Diligence and 'Reasonable Man,' Offshore." *Cultural Anthropology* 20(4): 474–505.

———. 2005b. "Finance." In *Handbook of Economic Anthropology*, ed. James G. Carrier, 176–193. Cheltenham, U.K.: Edward Elgar.

———. 2005c. *Mutual Life, Limited Islamic Banking, Alternative Currencies, Lateral Reason.* Princeton, N.J.: Princeton University Press.

———. 2006a. "The Anthropology of Money." *Annual Review of Anthropology* 35: 15–36.

———. 2006b. *Pious Property: Islamic Mortgages in the United States.* New York: Russell Sage Foundation.

Mauss, Marcel. (1950) 1990. *The Gift: The Form and Reason for Exchange in Archaic Societies.* Trans. W.D. Hall. New York: Norton.

McMoneagle, Joseph. 1998. *The Ultimate Time Machine: A Remote Viewer's Perception of Time, and Predictions for the New Millennium.* Charlottesville, Va.: Hampton Roads Publishing.

Mentz, Steven R. 2003. "The Fiend Gives Friendly Counsel: Launcelot Gobbo and Polyglot Economics in *The Merchant of Venice.*" In *Money and the Age of Shakespeare: Essays in New Economic Criticism*, ed. Linda Woodbridge, 177–187. New York: Palgrave Macmillan.

Merlan, Francesca, and Alan Rumsey. 1991. *Ku Waru: Language and Segmentary Politics in the Western Nebilyer Valley, Papua New Guinea.* Cambridge: Cambridge University Press.

Mikami, Yoshihiro, and Toshiki Yotsuzuka. 2000. *Hejji fando tekunoroji: Kin'yu gijutsu to toshi senryaku no furontia* [Hedge fund technology: The frontiers of financial technology and investment strategy]. Tokyo: Toyokeizai.

Miller, Daniel. 1998. "Conclusion: A Theory of Virtualism." In *Virtualism: A New Political Economy*, ed. James G. Carrier and Daniel Miller, 187–215. Oxford: Berg.

———. 2002. "Turning Callon the Right Way Up." *Economy and Society* 31(2): 218–233.

Miller, Merton H. 1997. *Merton Miller on Derivatives.* New York: John Wiley and Sons.

Mirowski, Philip. 1994. "A Visible Hand in the Marketplace of Ideas: Precision Measurement as Arbitrage." *Science in Context* 7(3): 563–589.

Mitchell, Timothy. 2002. *Rule of Experts: Egypt, Techno-politics, Modernity.* Berkeley: University of California Press.

Miyazaki, Hirokazu. 2000. "Faith and Its Fulfillment: Agency, Exchange and the Fijian Aesthetics of Completion." *American Ethnologist* 27(1): 31–51.

———. 2002. "Kaikaku to kibo: Shoken toreda no tenshoku" [Reform and hope: Securities traders' career change]. In *Kane to jinsei* [Money and life], ed. Toru Konma, 268–280. Tokyo: Yuzankaku.

———. 2003. "The Temporalities of the Market." *American Anthropologist* 105(2): 255–65.

———. 2004a. "Delegating Closure." In *Law and Empire in the Pacific: Fiji and Hawai'i,* ed. Sally Merry and Donald Brenneis, 239–259. Santa Fe, N.M.: School of American Research Press.

———. 2004b. *The Method of Hope: Anthropology, Philosophy, and Fijian Knowledge.* Stanford, Calif.: Stanford University Press.

———. 2005a. "From Sugar Cane to 'Swords': Hope and the Extensibility of the Gift in Fiji." *Journal of the Royal Anthropological Institute* 11(2): 277–95.

———. 2005b. "The Materiality of Finance Theory." In *Materiality,* ed. Daniel Miller, 165–181. Durham, N.C.: Duke University Press.

———. 2006a. "Documenting the Present." In *Documents: Artifacts of Modern Knowledge,* ed. Annelise Riles, 206–225. Ann Arbor: University of Michigan Press.

———. 2006b. "Economy of Dreams: Hope in Global Capitalism and Its Critiques." *Cultural Anthropology* 21(2): 147–172.

———. 2007. "Between Arbitrage and Speculation: An Economy of Belief and Doubt." *Economy and Society* 36(3): 397–416.

———. 2009. Review of *Kinship, Law, and the Unexpected: Relatives Are Always a Surprise,* by Marilyn Strathern. *Journal of the Royal Anthropological Institute,* n.s., 15 (1): 195–196.

———. 2010a. "Gifts and Exchange." In *The Oxford Handbook of Material Culture Studies,* ed. Dan Hicks and Mary Beaudry, 246–264. Oxford: Oxford University Press.

———. 2010b. "The Temporality of No Hope." In *Ethnographies of Neoliberalism,* ed. Carol Greenhouse, 238–250. Philadelphia: University of Pennsylvania Press.

Miyazaki, Hirokazu, and Annelise Riles. 2005. "Failure as an Endpoint." In *Global Assemblages: Technology, Politics and Ethics as Anthropological Problems,* ed. Aihwa Ong and Stephen Collier, 320–331. Malden, Mass.: Blackwell.

Miyazaki, Yoshikazu. 1992. *Fukugo fukyo: Posuto-baburu no shohosen wo motomete* [Manifold depression: In search of a remedy for the post-bubble economy]. Tokyo: Chuokoronsha.

Mizuno, Takanori. 1998. *Beikoku kin'yu meja no Nihon senryo* [The occupation of Japan by American multinational financial firms]. Tokyo: Jitsugyo no Nihonsha.

Munn, Nancy. 1986. *The Fame of Gawa: A Symbolic Study of Value Transformation in a Massim (Papua New Guinea) Society.* Cambridge: Cambridge University Press.

———. 1990. "Constructing Regional Worlds in Experience: Kula Exchange, Witchcraft and Gawan Local Events." *Man,* n.s., 25(1): 1–17.

———. 1992. "The Cultural Anthropology of Time: A Critical Essay." *Annual Review of Anthropology* 21: 93–123.

Murphy, John. 1986. *Technical Analysis of the Futures Markets: A Comprehensive Guide to Trading Methods and Applications.* New York: New York Institute of Finance.

Myers, Fred R. 2001. "Introduction: The Empire of Things." In *The Empire of Things: Regimes of Value and Material Culture,* ed. Fred R. Myers, 3–61. Santa Fe, N.M.: School of American Research Press.

Nadauld, Taylor D., and Shane M. Sherlund. 2009. "The Role of the Securitization Process in the Expansion of Subprime Credit." Finance and Economics Discussion Series, Divisions of Research & Statistics and Monetary Affairs, Federal Reserve Board, Washington, D.C., www.federalreserve.gov/pubs/feds/2009/200928/200928pap.pdf. Accessed November 14, 2010.

Nakamaki, Hirochika. 2006. *Kaisha no kami hotoke: Keiei to shukyo no jinruigaku* [Gods and ancestral souls of companies: An anthropology of management and religion]. Tokyo: Kodansha.

Nakanishi, Hiroshi. 2002. "Japanese Relations with the United States." In *The Golden Age of the U.S.-China-Japan Triangle, 1972–1989,* ed. Ezra F. Vogel, Yuan Ming, and Tanaka Akihiko, 164–188. Cambridge, Mass.: Harvard University Asia Center.

Neftci, Salih N. 2000. *An Introduction to the Mathematics of Financial Derivatives.* 2nd ed. San Diego, Calif.: Academic Press.

Netzloff, Mark. 2003. "The Lead Casket: Capital, Mercantilism, and *The Merchant of Venice.*" In *Money and the Age of Shakespeare: Essays in New Economic Criticism,* ed. Linda Woodbridge, 159–176. New York: Palgrave Macmillan.

Newman, Karen. 1987. "Portia's Ring: Unruly Women and Structures of Exchange in *The Merchant of Venice.*" *Shakespeare Quarterly* 38(1): 19–33.

Nihon Keizai Shinbunsha, ed. 1999. *Shinshihonshugi ga kita: 21 seiki shosha no joken* [New capitalism has arrived: Conditions for winners in the twenty-first century]. Tokyo: Nihon Keizai Shinbunsha.

———. 2005. *Shinso Raibudoa vs. Fuji: Nihon wo yurugashita 70 nichi* [The truth of Livedoor vs. Fuji: Seventy days that shook Japan]. Tokyo: Nihon Keizai Shinbunsha.

Nocera, Joe. 2009. "Propping Up a House of Cards," *New York Times,* February 27. www.nytimes.com/2009/02/28/business/28nocera.html, accessed October 30, 2010.

Noguchi, Takuro. 1998. "Anata no nedan wa ikura? Tenshoku shijo ga suru handan [What is your worth? The verdict of the job market]. *AERA,* February 9: 21–24.

Nonaka, Ikujiro, Noboru Konno, and Ryoko Toyama. 2001. "Emergence of 'Ba': A Conceptual Framework for the Continous and Self-transcending Process of Knowledge Creation." In *Knowledge Emergence: Social, Technical, and Evolutionary Dimensions of Knowledge Creation,* ed. Ikujiro Nonaka and Toshihiro Nishiguchi, 13–29. New York: Oxford University Press.

Nonaka, Ikujiro, and Hirotaka Takeuchi. 1995. *The Knowledge-Creating Company: How Japanese Companies Create the Dynamics of Innovation.* New York: Oxford University Press.

O'Barr, William M., and John M. Conley. 1992. *Fortune and Folly: The Wealth and Power of Institutional Investing.* Homewood, Ill.: Business One Irwin.

Ochs, Elinor, and Lisa Capps. 1996. "Narrating the Self." *Annual Review of Anthropology* 25: 19–43.

Okamoto, Toru, Atsunori Namiki, Yuri Takahashi, and Jun Fukui. 1998. "Towareru jibun no 'nedan'" [One's own "price" in question]. *Shukan Toyo Keizai*, September 12, 96–98.

Omae, Ken'ichi. 1995. *Kin'yu kiki kara no saisei* [Recovery from a financial crisis]. Tokyo: Purejidentosha.

Ong, Aihwa. 2006. *Neoliberalism as Exception: Mutations in Citizenship and Sovereignty.* Durham, N.C.: Duke University Press.

Osaka Shoken Torihikijo (Osaka Stock Exchange). 2011. *Nikkei 225 sakimono torihiki no subete* [A comprehensive guide to Nikkei 225 futures trading]. Osaka: Osaka Shoken Torihikijo. www.ose.or.jp/f/general_cms_pages/11272/wysiwyg/pu_sa.pdf, accessed June 7, 2012.

Oshika, Yasuaki. (2006) 2008. *Hiruzu mokushiroku: Kensho Raibudoa* [The apolcalypse of the (Roppongi) Hills: An examination of Livedoor]. Tokyo: Asahi Shinbun Shuppan.

Oshita, Eiji. 1998. *Shosetsu Nihon baishu* [Buying out Japan: A novel]. Tokyo: Shodensha.

Osteen, Mark. 2002. "Introduction: Questions of the Gift." In *The Question of the Gift: Essays across Disciplines,* ed. Mark Osteen, 1–41. London: Routledge.

Osteen, Mark, and Martha Woodmansee. 1999. "Taking Account of the New Economic Criticism: An Historical Investigation." In *The New Economic Criticism: Studies at the Intersection of Literature and Economics,* ed. Martha Woodmansee and Mark Osteen, 3–50. London: Routledge.

Otsuka, Hisao. 1966. *Shakaikagaku no hoho: Veba to Marukusu* [The method of social science: Weber and Marx]. Tokyo: Iwanamishoten.

———. 1994. *Shakaikagaku to shinko to* [With social science and faith]. Tokyo: Misuzushobo.

Parry, Jonathan. 1986. "The Gift, the Indian Gift and the 'Indian Gift.'" *Man,* n.s., 21 (3): 453–473.

Parsons, Talcott. 1937. *The Structure of Social Action: A Study in Social Theory with Special Reference to a Group of Recent European Writers.* New York: McGraw-Hill.

Pettet, E.D. (1945) 1969. "*The Merchant of Venice* and the Problem of Usury." In *Shakespeare, "The Merchant of Venice": A Case Book,* ed. John Wilders, 100–113. Nashville, Tenn.: Aurora.

Pickering, Andrew. 1995. *The Mangle of Practice: Time, Agency, and Science.* Chicago, Ill.: University of Chicago Press.

Polanyi, Karl. (1944) 1957. *The Great Transformation: The Political and Economic Origins of Our Time.* Boston: Beacon.

———. 1957. "The Economy as Instituted Process." In *Trade and Market in the Early Empires: Economies in History and Theory,* ed. Karl Polanyi, Conrad M. Arensberg, and Harry W. Pearson, 243–270. New York: Free Press.

Poovey, Mary. 1998. *A History of the Modern Fact: Problems of Knowledge in the Sciences of Wealth and Society.* Chicago, Ill.: University of Chicago Press.

———. 2008. *Genres of the Credit Economy: Mediating Value in Eighteenth- and Nineteenth-century Britain.* Chicago, Ill.: University of Chicago Press.

Preda, Alex, 2009. *Framing Finance: The Boundaries of Markets and Modern Capitalism.* Chicago, Ill.: University of Chicago Press.

RECOF Corporation. 2010. "M&A Markets in 2009." *RECOF Newsletter,* February 15. www.recof.co.jp/column/pdf/20100215.pdf. Accessed November 16, 2010.

Riles, Annelise. 2000. *The Network Inside Out.* Ann Arbor: University of Michigan Press.

———. 2001. "Encountering Amateurism: John Henry Wigmore and the Uses of American Formalism." In *Rethinking the Masters of Comparative Law,* ed. Annelise Riles, 94–126. Oxford: Hart.

———. 2004a. "Property as Legal Knowledge: Means and Ends." *Journal of the Royal Anthropological Institute* 10(4): 775–795.

———. 2004b. "Real Time: Unwinding Technocratic and Anthropological Knowledge." *American Ethnologist* 31(3): 392–405.

———, ed. 2006. *Documents: Artifacts of Modern Knowledge.* Ann Arbor: University of Michigan Press.

———. 2010. "Collateral Expertise: Legal Knowledge in the Global Financial Markets." *Current Anthropology* 51(6): 795–818.

———. 2011. *Collateral Knowledge: Legal Reasoning in the Global Financial Market.* Chicago, Ill.: University of Chicago Press.

Robbins, Joel, 2001. "Secrecy and the Sense of an Ending: Narrative, Time, and Everyday Millenarianism in Papua New Guinea and in Christian Fundamentalism." *Comparative Studies in Society and History* 43(3): 525–551.

Robertson, Jennifer. 1998. *Takarazuka: Sexual Politics and Popular Culture in Modern Japan.* Berkeley: University of California Press.

Rohlen, Thomas. 1973. "'Spiritual Education' in a Japanese Bank." *American Anthropologist* 75(5): 1542–1562.

———. 1974. *For Harmony and Strength: Japanese White-Collar Organization in Anthropological Perspective.* Berkeley: University of California Press.

———. 1992. "Learning: The Mobilization of Knowledge in the Japanese Political Economy." In *Cultural and Social Dynamics,* vol. 3 of *The Political Economy of Japan,* ed. Shumpei Kumon and Henry Rosovsky, 321–363. Stanford, Calif.: Stanford University Press.

Rohlen, Thomas, and Gerald LeTendre. 1996. "Introduction: Japanese Theories of Learning." In *Teaching and Learning in Japan,* ed. Thomas Rohlen and Gerald Le Tendre, 1–15. New York: Cambridge University Press.

Roitman, Janet. 2005. *Fiscal Disobedience: An Anthropology of Economic Regulation in Central Africa.* Princeton, N.J.: Princeton University Press.

Rosenbluth, Frances M. 1989. *Financial Politics in Contemporary Japan*. Ithaca, N.Y.: Cornell University Press.

Ross, Stephen A. 2005. *Neoclassical Finance*. Princeton, N.J.: Princeton University Press.

Royama, Shoichi, ed. 1997. *Shoken shijo dokuhon* [Handbook on securities markets]. Tokyo: Toyokeizai.

Rubenfeld, Jed. 2001. *Freedom and Time: A Theory of Constitutional Self-government*. New Haven, Conn.: Yale University Press.

Sahlins, Marshall. 1972. *Stone Age Economics*. New York: Aldine.

Saito, Takao. (1997) 2000. *Karuto shihonshugi* [Cult capitalism]. Tokyo: Bungeishunju.

Sakai, Naoki. 1997. *Translation and Subjectivity*. Minneapolis: University of Minnesota Press.

Schaede, Ulrike. 1991. "The Development of Organized Futures Trading: The Osaka Rice Bill Market of 1730." In *Japanese Financial Market Research*, ed. William T. Ziemba, Warren Bailey, and Yasushi Hamao, 339–366. Amsterdam: Elsevier Science.

Schumpeter, Joseph A. (1934) 1983. *The Theory of Economic Development: An Inquiry into Profits, Capital, Credit, Interest, and the Business Cycle*. Trans. Redvers Opie. New Brunswick, N.J.: Transaction.

———. (1942) 1975. *Capitalism, Socialism and Democracy*. New York: Harper and Row.

Schwager, Jack D. (1989) 1993. *Market Wizards: Interviews with Top Traders*. New York: Harper Business.

———. (1992) 2005. *The New Market Wizards: Conversations with America's Top Traders*. New York: Collins Business.

Scott, William O. 2004. "Conditional Bonds, Forfeitures, and Vows in *The Merchant of Venice*." *English Literary Renaissance* 34(3): 286–305.

Sen, Amartya. 1977. "Rational Fools: A Critique of Behavioral Foundations of Economic Theory." *Philosophy and Public Affairs* 6(4): 317–344.

Shakespeare, William. 2000. *The Norton Shakespeare, Based on the Oxford Edition: Comedies*. Ed. Stephen Greenblatt, Walter Cohen, Jean E. Howard and Katharine Eisaman Maus. New York: W.W. Norton.

Sharp, Ronald A. 1986. "Gift Exchange and the Economies of Spirit in *The Merchant of Venice*." *Modern Philology* 83(3): 250–265.

Shell, Marc. (1982) 1993a. *Money, Language, and Thought: Literary and Philosophical Economies from the Medieval to the Modern Era*. Baltimore: Johns Hopkins University Press.

———. (1982) 1993b. "The Wether and the Ewe: Verbal Usury in *The Merchant of Venice*." In *Money, Language, and Thought: Literary and Philosophical Economies from the Medieval to the Modern Era*, 47–83. Baltimore: Johns Hopkins University Press.

Shiller, Robert J. (2000) 2001. *Irrational Exuberance*. New York: Broadway Books.

Shimada, Masahiko, Mutsumi Yamashiro, and Kojin Karatani. 2000. "Gurobaru shihonshugi kara komyunizumu e" [From global capitalism to communism]. In *Kanonaru komyunizumu* [Possible communism], ed. Kojin Karatani, 51–87. Tokyo: Ota Shuppan.

Shimazono, Susumu. 1996. *Seishinsekai no yukue: Gendai sekai to shin reisei undo* [The direction of the spiritual world: The contemporary world and the new spiritual movement]. Tokyo: Tokyodo-shuppan.

———. 2000. "Gendai shukyo to kokyo kukan: Nihon no jokyo wo chushin ni." [Contemporary religion and public space: Taking the case of Japan]. *Shakaigaku Hyoron* [Sociological Critiques] 50(4): 541–555.

———. 2007. *Supirichuariti no koryu: Shin reisei bunka to sono shuhen* [The rise of spirituality: New spiritual culture and its surroundings]. Tokyo: Iwanamishoten.

Shleifer, Andrei, and Robert W. Vishny. 1997. "The Limits of Arbitrage." *Journal of Finance* 52(1): 35–55.

Shore, Chris, and Susan Wright. 1999. "Audit Culture and Anthropology: Neo-Liberalism in British Higher Education." *Journal of the Royal Anthropological Institute,* n.s., 5(4): 557–575.

Skodol, Andrew E., John G. Gunderson, Bruce Pfohl, Thomas A. Widiger, W. John Livesley, and Larry J. Siever. 2002. "The Borderline Diagnosis I: Psychopathology, Comorbidity, and Personality Structure." *Biological Psychiatry* 51(12): 936–950.

Smith, Robert J. 1983. *Japanese Society: Tradition, Self and the Social Order.* Cambridge: Cambridge University Press.

Sokol, B.J. 1992. "*The Merchant of Venice* and the Law Merchant." *Renaissance Studies* 6(1): 60–67.

Soros, George. (1987) 2003. *The Alchemy of Finance.* Hoboken, N.J.: John Wiley and Sons.

———. 1998. *The Crisis of Global Capitalism: Open Society Endangered.* New York: Public Affairs.

———. 2009. *The Crash of 2008 and What It Means: The New Paradigm for Financial Markets.* New York: Public Affairs.

Spinosa, Charles. 1994. "The Transformation of Intentionality: Debt and Contract in *The Merchant of Venice.*" *English Literary Renaissance* 24(2): 370–409.

Stewart, Kathleen. 1996. *A Space on the Side of the Road: Cultural Politics in an "Other" America.* Princeton, N.J.: Princeton University Press.

Stiglitz, Joseph. 2010. *Freefall: America, Free Markets, and the Sinking of the World Economy.* New York: W.W. Norton.

Strange, Susan. 1986. *Casino Capitalism.* Oxford: Blackwell.

Strathern, Andrew J. 1979. "Gender, Ideology and Money in Mount Hagen." *Man,* n.s., 14(3): 530–548.

Strathern, Marilyn. 1988. *The Gender of the Gift: Problems with Women and Problems with Society in Melanesia.* Berkeley: University of California Press.

———. 1992. *Reproducing the Future: Anthropology, Kinship and the New Reproductive Technologies.* Manchester: Manchester University Press.

———. 2000. *Audit Cultures: Anthropological Studies in Accountability, Ethics and the Academy.* London: Routledge.

Swedberg, Richard. 2005. *The Max Weber Dictionary: Key Words and Central Concepts*. Stanford, Calif.: Stanford University Press.

Tachibana, Takashi. 1994. *Rinshi taiken* [Near death experience]. Tokyo: Bungeishunju.

Taussig, Michael. 1997. *The Magic of the State*. New York: Routledge.

Taylor, Mark C. 2004. *Confidence Games: Money and Markets in a World without Redemption*. Chicago, Ill.: University of Chicago Press.

Tett, Gillian. 2009a. *Fool's Gold: How the Bold Dream of a Small Tribe at J.P. Morgan Was Corrupted by Wall Street Greed and Unleashed a Catastrophe*. New York : Free Press.

———. 2009b. "Icebergs and Ideologies: How Information Flows Fuelled the Financial Crisis." *Anthropology News* 50(7): 6–7.

Thomas, Nicholas. 1991. *Entangled Objects: Colonialism, Exchange and Material Culture in the Pacific*. Cambridge, Mass.: Harvard University Press.

Thrift, Nigel. 2005. *Knowing Capitalism*. London: Sage.

Tokyo Shoken Torihikijo (Tokyo Stock Exchange). 2002. *Tokyo Shoken Torihikijo 50 nenshi*. [Fifty years of the Tokyo Stock Exchange]. Tokyo: Tokyo Shoken Torihikijo.

Tomlinson, Matt. 2010. "Compelling Replication: Genesis 1:26, John 3:16, and Biblical Politics in Fiji." *Journal of the Royal Anthropological Institute*, n.s., 16(4): 743–760.

Traweek, Sharon. (1988) 1992. *Beamtimes and Lifetimes: The World of High Energy Physicists*. Cambridge, Mass.: Harvard University Press.

Treat, John Whittier. 1996. "Yoshimoto Banana Writes Home: The *Shojo* in Japanese Popular Culture." In *Contemporary Japan and Popular Culture*, ed. John Whittier Treat, 275–308. Honolulu: University of Hawaii Press.

Tsutsui, William M. 1998. *Manufacturing Ideology: Scientific Management in Twentieth-century Japan*. Princeton, N.J.: Princeton University Press.

Turner, Terence S. 1989. "A Commentary [on T.O. Beidelman's 'Agonistic Exchange: Homeric Reciprocity and the Heritage of Simmel and Mauss']." *Cultural Anthropology* 4(3): 260–264.

———. 2002. "Shifting the Frame from Nation-state to Global market: Class and Social Consciousness in the Advanced Capitalist Countries." *Social Analysis* 46(2): 56–80.

Uchida, Shigeo, 1995. *Nihon shokenshi* [A history of the Japanese securities markets]. Vol. 3. Tokyo: Nihon Keizai Shinbunsha.

United States Congress. 1987. "Program Trading: Public Policy Aspects of Index Arbitrage." A Report Prepared for the Use of the Subcommittee on Oversight and Investigations of the Committee on Energy and Commerce, U.S. House of Representatives, June. Washington, D.C.: U.S. Government Printing Office.

Vaihinger, Hans. (1924) 2000. *The Philosophy of "As If": A System of the Theoretical, Practical, and Religious Fictions of Mankind*. Trans. Charles Kay Ogden. London: Routledge.

Velasco, Jean-Jacques, and Nicolas Montigiani. 2008. *UFO wa . . . tondeiru: Furansu seifukikan no kansatsu to kenkyu.* Trans. Yuki Fukuda, Kaori Noda, Tetsuko Hatakeyama, and Wakana Saeki. Tokyo: Takarajimasha. Originally published as *Troubles dans le ciel* (Paris: Presses du Châtelet, 2007).

Viveiros de Castro, Eduardo. 1992. *From the Enemy's Point of View: Humanity and Divinity in an Amazonian Society.* Trans. Catherine V. Howard. Chicago, Ill.: University of Chicago Press.

Vogel, Ezra. 1979. *Japan as Number One: Lessons for America.* Cambridge, Mass.: Harvard University Press.

Wallerstein, Immanuel. 1991. "The Bourgeois(ie) as Concept and Reality." In *Race, Nation, Class: Ambiguous Identities,* by Etienne Balibar and Immanuel Wallerstein, 135–152. London: Verso.

Weber, Max. (1922) 1978. *Economy and Society.* Ed. Guenther Roth and Claus Wittich. Trans. Ephraim Fischoff, et al. Berkeley: University of California Press.

———. (1924) 2000. "Commerce on the Stock and Commodity Exchanges" [Die Börsenverkehr]. Trans. Steven Lestition. *Theory and Society* 29(3): 339–371.

———. (1930) 1992. *The Protestant Ethic and the Spirit of Capitalism.* Trans. Talcott Parsons. London: Routledge.

Weiner, Annette. 1976. *Women of Value, Men of Renown: New Perspectives in Trobriand Exchange.* Austin: University of Texas Press.

Westney, D. Eleanor. 1987. *Imitation and Innovation: The Transfer of Western Organizational Patterns to Meiji Japan.* Cambridge, Mass.: Harvard University Press.

Wilkins, Alan L. 1989. *Developing Corporate Character: How to Successfully Change an Organization Without Destroying It.* San Francisco: Jossey-Bass.

World Bank. 1993. *The East Asian Miracle: Economic Growth and Public Policy.* New York: Oxford University Press.

Yamada, Masahiro. 2004. *Kibo kakusa shakai* [Stratified hope society]. Tokyo: Chikumashobo.

Yamagishi, Toshio. 1998. *Sinrai no kozo: Kokoro to shakai no shinka gemu* [The structure of trust: The evolutionary games of mind and society]. Tokyo: Tokyo Daigaku Shuppankai.

Yamagishi, Toshio, Karen S. Cook, and Motoki Watabe. 1998. "Uncertainty, Trust, and Commitment Formation in the United States and Japan." *American Journal of Sociology* 104(1): 165–194.

Yamaichi Shoken Kabushikigaisha Shashi Hensan Iinkai. 1998. *Yamaichi Shoken no hyakunen* [One hundred years of Yamaichi Securities]. Tokyo: Yamaichi Shoken.

Yamamoto, Genpo. 1960. *Mumonkan teisho* [Lectures on *The Gateless Gate*]. Tokyo: Daihorinkaku.

Yamashita, Takeji. 1987. *Kabushikishijo no kagaku* [The science of stock markets]. Tokyo: Chuokoronsha.

Yanagisako, Sylvia Junko. 2002. *Producing Culture and Capital: Family Firms in Italy*. Princeton, N.J.: Princeton University Press.
Yoneyama, Lisa. 1999. *Hiroshima Traces: Time, Space, and the Dialectics of Memory.* Berkeley: University of California Press.
Young, Michael. 2004. *Malinowski: Odyssey of an Anthropologist, 1884–1920.* New Haven, Conn.: Yale University Press.
Zaloom, Caitlin. 2006. *Out of the Pits: Trading and Technology from Chicago to London.* Chicago, Ill.: University of Chicago Press.

Index